Pavilion Press

# PRESSING ISRAEL

## Media Bias Exposed - From A to Z

By Jerome R. Verlin and Lee S. Bender

D1450879

**PAVILION PRESS**

Philadelphia

*Bravo to Verlin and Bender: With a copy of* Pressing Israel *in hand, Americans can learn how to read mainstream media reporting on the Middle East rather as Soviet subjects once read Pravda- that is, picking out truth from distorted coverage*
- **Daniel Pipes**- Director, Middle East Forum

*Finally, an exciting expose' of the whole truth about the Muslim Arab war against the Jewish State of Israel. This book will make you an expert, able to defend against any arguments hostile to Israel. One can use the facts presented here to write letters, Op-Eds, or verbally make a powerful case in defense of Israel and against the rampant and persistent anti-Israel media bias. The facts in this book will enable you to win over ill-informed Israeli critics, be they professors, journalists, congressmen, friends; and to read any article or report about Israel with powerful new insights that will make it impossible for you to be misled. Run, don't walk to get this book.*
- **Mort Klein**- President, Zionist Organization of America

*This seminal book provides someone who follows news from the Middle East with insight into the subtle ways in which the mainstream media will provide skewed coverage of events in the Middle East, giving you the reader the ability to discern the tendentious headlines, pejorative descriptions, and one-sided news stories. Once you have read* Pressing Israel: Media Bias Exposed form A-Z, *the reader will have the ability to know how to confront editors, publishers and journalists to tone done the inherent media bias in the western media.*
- **David Bedein**- Director Israel Resource News Agency, and Center for Near East Policy Research

Pressing Israel *by Lee Bender and Jerry Verlin confronts the mainstream media's biased coverage of Israel. The presence of a multitude of foreign reporters who prefer to be based in Jerusalem rather than in Gaza, Ramallah, Damascus, or elsewhere in the Middle East, due to the freedoms and comforts Israel provides is used against this open democracy in the most vicious and inaccurate ways. Lee Bender and Jerry Verlin deal accurately and effectively with the buzz words that dominates the media's discourse on the Arab Palestinian-Israeli conflict. Provocative terms such as "Apartheid state" and "Occupied Territories" are debunked by this useful book. Pressing Israel is an excellent primer for students on campus dealing with the Arab/Muslim/leftist propagandists.*
- **Joseph Puder**- Founder and Director, Interfaith Taskforce for America and Israel (ITAI)

*The mainstream media's misinformation and vilification of Israel is the Trojan Horse in the modern-day war against the Jewish People. But this horse does not just enter through the gates, it has vaporized and flows through the printing presses, the bandwidths and the aural passages of every sentient human being. Each of us are continuously assaulted with that noxious gas of anti-Israel vitriol masquerading as facts. Kudos to Messrs Verlin and Bender for creating an easily accessible and fact-filled source for decoding the major organs and language of this potent weapon. From the A-Z section laying out the key terms behind which the weapon enters our consciousness, to the just as vital antidote section which lays out the necessary background tools of truth with which we can immunize ourselves from this weapon,* Pressing Israel *is a must-have and must-read for all who want to attain a healthy understanding of the truth about what is happening in and to Israel.*

- **Lori Lowenthal Marcus**- President, Z STREET

Pressing Israel *is an important book that everyone who cares about Israel should read. It reveals the depth of media bias and exposes how the starting point for conversation about Israel is inherently biased due to the media's repeated use of misleading terms and inaccurate facts. Read it, digest it, and then act upon it so you can speak the truth to the propaganda.*
- **Amy Holtz** – President, JerusalemOnlineU.com

*The authors of* Pressing Israel *understand that whoever controls the language controls the debate. They have painstakingly constructed a lens through which to see how media coverage of the Mideast, specifically careless use of language and systematic errors of description, undermines the legitimacy of Israel, the only true democracy in the region.*
- **Stu Bykofsky** - Columnist, Philadelphia Daily News

Pavilion Press, Inc.

Philadelphia • New York •

Copyright ©2012 by Pavilion Press, Inc.

Pressing Israel:   Media Bias Exposed - From A to Z

By Jerome R. Verlin and Lee S. Bender

ISBN: .   Paperback  1-4145-0727-5

Hardcover 1-4145-0728-3


Library of Congress

Cataloging-in-Publication Data

1. Current Events  2. Mideast•
3. Israel • 4. Media • 5. Judaism


Composition by Pavilion Press, Inc. Philadelphia, PA

www.pavilionpress.com

What you've read about the Arab-Israeli
conflict in the mainstream media may have misled you.
Do you know –

◄ That the term "**West Bank**," which the media incessantly uses, was never a place name known to history, that for thousands of years, up through the U.N.'s partition resolution in 1947, the land of Israel's Judea-Samaria heartland was still known by its biblical names, "Judea" and "Samaria"?

◄ That what the media insistently calls "**East Jerusalem**," even "Arab East Jerusalem," existed only between 1948 and 1967; that Palestinian Arabs have never ruled any part of Jerusalem for one day in history; that foreign Arabs ruled it only from 638 until the Crusade of 1099 and only part of the city from Jordan's invasion in 1948 until 1967; that Jerusalem has been the capital of three states in the past 3,000 years, all of them Jewish; and that Jerusalem has again had a Jewish majority since 19th century Turkish rule?

◄ That when Rome renamed Judaea as "**Palestine**" in 135 to disassociate it from Jews, the Romans were referring to the long-gone "sea people" Philistines, not Arabs, who didn't invade the land until half a millennium later?

◄ That the Jews, through 3,000 years' continuous physical presence and 20th century international recognition including the San Remo Conference and Palestine Mandate for reconstituting the Jewish National Home, have a legitimate, albeit Arab-contested, claim to their homeland; that Jewish Israel in 1948 became the land's next native state after Jewish Judaea, defeated by Rome in 135, so Jews in Judea, Samaria and "east" Jerusalem are not the outside "**settlers**" and "**occupiers**" the media incessantly calls them?

◄ That the UN's 1947 partition resolution sought Palestine's division into a "Jewish state" and "Arab state," not "Palestinian state," and that it wasn't until after the 1967 Six Day War that Palestinian Arabs came to be known as "**the Palestinians**"?

◄ That during the 1948 Arab-Israeli war and its aftermath more Middle Eastern Jews were displaced from vast Muslim lands than Arabs left tiny Israel; that most of these indigenously Middle-eastern Jews fled to Israel, which absorbed them with no help from the UN, which still supports the Arab refugees and their descendants in "refugee camps" in which their Arab "hosts" (including the Palestinian Authority) keep them; and that the Arab-Israeli conflict's refugee issue embraces these media-unmentioned Jewish as well as **"Palestinian refugees"**?

◄ That Palestinian Arabs who bomb, shoot, stab and relentlessly rocket civilians in towns and cities in Israel are terrorists, not the media's **"militants,"** and that Israel's response against terrorists is in legitimate defense of its citizens, not the tit-for-tat **"retaliation"** the media calls it?

The mainstream Western media is selling out our Judeo-Christian heritage in the Mideast. Read this book which lays out this misreporting from A-to-Z, followed by the background information you need to participate in setting the media straight.

~~

Dedicated to the memory of David Bar-Illan, Editor of *The Jerusalem Post* and its ground-breaking "Eye On The Media" column. He was a role-model, a brilliant concert pianist who dedicated his life to enhancing self-respect for the Jewish soul, in Israel and in the Diaspora.

We invite reader comment through our publisher's website, www.pavilionpress.com on this or any other Pavilion book. Go to the website and to the book page. Click on "Product Reviews" and give us your thoughts.

Jerome R. Verlin (Washington & Lee Univ., B.S., 1961, Univ. of Pennsylvania, LLB, 1964) is the author of *Israel 3000 Years* (Pavilion Press, 2011), and the weekly Brith Sholom Media Watch. He is a past national president of the fraternal order Brith Sholom and a vice-president of the Greater Philadelphia District of the Zionist Organization of America. He is the president of a custom software developing firm. He and his wife, Eileen, reside in suburban Philadelphia, and have two sons and two grandsons.

Lee S. Bender (Cornell, B.A. 1984; William & Mary, J.D. 1988), a former Philadelphia Assistant District Attorney, has been in private practice as a trial attorney since 1995. He is Co-President of the Zionist Organization of America-Greater Philadelphia District, a board member of the Jewish Community Relations Council of Greater Philadelphia, and chairman of the Israel Advocacy Committee of Temple Beth Hillel-Beth El, among many other organizations. He lives with his wife, Jane, and two sons in the Philadelphia region.

"Rock of Israel, arise to Israel's defense! Fulfill Your promise to deliver Judah and Israel. Our Redeemer is the Lord of Hosts; He is the Holy One of Israel. Blessed are You, Redeemer of your people Israel."

    – Tzur Yisrael prayer from the Siddur (Hebrew Prayer Book)


"The great enemy of truth is very often not the lie – deliberate, contrived and dishonest but the myth – persistent, persuasive and unrealistic. Too often...we enjoy the comfort of opinion without the discomfort of thought."

    – President John F. Kennedy, Commencement Address, Yale
      University, 1962


"...bias and distortion are expressed by patterns of subtle details (the wording of headlines, the use of prejudicing adjectives, the balance of 'pro' and 'con' experts, and the like)...."

    – Stephanie Gutmann, *The Other War: Israelis, Palestinians*
      *and the Struggle for Media Supremacy,* p. 259

# Table of Contents

Preface

Section 1: Media Bias Exposed - From A to Z

Section 2: Background for Understanding the Misreporting of News    126

# Preface

Israel, the tiny nation-state of the Jewish people, is an oasis of Western Democracy and Judeo-Christian morality amidst an otherwise totalitarian Arab/Muslim Middle East bent on her destruction. Israel has sought peaceful coexistence with her neighbors since before her re-establishment in 1948, merely seeking recognition as a co-equal within the family of nations and fair treatment.

Instead, Israel is continually vilified in most areas of the world, less perhaps by people or governments, but more by local media and academia. Journalists routinely convey the impression that Israel's daily fare consists of "chaos, war, and terror." Yet, citizens of this sun-soaked country achieve mind-boggling technological advances; the number of Israeli start-ups outweighs that of all of Western Europe combined, and Israeli innovations find their way across the globe…even to countries with which Israel does not enjoy diplomatic relations.

Anti-Zionism has, however, become the mask behind which journalists (who often harbor a political agenda) vent covert anti-Semitism by manifesting, at their cores, engrained moral-relativism; they resent the success of the state run by Jews functioning within a representative democracy in the face of unrelenting hostility, terrorism and war by Palestinian Arabs and state-sponsored terrorist proxy groups. For example, the Palestinian Authority {"P.A."}—consistently dubbed as Israel's potential "peace partner"—has constantly tried to excommunicate Israel from some of the holiest Jewish sites, indeed, to divorce any linkage of the Jewish people to the land. Witness, for example, the recent invocation of newly-acquired membership status in UNESCO to designate regions harboring the greatest Biblical heritages—such as the Temple Mount and the Cave of the Patriarchs in Hebron—as "world heritage sites," to be governed exclusively by Palestinian Arabs.

Meanwhile, news outlets incessantly portray Israel as the aggressor, the "Goliath," in her existential struggle against the mammoth Arab/Muslim world when, in reality, she is the "David." Israel is under attack from all quarters both by the usual suspects (Islamofascists, Islamists, Jihadists, and Arab states) and by parties that are self-proclaimed to be "neutral" (the U.N., European Union, non-governmental organizations {"NGOs"}, "western" elites, progressives, commentators). Israel is continually pressed to concede unilaterally while Palestinian Arabs continue their armed struggle and shun negotiations that might end the conflict by effecting a peaceful two-state solution. Indeed, during recent years, they have revved up the war to delegitimize Israel in diplomatic circles by pursuing lawfare, boycotts, divestments and sanctions against Israel. Functioning in a non-critical environment, Palestinian Arabs increasingly feel they have license to fail to abide by international law, to fail to recognize Israel as the Jewish state, and to persist in initiating and continuing violence against Israel…all the while inciting hatred of Israel and of the Jewish people.

History is clear: Israel accepted the U.N.'s 1947 Partition Plan of "Palestine" as delineated by the British Mandate, but the Arabs rejected it and initiated a war which they lost. Had they accepted Partition, the state of Palestine would have been created alongside Israel. Omitted from dispatches from the Middle East is the fact that the motivation for Israel's actions in Judea/Samaria (the so-called "West Bank") and Gaza is predicated on her need to fight to exist— a right honored by every past and present country—for Israel is under siege; there is no intent (nor has there ever been) to acquire another country's territory.

Unfortunately, Israel's critics continually gloss-over the terrorism, violence, human rights abuses, and anti-democratic practices promulgated by surrounding Arab regimes; they eschew objective analysis of these ideologies, substituting accusations that these critics are bigots. The Mainstream Media {"MSM"} rarely reports how the P.A.—through its controlled media, schools, and mosques—poisons and brainwashes its population, especially youth, thereby inciting chronic violence, terrorism and hatred of Jews and Israel. Moreover, despite the recent "on again, off again" Hamas-P.A. confederation, Israel is incessantly pushed to concede territory and to sacrifice her safety/security, empowering enemies wishing nothing less than her destruction; abiding by such advice would not lead to peace, for it would signal weakness and invite more violence, war and terrorism to deliver the final knock-out. Fundamentally overlooked is the realization that Israel's struggle to survive is part of a religious war against the Judeo-Christian Ethic, initiated over the centuries and sustained by the Arab-Muslim world as a manifestation of the larger "clash of civilizations" articulated by Bernard Lewis and Samuel Huntingdon. Israel is the "canary in the coal mine," for the true target cannot be denied: Western Civilization.

This book counters such inherent bias, to set the record straight regarding key facets of the seemingly-permanent anti-Israel imbalance promoted by the M.S.M. prominent in the West (America and Europe); an "A-to-Z" format (supplemented by a distilled Background) is used to show how the Fourth Estate has so misinformed the American public. Effectively countering press misportrayal of Israel mandates appreciation of patterns of mischaracterization of historical facts, for such instances are too frequent to be dismissed as "random." Their implications must be unambiguously confronted; only then will they become susceptible to being stopped in real-time, countered effectively, and prevented as much as is feasible.

Sometimes, this daunting task feels particularly burdensome when one is forced to wonder whether the Jewish community cares about its own survival. Journalist Stephanie Guttman recounts a mid-1970's dinner conversation between Saul Bellow and Yitzhak Rabin (*The Other War: Israelis, Palestinians and the Struggle For Media Supremacy*, p. 140), in which Rabin grew bored after hearing Bellow advise that this Western misperception required correction:

> "Very few Americans," he pointed out, "seem to know, for instance, that when the U.N. in 1947 proposed the creation of two separate states, Jewish and Arab, the Jews accepted the provision for the political independence of the Palestinian Arabs. It was the Arab nations which rejected the U.N. plan... (but) the Arabs have succeeded in persuading American public opinion that the Jews descended upon Palestine after World War II and evicted the native population with arms."

## HOW TO SPOT MEDIA BIAS REGARDING ARAB-ISRAEL CONFLICT

◄ Is the news headline accurate, focused on the heart of the story?

◄ Are the photographs relevant, accurate and fair to the subject matter?

◄ Are Arabs quoted without response from Israelis, especially Israeli officials, (*i.e.*, not merely quotes from outside-the-mainstream extremist, left-leaning Anti-Zionist Israelis)?

◄ Does the article put key pro-Israel facts at the end or omit them?

◄ Are important articles and features about Israel's positive achievements squarely noted, acknowledged, placed in prominent positions in newspapers/articles, or buried?

◄ Is there "code" language for anti-Semitism masquerading as Anti-Israel sentiment?

◄ Is Israel being singled-out by being held to an impossibly high standard not applied to other nations, including Palestinian Arab behavior?

◄ Is Israel being denied the right of self-defense possessed by every other nation?

◄ Is moral equivalence or moral relativism being applied, unfairly equating Israel's response to terrorism with the perpetrators initiated violence (*i.e.*, conflating the arsonist with the firefighter)?

◄ Is Israel being demonized and delegitimized?

◄ Is there an abdication of all responsibility in assigning moral judgment regarding a brutal murder, terrorist attack, etc., leaving such issues "for philosophers to wrestle with"?

# NOTE ON SOURCES AND EMPHASIS

For the past decade, one of this book's authors (J.V.) has composed and e-mailed (under the auspices of Brith Sholom) a weekly "media watch" exposé focused on Israel-related coverage by the *Philadelphia Inquirer* {"*Inq.*"}. Most citations of pieces by-lined by national news services – such as the Associated Press {"*A.P.*"}, the New York Times {"*N.Y. Times*"}, and the Los Angeles Times {"*L.A. Times*"} – are cited as the articles appeared in the *Inq.*; therefore, date and page-number designations refer to their placement in that newspaper. The term {"M.S.M."} references the mainstream Western media. "Lede" is a media term for the introductory top of a news article. Wire service news articles' headlines are crafted by the newspaper running the articles. Capitalization, boldface and italics have been added by this book's authors for emphasis, except where "emphasis original" has been inserted in brackets.

The authors are deeply grateful for numerous comments and suggestions and tireless editing efforts by Steve Feldman and Robert ("Dr. Bob") Sklaroff, M.D., in strengthening the content, layout and formatting of *Pressing Israel*. Any remaining errors, of course, are our own. We express our deep appreciation to our families for patient and understanding endurance through this book-writing process. Our publisher, Steve Crane, has been an inspiration, encouraging and pushing this project along. We invite reader comment through our publisher's website, www.pavilionpress.com.

# Section 1
# Media Bias Exposed - From A to Z

## A
## "Apartheid" – A False Charge Against Israel

The competing terms "Security Fence" and "Apartheid Wall" swirled around Israel as she commenced construction of a separator between most Israelis and most Palestinian Arabs in 2004. It is a fence for almost all of its length, but "wall" got more play in the M.S.M. [*See* Section 2 IX.] This bias was particularly manifest through editorial treatment of this manufactured controversy.

◄ On February 20, 2004, the *Philadelphia Inquirer* headlined a pair of op-eds: "A **Wall** Between Two Sides Who Don't Talk." One contained the sub-headline "It Is a Temporary Effort at Passive Defense" and began: "Israel's antiterrorist security fence...." The other, topped by "THE WALL" in block-letters, was sub-headlined "It Exists Not For Security But For **Apartheid**" and led off: "On Monday, the International Court of Justice at the Hague will begin hearings on the *wall* Israel is building *around* Palestinian cities and villages."

◄ On July 31, 2003, the *Inquirer* published an editorial cartoon by its in-house illustrator, Tony Auth. It portrayed huddled groups of Palestinian Arabs compartmentalized within the sections of the six-pointed Star of David, a universally-recognized symbol of the Jewish people that appears on Israel's flag. This cartoon inaccurately depicting Israel's linear separation fence as six closed triangles imprisoning groups of Palestinian Arabs evoked memories of Nazi propagandists' misuse of this Jewish symbol, including similarly to the *Inquirer's* 7/31/03 cartoon. The Greater Philadelphia District of the Zionist Organization of America held a formal press conference denouncing the *Inquirer's* cartoon, and an appeal was made to the Society of Professional Journalists, which declined to pursue it.

Sinister misuse of the "Mogen David" symbol of the Jewish people in political cartoons falsely depicting Israeli treatment of Arabs as comparable to how Jew-exterminating Nazis had maltreated Europe's Jews is "widespread." Examples are included in Tal, *Israel in Medialand* (rev. ed., 1989, pp. 44-47, 64, 70). One example in Tal's 1989 book is a *Miami News* cartoon, labeled "The Palestinians," showing them tightly packed in the center section of a barbed-wire Mogen David.

"Apartheid," which refers to segregated discrimination against ethnic elements of a society, is actually the most inapt of all accusations for Palestinian

Arabs to hurl at Israelis. Israeli Arabs are part of Israel's integrated democratic society, which respects human rights. [*See* section 2 IX.] And also part of Israeli society are Black Jews from north Africa. *A.P.* (9/14/08, *Inq.*, A21): "Starting in the early 1980's, Israel clandestinely airlifted 80,000 members of Ethiopia's ancient Jewish community, nearly 15,000 of them in just two days in 1991." But as Caroline Glick reported in her August 13, 2009, *Jerusalem Post* column, "Fatah's Message," one resolution which Abbas' "moderate" Fatah movement adopted at its 2009 General Assembly "demanded that all Jews be *expelled* from Judea, Samaria and Jerusalem ahead of the establishment of a *Jew-free* Palestinian state."

# B

## Borders?  Just 1949 Ceasefire Lines

The terms "1949 ceasefire lines" and "1967 borders" refer to the same line on a map, the so-called "Green Line" (so named because it was drawn with a green marker) that snakes through Judea, Samaria and Jerusalem, marking the front between Israeli and invading Jordanian forces at the ceasefire in fighting in 1949.  The land on the Israeli side was only nine miles wide in critical places, prompting the diplomat Abba Eban to call it an "Auschwitz line."  During the 1967 Six Day War, Israel drove the Jordanian army back across the Jordan River, creating a successor ceasefire line.

The current "peace process" entails delineating a border between Israel and a new Palestinian Arab state to be created west of the Jordan River.  The two sides disagree on whether the 1949 or post-1967 war lines should be the starting point for border talks, and on how the 1949 lines should be viewed.  Incorrect M.S.M. reference to the old narrow, perilous-to-Israel 1949 ceasefire line as Israel's "1967 borders" gravely prejudices public perception of that line's actual significance.  In diplomatic parlance, a "border" carries gravitas – a legal standing and permanence – that a "ceasefire line" lacks.  And "1967" seems more proximate and thus pertinent to the present than does "1949."

### The Arab Position:  "The 1967 Border"

The Palestinian Arabs want the border between Israel and the new Palestinian Arab state, except for any "agreed swaps," to be the old 1949 ceasefire lines, which they call "the 1967 border."

◄  *A.P.* (10/18/10, *Inq.*, A3):

> In an apparent attempt to reach out to Israeli public opinion, Abbas said that, once the Palestinians establish their state in

**the 1967 border**, there is another important thing to end, the conflict, and we are ready for that, to end the historic demands.

◄ *Jerusalem Post* (1/10/10) quoting "top Palestinian negotiator Saab Erekat": "We want a clear recognition of the two-state solution and **the 1967 borders**," Erekat said.

## The Israeli Position: 242's "secure and recognized boundaries"

Israel points out that the 1949 armistice agreement specifically stated that the "Green Line" was not to be construed as a border, and wants the border-drawing to take into account the emergence of post-1967 communities and the reality of Israel's security needs. Elevating the "Green Line" to a political border would cut Israel off from the Jewish homeland's Judea-Samaria historical heartland, the strategic defensible hill country. It would sever the Jewish people from treasure-troves of archeological remains of ancient Israel in the heart of Jerusalem: from the City of David and from the Old City with its Jewish Temple Mount, Western Wall and Jewish Quarter.

Israel wants negotiations to start from the post-1967 war lines, which encompass all of historic western Palestine, and is prepared to negotiate a fallback from there to what post-1967 war U.N. Security Council Resolution 242 called "secure and recognized boundaries." Israel rejects redividing Jerusalem.

## The U.S. Position: Shifting Over Time

The U.S. was deeply involved in the framing of U.N. Security Council Resolution 242, adopted after the 1967 Six Day War, which calls for Israel's withdrawal from "territory"– *intentionally* not specified as "the" territory or "all" territory – captured in the 1967 war, back to "secure and recognized boundaries." [*See* Section 2 I]

In 2009, the U.S. State Department spoke of the parties themselves negotiating a conflict-ending agreement setting a boundary that *reconciled* the *Palestinian* goal of a state on "the 1967 lines, with agreed swaps," with the *Israeli* goal of secure and recognized borders reflecting post-1967 demographic developments, the so-called "settlements." Every word in that U.S. State Department statement is charged with meaning:

> We believe that, through good-faith negotiations, the parties can mutually agree on an outcome which ends the conflict and reconciles the Palestinian goal of an independent and viable state based on the 1967 lines, with agreed swaps, and the Israeli goal of a Jewish state with secure and recognized borders that reflect subsequent developments and meet Israeli security requirements.

On May 19, 2011, however, President Obama made the following statement at the U.S. State Department:

> I believe the borders of Israel and Palestine should be based on the 1967 lines with mutually agreed swaps, so that secure and recognized borders are established for both sides.

There is no sugar-coating that this constituted a *significant* U.S. policy shift. In adopting as the position of the President of the United States that the Israel-Palestinian Arab border "should be based on the 1967 lines with mutually agreed swaps," the President was adopting **verbatim** what the State Department had described in 2009 as "the Palestinian goal" of "the 1967 lines with agreed swaps" that **needed to be "reconciled"** with "the Israeli goal of a Jewish state with secure and recognized borders that reflect subsequent developments and meet Israeli security requirements."

The A.P. report on President Obama's statement acknowledged

> President Barack Obama on Thursday **endorsed a key Palestinian demand for the borders** of its future state. Obama's urging that a Palestinian state be based on the 1967 lines was a **significant shift** in the U.S. approach.

## The M.S.M. Routinely Uses the Incorrect "1967 Border" Term

The M.S.M. occasionally acknowledges the difference in meaning of those two terms, "1949 ceasefire lines" and "1967 borders."

◄ The *Inquirer*'s former Jerusalem Bureau Chief, Michael Matza (5/21/11, A4) asked rhetorically whether these terms ("lines," "borders" and "boundaries") were interchangeable; his conclusion was: "not legally, and certainly not in the Middle East."

◄ Yet, on the preceding day (5/20/11, A10), this same *Inquirer* carried an *A.P.* article using the incorrect term "1967 borders." In quoting President Bush's 2004 statement that "it is unrealistic to expect that the outcome of final status negotiations will be a full and complete return to the armistice lines of 1949," the *A.P.* appended—on its own—that that term, "the armistice lines of 1949," is "a term *synonymous* with the **pre-1967 borders.**"

◄ And on that same day (5/20/11, A1), the *Inquirer* carried a Tribune Washington Bureau piece stating:

> But immediately, it was the Israelis who reacted more negatively, focusing on Obama's declaration that the starting point of the negotiations should be Israel's **borders** prior to the 1967 war. [*N.B.*, the President had used the word "lines," not "borders."]

The *Inquirer* headlined and sub-headlined this front-page article:

Obama Maps a Peace Path; In a major speech, he said a starting point for Israeli-Palestinian talks should be the **borders** set before the 1967 war. Netanyahu criticized the idea.

◄ In a "Worldview" op-ed column (11/11/10), *Inquirer* in-house world affairs columnist Trudy Rubin wrote that Israel's decisions to build new homes "in Jewish settlements on the West Bank and in suburbs of Jerusalem beyond **Israel's 1967 borders**" is "insulting" and evince "disrespect the Israeli government has shown Obama."

◄ The *A.P.* (10/11/07, *Inq.*) wrote incredibly "the Palestinians want **the old** [pre-Six Day War] **Israeli-Palestinian frontier**," quoting P.A. negotiator Qureia that any modifications must be "based on the principle that the Palestinians end up with as much land as *they* lost in 1967," and quoted "Qureia's Boss," Abbas, telling Palestinian TV that "the Palestinians wanted to **get back** 2400 square miles of territory."

### Jews Also Use the Incorrect "1967 Border" Term

A June 12, 2011, *J.T.A.* article in Philadelphia's *Jewish Exponent* twice used the incorrect term, "the 1967 borders":

> Palestinian supporters of the U.N. gambit [for U.N. recognition of Palestinian Arab statehood], like Abbas and his chief negotiators Saeb Erekat and Nabil Shaath, are proposing sending an accompanying letter to the U.N., recognizing Israel in *the 1967 borders* and committing to resuming negotiations immediately on a state-to-state basis.

> .:.Netanyahu has been warning European leaders that a U.N. resolution that enshrines *the 1967 borders* will kill off the peace process.

Even before President Obama's May 19, 2011, pronouncement, there was division among some Israeli and diaspora Jews on the wisdom of Israel negotiating borders based on the "Green Line." For example, an April 20, 2011, Ethan Bronner *N.Y. Times* article (*Inq.* A20) quoted Israeli intellectuals advocating that Israel accept borders based on the "1967 lines." The *Inquirer's* headline to its *N.Y. Times* article upped the ante a bit: "Israeli Savants Urge Peace Based on **1967 Borders**."

But not all Jewish liberals abide by this liberal view on Israel's borders. In a *Jerusalem Post* op-ed (12/16/11), Harvard University Professor Alan Dershowitz, in commenting upon Iceland adopting the Arab view, explained its implications upon Jewry. And he cautioned Jews by using terminology mirroring what they use:

> Now even Iceland, a country with fewer people than Boston, has put in its much deflated two cents. It has decided

to become the first European country to recognize Palestine as a state on the 1967 "**borders.**" [emphasis original]

Thus, according to the wise men and women of Iceland, every Jew who prays at the Western Wall is trespassing on Palestinian territory. Every Israeli student who makes his or her way to the Hebrew University on Mount Scopus is an unlawful occupier. And every Israeli who lives in the Jewish Quarter of Jerusalem must be moved out of his home, despite the reality that Jews have lived in the Jewish Quarter for more than 2,000 years. There is no shortage of stupidity when it comes to international expression of opinion about Israel.

So let Israelis continue to debate vigorously every issue under the sun, but let them realize that every insult they hurl at each other is heard through a megaphone around the world and becomes part of the international effort to delegitimize the Jewish state. So cool it, please.

He was referring to insults that Israelis "hurl at each other," but even greater damage is done by Israelis and diaspora Jews who – out of ignorance or intent – themselves mouth terms ("1967 borders" being one) designed to delegitimize the Jewish homeland connection to Israel. Israelis and Israel's supporters should shun such terms, and the M.S.M. should use them only in direct quotes attributed to the parties who used them.

# C

## "Creation-of-Israel"

### Historical Facts vs. M.S.M. Misportrayal

Compare the historical facts of what transpired in 1947 and succeeding years with the M.S.M.'s portrayal to readers:

Historical Fact: The Arabs rejected the U.N.'s partition plan.

M.S.M. Misportrayal: The M.S.M. rarely notes that the Arabs rejected partition.

Historical Fact: Israel declared independence effective upon the British Mandate's expiration on May 15, 1948, the natural culmination of a legal process, recognized by international conferences and documents, that reflected the Jews' three-millennia presence in the land.

M.S.M. Misportrayal: The M.S.M. persistently misdescribes Israel's natural attainment of independence as "the 1948 creation [or founding] of Israel," as though artificially, arbitrarily and out-of-the-blue.

Historical Fact:  Neighboring Arab states immediately invaded to destroy Israel.

M.S.M. Misportrayal:  The M.S.M. misdescribes the war begun by that Arab invasion as "the war that followed Israel's creation," without the invading Arab states even named.

Historical Fact:  During and after that Arab-Israeli war, many more Middle Eastern Jewish refugees left vast Muslim lands than Arabs left tiny Israel.

M.S.M. Misportrayal:  The M.S.M. cites only "Palestinian" refugees; the Jewish refugees from Arab and other Muslim lands are ignored.

Historical Fact:  The invading Arab states encouraged Palestinian Arabs to leave "temporarily."

M.S.M. Misportrayal:  The M.S.M. attributes seemingly exclusively "Palestinian" refugees to that "war that followed Israel's creation."

Historical Fact:  Whereas most of the Jewish refugees expelled from Arab lands fled to Israel, where they were absorbed, "host" Arab countries, including what are today areas of Palestine controlled by the P.A., keep the Arab refugees and their descendants confined in Western-supported "refugee camps" run by a Dr. Palestine U.N., where they have multiplied into Dr. Palestine's Monster.

M.S.M. Misportrayal:  The M.S.M. (which fails to mention the Jewish refugees and hence not Israel's absorption of them) doesn't mention Arab "hosts'" exclusion of the Arab refugees from their societies [now *there's* apartheid], or the indoctrination of children in these "refugee camps" with anti-Israel, anti-Jewish and anti-Western incitement in the Western-supported U.N. agency's schools.  The U.N. does not recognize descendants of the millions of other refugees as themselves "refugees."

Historical Fact:  Palestine's entire 1947 population was about 1 to 1.2 million Arabs and 600,000 Jews.  About a half-million Arabs left tiny Israel.  Almost a million Jews left vast Muslim lands.

M.S.M. Misportrayal:  For years [*see* "Refugees" below] the M.S.M. carried on about "*millions* of Palestinian refugees and their descendants" from "the war that followed Israel's creation," while ignoring the Jewish refugees from Muslim lands.


**M.S.M. on "Palestinian Refugees From 1948 Creation of Israel"**

Among the M.S.M.'s gravest misportrayals of Israel is its attributing Palestinian Arabs' displacement to "Israel's creation in 1948."  A classic instance was this article (*Knight-Ridder*, 1/4/01, *Inq.*, A1):

> [Under President Clinton's plan] Palestinians would have to scale-back demands that nearly four million Palestinian

refugees and their descendants be able to exercise a right of return to land they fled or were forced to leave in 1948 during **the creation of Israel**. In exchange, Palestinians would gain....

(Of course, there weren't "four million," that's not why they left, and that's not what happened, in any event.)

The following are recent instances of the media mis-describing Palestine's attempted partition as Israel's "establishment," "creation," "founding," and attributing seemingly exclusively "Palestinian" refugees to that "creation" or "founding."

◄ *N.Y. Times* (Isabel Kershner, (6/6/11, *Inq.*, A6): "...the confrontations Sunday echoed the events of May 15, the day Palestinians mark as the 'Nakba,' or *catastrophe*, of **Israel's establishment in 1948**."

◄ *A.P.* (5/15/11, *Inq.*, A22): "Palestinian commemorations of their *uprooting* during **Israel's 1948 creation**."

◄ *A.P.* (9/13/10, *Inq.*, A2): "the *wars and grievances* that flowed from **Israel's 1948 founding** as a Jewish state."

◄ *A.P.* (9/9/09, *Inq.* A4): "the e*xpulsion and exile* of hundreds of thousands during the war that followed **Israel's creation in 1948**."

◄ *A.P.* (9/1/09, *Inq.*): "the two-year war that followed **Israel's creation**, when about 700,000 Palestinians fled or were *forced from their homes*."

◄ *A.P.* (8/4/09, *Inq.*, A4): "[Palestinian Arabs'] demand for 'the right of return' of Palestinians *displaced* after the 1948 Mideast war **over Israel's creation**."

◄ *A.P.* (6/16/09): "Palestinian refugees *displaced* by **Israel's 1948 creation**."'

◄ *L.A. Times* (9/30/08, *Inq.*, A5): "[UN troops' Mideast presence] began 60 years ago, on May 29, 1948, when the fledgling world body dispatched its first batch of blue-helmeted troops to maintain a truce between the **newly-founded** state of Israel and its Arab neighbors." [some "neighbors"]

◄ *N.Y. Times* (8/1/08, *Inq.* A9): "the fate of [1948] Palestinian refugees who left or were *forced to leave* their homes."

◄ McClatchy, commemorating Israel's 60th independence anniversary, 5/8/08 (*Inq.*):

> Jews proclaimed the state of Israel; fighting between Jews **and Palestinians** caused two-thirds of Palestinian population to flee. [Not exactly]

◄ *A.P.* (5/16/08, *Inq.*, A2): "...day mourned by Palestinians as the 60th anniversary of *their uprooting* **by Israel's independence**."

◀ *A.P.* (11/29/07, *Inq.*, A2):

> The Palestinians want refugees and their descendants to be able to return to homes they left, or were *forced out* of, in the war that accompanied Israel's **creation,** That is a deal-breaker for Israel, which sees it as a threat to its Jewish character.
>
> In the end, it seems the Palestinians will have little choice but to give up their dream of returning home. But that still leaves open the question of whether Israel will meet Palestinian demands that it **acknowledge responsibility for the refugees' plight.**

The *A.P.* here utterly begged the open (*i.e.*, contested) question here, which is not whether Israel will "*acknowledge* responsibility" for the Arab refugees' plight, but rather *which side* is responsible for Arab refugees' plight, and for that of the Jewish refugees from Arab lands.

## The Anglo-Jewish Press Has at Times Succumbed to "Creation-of-Israel"

The *J.T.A.*'s 1/16/08 article in Philadelphia's *Jewish Exponent* referred to "Palestinians dispersed after the **creation** of Israel in 1948" and to "Palestinians who fled or *were chased* from their homes upon Israel's **creation.**" [Not even the *A.P.* had come up with "were chased."]

## Other Places "Win Independence Without Becoming "Created" or "Founded"

**India and Pakistan:** In stark contrast to the M.S.M. consistently labeling Israel's attainment of independence as Israel's 1948 "creation" and "founding," an August 14, 2007. *A.P.* article (*Inq.*) led: "Sixty years ago this week, India and Pakistan **won their independence.**" The article proceeded to report "about *10 million* people moved across borders in one of history's largest mass migrations," and "estimates of the dead" in "the sectarian riots and fighting surrounding partition" ranged "from *200,000 to more than a million.*" The article text used the historically accurate terms "independence" and "partition." Imagine the impression readers would have gleaned from the media insistently attributing displacement of 10 million people and 200,000 to one million killed to "Pakistan's creation" or "the war that followed."

**Israel's Arab Neighbors:** "Lebanon and Syria have not had diplomatic relations since they **gained independence** from France more than 60 years ago" (*A.P.*, 8/13/08; *Inq.*, A4).

"Lebanon and Syria formally established diplomatic relations yesterday for the first time since they **won their independence** in the 1940's....Syria, whose territory included Lebanon until the two countries were **given independence** by France, had long refused to establish relations with its neighbor." (*Chicago Tribune*, 8/14/08; *Inq.*, A1, 8, front-page article lead):

## What Happened After One Newspaper's Israel-Supporting Readers Stood Up

For the past 11 years, one of this book's co-authors has written a weekly media watch, focusing on the *Inquirer's* Israel coverage. In 2008, in anticipation of the *Inquirer's* coverage of Israel's upcoming 60$^{th}$ independence anniversary, he sent the *Inquirer's* editor and publisher a 60-page dossier of *Inquirer* reporting citations enclosed with a letter with over 150 readers' endorsements. The letter called for four conceptual *Inquirer* Israel-coverage corrections:

◄ stop calling attempted partition of the Palestine Mandate between its two populations "Israel's creation" and "founding";

◄ stop calling the 1948 multi-nation Arab invasion for Israel's destruction "the war that followed Israel's creation," without the invading Arab states so much as named;

◄ stop blaming seemingly-exclusively Arab refugees on "Israel's creation" or "war that followed Israel's creation"; and

◄ start mentioning equally persistently and prominently that era's greater number of Jewish refugees expelled from vast Muslim lands, most of whom went to Israel and were absorbed.

The *Inquirer* did not favor these callers for coverage change with a direct reply. But its May 8, 2008, front-page article on Israel's commemoration of its independence, authored by its former Jerusalem bureau chief, Michael Matza, referred to the "United Nations partition vote," and referenced 1948 as when "Israel gained its independence from the British," and as "when the armies of Egypt, Syria, Transjordan, Lebanon and Iraq invaded the land Israel claimed as its home." It wasn't until that article's very tail-end last sentence that Mr. Matza signed off with a signature "the creation of Israel and war that followed."

# D

## Denial of Ancient Jewish History

Incredible as it may seem to Westerners living in a society built on Judeo-Christian foundations, even "moderates" among Palestinian Arabs deny not only that the Jewish Temples ever existed and that the still-standing Western

Wall was part of the Temple Mount's structure, but also that Biblical history ever occurred. The M.S.M. has, on occasion, treated such delegitimizing seriously, and has joined in calling Israel's demand to be recognized as the Jewish state "a new stumbling block" to peace talks' resumption. [*See* Section 2 VI, XII] and point (1) under "Killing the Peace Process" below.]

## *New York Times*: "A Myth Used to Justify Conquest and Occupation?"

The August 5, 2005, *N.Y. Times* and *International Herald Tribune* reported on Israeli archeologist Eilat Mazar having unearthed in the City of David area of Jerusalem an enormous well-preserved public building dating back to the 10th century B.C.E. that may have been King David's palace.

*N.Y. Times*: "The find will also be used in the broad political battle over Jerusalem – whether the Jews have their origins here and thus have some special hold on the place, or whether, as many Palestinians have said, including the late Yasser Arafat, the idea of a Jewish origin in Jerusalem is **a myth used to justify conquest and occupation.**"

*International Herald Tribune*'s language went even further, ending that "many Palestinians believe – including the late Yasser Arafat – that the notion of a Jewish origin in Jerusalem is **a religious myth used to justify occupation and colonialism.**"

## The Palestinian Authority's Cut & Paste Propagation of "No Western Wall"

The November 22, 2010, *Jerusalem Post* headlined a Khaled Abu Toameh article "Jews Have No Right To Western Wall, P.A. 'Study' Claims." A week later (11/29/10), the *Jerusalem Post* op-ed by Israeli Deputy Foreign Minister Danny Ayalon, "Palestinian Revisionism is the Only Obstacle To Peace," placed the "study" into context, calling it "sadly, yet another attempt at political historical revisionism":

> The recent "study"…attempting to "refute" the Jewish claim to the Western Wall is merely the latest in a series of efforts, stretching back more than 100 years, to deny the Jewish people's connection with its homeland.

Israeli Prime Minister Netanyahu issued a statement on December 1, 2010:

> A few days ago, I heard that the Palestinian Information Ministry was publishing a study that claims that the Jewish people has no connection to the Western Wall.…It is not only a religious bond, it is a religious and a national bond, a historic link of the highest level that has been going on for thousands of

years, and that too is not trivial because there is a test point here. I say to Abu Mazen to condemn this, denounce the study, turn to your people and tell them: "There is a Jewish people here, it has been here for close to 4,000 years, we recognize this people, we recognize their historic bond with this land and this city." We want to make peace with you, but a real peace. Real peace is based on the truth, not on spin, not on lies, not on half-truths or non-truths. It is based on the truth. I call upon Abu Mazen to promote peace; tell your people the truth (Israel Prime Minister's Office, 12/1/10).

The U.S. joined in this reaction (*J.T.A.* in the *Jerusalem Post*, 11/30/10, "U.S. Condemns P.A. Denial of Jewish Ties to Western Wall"):

> The U.S. called the P.A. study de-legitimization of Israel. U.S. State Dept. spokesman Crowley on Tuesday this week: "We have repeatedly raised with Palestinian Authority leadership the need to consistently combat all forms of de-legitimization of Israel, including denying historic Jewish connections to the land."

Then, a December 1, 2010, *Jerusalem Post* article reported that "a Palestinian Authority 'study' that rejects Jews' claim to the Western Wall" had "disappeared…from the official website of the Palestinian Ministry of Information," and that "a senior P.A. official in Ramallah revealed that the controversial report was **cut** at the request of the United States."

What actually transpired, however, was not "cut," but "**cut and paste.**" Three days later (12/4/10), the *Jerusalem Post* headlined:

> Study Denying Jews' Right to Kotel Resurfaces; Document which sparked strong condemnations from Israel and the US, returns on official website of the P.A.'s news agency Wafa.

That *Jerusalem Post* article led:

> Only days after it was removed from the Palestinian Authority Ministry of Information website, a "study" denying Jews' rights to the Western Wall has resurfaced, this time on the official website of the PA's news agency, Wafa.
>
> By publishing the document on Wafa's website, the official mouthpiece of the Palestinian Liberation Organization and P.A., the authority has sent a message that it has officially endorsed its findings.

Denial hadn't always been the Arab position. In 1924, the Supreme Muslim Council, at the time headed by Grand Mufti of Jerusalem Haj Amin al-Husseini, published "A Brief Guide to Al-Haram Al-Sharif" (reproduction by Simon

Wiesenthal Center) stating:

> The site is one of the oldest in the world. Its sanctity dates from the earliest (perhaps pre-historic) times. Its identity with the site of Solomon's Temple is beyond dispute. This, too, is the spot, according to the universal belief, on which "David built there an altar unto the Lord, and offered burnt offerings and peace offerings." (citing 2 Samuel XXIV, 25).

It also states, regarding the subterranean chamber called "Solomon's Stables":

> Little is known for certain of the early history of the chamber itself. It dates probably as far back as the construction of Solomon's Temple. According to Josephus, it was in existence and was used as a place of refuge by the Jews at the time of the conquest of Jerusalem by Titus in the year 70 A.D.

## Palestinian Authority: "If I Forget Thee, O Jerusalem" Phony Too

◄ *Arutz Sheva* reported (6/10/11):

> Continuing its policy of denying Jerusalem's Jewish heritage, the P.A. publicized the claims of an Arab researcher that the well-known ancient Hebrew psalm, "If I forget thee, Jerusalem, may my right hand forget its skill," is not Jewish at all, the Israeli research institute Palestinian Media Watch reports.
>
> Instead, Dr. Hayel Sanduqa insists the words were uttered by a Christian Crusader, and have only recently been "borrowed" by Jews and "falsified in the name of Zionism."
>
> The verse in question, from Psalm 137 of the Hebrew Bible, opens with the words: "By the rivers of Babylon, there we sat, yea, we wept when we remembered Zion." The researcher did not inform listeners of that fact.
>
> Psalm 137, which mourns the destruction of Jerusalem by the Babylonian army in 586 B.C.E., is part of Jewish tradition and liturgy since then and has appeared in Jewish sources for thousands of years.

## Real Peace Obstacle: Not "Settlement" Expansion, but Denial of Jewish Place in Mideast

The M.S.M. frequently cites "Israel's refusal to stop building settlements" as the prime impediment to achieving peace. [*See* "Killing the Peace Process" below]. The real impediment is Palestinian Arab refusal to recognize Israel as the Jewish state. [*See* "Jewish State – Fundamental Part of Two-State Soluton" below]. At the core of this is denial that Jewish biblical history happened.

# E

## Exhortation – Anti-Israel Incitement as Intense and Ignored as Ever

### Palestinian Authority Involvement in Anti-Israel Incitement

Under "Hot Topics," the media watchdog group "HonestReporting" states on its website:

> Israel repeatedly comes under fire in the media for allegedly promoting policies that are "obstacles to peace" or "undermining trust" with the Palestinians....The media, however, ***virtually ignores*** a very real obstacle to peace – the demonization and incitement against Israel in the Palestinian media and education system and the glorification of terrorism through the naming of public works and streets after the killers of Israeli women and children. (http://honestreporting.com/hot-topics/palestinian-incitement)

Phase I of the U.S.-promulgated 2003 "Road Map," mandated mutual efforts to end incitement. (http://judaism.about.com/od/peaceprocess/a/roapmap_text_2.htm), but P.A. anti-Israel incitement has not abated, as the monitoring reports of both the Israeli government and an NGO show. On March 13, 2011, Israel's Ministry of Foreign Affairs published a compendium of "Recent Examples of Palestinian Authority Incitement" and concluded:

> Incitement against Israel, which frequently turns into genuine anti-Semitic incitement, is an inseparable part of the fabric of life in the Palestinian Authority. Thus, anti-Israel and anti-Semitic messages are regularly heard in both the private and official media and in mosque sermons, and are studied in school textbooks.
>
> Terrorists are given an honored status and become models for emulation in Palestinian society, both in the media and via ceremonies held by institutions affiliated with the P.A.
>
> Institutionalized and systematic incitement against Israel has never ceased in the P.A., even during the height of the diplomatic process in the 1990's.

Examples which this March 2011 report cited included: a 3/9/11 Abbas' advisor's speech emphasizing that "Palestinian weapons must be turned towards Israel," and that a public square should be named for the 1978 coastal highway massacre's perpetrators; a 3/6/11 item in "the P.A.'s official newspaper" on naming a youth club soccer tournament for a "suicide bomber"; a 2/9/11 "official Palestinian television broadcast" extolling a female 1978 coastal highway massacre perpetrator for whom "several children's camps were named" in 2010; a 12/30/10 official P.A. newspaper claim "that Israel aspired to destroy the al-Aqsa Mosque"; a 10/26/10 P.A. TV broadcast of "a fictitious scene in which an Israel soldier shoots a Palestinian in the head"; a 10/6/10 P.A. newspaper interview with a government minister calling Israel "an apartheid state that carries out state terrorism against the Palestinians"; a 9/10/10 P.A. TV broadcast that "Jewish prayer at the Western Wall is 'a sin and impurity'"; and a 6/6/10 P.A. TV children's program that said "the Jews are our enemies" and "Israeli soldiers are wild animals."

Palestinian Media Watch (PalWatch.org) includes on its website a comprehensive "Choose By Topic" classification of Palestinian Arab activity, including incitement, which it monitors. Topics include: "Demonization of Jews/Israelis," "P.A. Depicts a World Without Israel," "Suicide Terror and Shahada," "Children as Combatants," "Rewriting History" and "Holocaust Denial and Distortion." The site includes a section "Choose By Genre," including, among others, "Sermons/Mosques," "Putting Murder to Music," "Children's Programs" and "Academics." There's a "Choose By Year" section with 1997 through 2011 selections.

Regarding "Children's Programs," consider this M.S.M. report (3/17/01, *Inq.*, A4) of an assembly of **4th grade** Palestinian Arab children "holding toy guns and dressed like suicide bombers" under the direction of an adult, that had been organized by "Islamic *militants.*"

A January 1, 2012, *New York Daily News* column by veteran op-ed writer Richard Chesnoff cited a new study, *Deception: Betraying the Peace Process*, by Palestinian Media Watch's Itamar Marcus and Nan Jacques Zilberdik. Chesnoff wrote that this new study:

> carefully analyzes a full year's worth of cultural, educational and general media clippings and resources in which the Palestinian Authority is seen systematically promoting messages of hate – not the need for negotiations with its neighbor. Indeed, says co-author Marcus, "their purpose is to undermine the peace process with Israel."

One of the ways in which the M.S.M. claims Israel undermines the peace process [*See* "'Killing the Peace Process'" below] was in an *A.P.* article (11/4/10, *Inq.* A2), which reported that it was Israel's "announcement" that it

30

would "monitor" Palestinian Arab anti-Israel incitement, not the incitement it-self, that "**further strained**" the "increasingly tense" atmosphere following breakdown of peace talks. The *Inquirer* headlined: "Israel To Monitor Pales-tinian 'Incitement', " with the word "Incitement" in *Inquirer* quotation-marks.

## Jenin – The "Massacre" that Wasn't

During Israel's spring 2002 "Operation Defensive Shield" to stop terrorism, Palestinian Arab leaders used the M.S.M. to issue wildly inflated figures of civilians "massacred" by the I.D.F. in the "refugee camp" in Jenin. The media watchdog group CAMERA complained that the M.S.M. was allowing itself to be so used by spreaders of such "massacre" claims, and took insufficient cor-rective action when the truth ("U.N. Report: No Evidence of a Massacre in Jenin") was confirmed by the U.N.

An August 2002 CAMERA "Backgrounder: A Study in Palestinian Duplicity and Media Indifference" complained:

> [D]espite copious evidence of [Palestinian Arab spokesmen's] blatant lying – the latest proof being United Nations Secre-tary-General Kofi Annan's August 1, 2002 report refuting their fictitious "massacre" – the credibility of these spokesmen with the American press is apparently unaffected. They enjoy al-most unlimited media access to propagate myths about Israel.

As examples of misreporting of the number of civilians allegedly killed, CAMERA cited, among others, P.A. leader Saab Erekat making four state-ments, carried on CNN on one day, April 10, 2002, including:

> I think the real terror is being practiced against the Palestini-ans....When we were in the president's office it came to our knowledge that the numbers of people **massacred** in the refugee camp....They have committed a major crime today in the old city of Nablus and in the Jenin refugee camp. We be-lieve the number of killed is more than 500 people there.

On April 12, Abdel Rahman told CNN:

> [E]veryone in this world knows that Israel committed a **mas-sacre** in Jenin in the last week, 400 to 500 people, mostly civilians, that were killed by the Israeli army.

The *Inquirer*, for one, buried its August 2002 article "U.N. Report: No Evi-dence of a Massacre In Jenin" on **page 20**.

The I.D.F.'s decision to bar journalists from Jenin for several days contributed to media delay in questioning the Arab claims. In his book *This Burning Land,* co-authored with spouse Fox journalist Jennifer Griffin (p. 90 ff), *NPR*'s Greg Myre – then with the *A.P.* – recounted his own experience getting into Jenin.

Myre wrote that he "piled into the Associated Press's armored car with three supremely talented photographers" and made it, a first for a journalist, into Jenin despite the I.D.F. ban until the following week on reporters. He wrote that "in my story, I noted the wild discrepancies and did not claim to have all the answers." He added: "Eventually, the picture became clear. About fifty-five Palestinians had been killed, most of them combatants, although some were civilians."

### **"Whistle-blower" – "one who informs on a wrongdoer." Webster**

The M.S.M. has gone beyond being used. E.g., it insistently euphemizes Israeli Mordechai Vanunu, who betrayed and endangered his countrymen by revealing Israel's military secrets, as a "whistle-blower." A real whistle-blower is a patriot who protects his country by reporting defense contractor fraud to his government. Euphemizing treason as "whistle-blowing" cynically inserts anti-Israel partisanship into news articles, mocking Israel's arming herself against enemies many times her size that are openly sworn to her annihilation, and through lauding such disloyalty incites its repetition by others.

◄ *Inquirer* (8/9/10, A10):

> Israeli nuclear **whistle-blower** Mordechai Vanunu was released Sunday after serving three months for violating the terms of his release from an earlier 18-year prison term for leaking pictures of a top-secret nuclear reactor to a British newspaper in 1986.

◄ *A.P.* (4/10/10, *Inq.*, A2):

> But officials and experts from various countries, in addition to a well-known Israeli **whistle-blower**, have all said [that Israel has nuclear weapons]

Less than a week later (*A.P.*, 4/16/10, *Inq.* A8), this same newspaper headlined:

> Hamas Executes 2 Suspected *Informers*

It was these people, whom the M.S.M. called "informers," who helped prevent terrorist attacks on civilians, who were the real whistle-blowers.

◄ *Inquirer* (7/3/07, A8):

> An Israeli court ordered nuclear **whistle-blower** Mordechai Vanunu to return to jail for six months for violating an order restricting his contact with foreigners.

◄ The 4/13/05 *Inquirer* headlined: "Israeli **Whistle-Blower** Returns to Court" and reported: "Nuclear **whistle-blower** Mordechai Vanunu appeared in court in Israel yesterday".

◄ *Reuters* (3/18/05, *Inq.*, A20, *Inquirer*-headlined as "Israel Files Charges

Against Nuclear **Whistle-Blower**"): "Israeli authorities yesterday charged nuclear **whistle-blower** Mordechai Vanunu...."

◄ *Inquirer* (7/27/04, *Inq.* headlined as "Israel's Top Court Rejects **Whistle-Blower's** Bid To Leave": "...the **whistle-blower** freed in April after 18 years in jail."

◄ *Inquirer* (5/28/04, *Inq.*-headlined "Israel Detains Journalist Who Sought **Whistle-Blower**"): "...nuclear **whistle-blower** Mordechai Vanunu."

◄ *Inquirer* staff-writer Matza article (2/9/04) front page lede: "Mordechai Vanunu, the controversial nuclear **whistle-blower** who revealed years ago in a British newspaper interview that Israel in fact has atomic bombs...."

On July, 14, 2005, that same *Inquirer* staff-writer, Jerusalem Bureau Chief Matza, wrote an article about an Israeli-protected Gaza village housing Arabs who'd helped Israel against terror attacks from Gaza. "Whistle-blower" didn't make it into that *Inquirer* article, but Arabs' descriptions of that village – "nest of snitches and spies...traitors' haven...hideout for informers...collaborated with the [Israeli] military forces" – did.

# F

## "**F**ounded" in 1948? – Not Exactly

The M.S.M. typically describes Israel as having been "created" or "founded" in 1948, as though artificially and without prior foundation. Neither of these media-purveyed perceptions is true. [See "**C**reation of Israel" above Section 2 VII.] But they have greatly prejudiced people's perception of Arab-Israeli conflict rights and wrongs:

> It is easy to point fingers, for Palestinians to point to the displacement brought by Israel's **founding**. (U.S. President Barack Obama, Cairo, Egypt, 6/4/2009)

### Holocaust – Not the Cause of Israel's "Creation"

The Jewish people have lived in the land of Israel continuously for 3,000 years, sovereign twice in ancient times and surviving foreign rule during the centuries between the crushing of Judaea by Rome in the year 135 C.E. until modern Israel's attainment of independence in 1948, when it became the land's next native state after Judaea. This historical connection to Palestine and the Jewish people's right to reconstitute their Jewish National Home in that land has been recognized by international conferences and documents that *preceded* the Holocaust. Israel was not "created" at all, for she comprises the natural evolution into statehood of the Jewish people's homeland presence. [*See* Section 2 III.]

Israel's enemies include Holocaust deniers and doubters who question why Palestinians should suffer, "even if" a calamity befell the Jewish people in Europe. They claim that any recompense due to the Jews should be provided in the place where the presumed injustice was perpetrated; all the while, they spew forth propaganda rather than newsworthy statements. The response to the Holocaust-denial canard is not to recite the evidence documenting that the Holocaust happened. Incontrovertibly, the Holocaust happened. The response is to make clear that Israel was not "created because of the Holocaust," to cite the historical record – the Balfour Declaration, the San Remo Conference, the League of Nations Palestine Mandate.

Here's the M.S.M. providing a megaphone for Israel-Because-of-the-Holocaust claimers:

◀ *A.P.* (12/9/05, *Inq.*):

> Speaking to reporters at an Islamic summit in the Muslim holy city of Mecca, Iranian President Mahmoud Ahmadinejad implied that European countries backed the founding of Israel in the Middle East in 1948 out of guilt over the Holocaust… .They [the Jews] faced an injustice in Europe, so why do the repercussions fall on the Palestinians?"

◀ *A.P.* on 12/10/05 (*Inq.* A2) characterized the Iranian leader as "casting doubt on whether the Holocaust took place and suggesting Europe give land for a Jewish state if it felt guilty about it." The *Inquirer's* headline had him calling "for Israel to be moved to Europe."

◀ *A.P.* (12/14/05) quoted the Iranian leader asking "Why should the Palestinian nation pay the price?"

◀ *Reuters* (9/18/09) lede: "President Mahmoud Ahmadinejad called the Holocaust a lie Friday.…" The article quoted him: " 'The pretext [Holocaust] for the creation of the Zionist regime is false.…It is a lie based on an unprovable and mythical claim.' "

Many in the West see a *post-hoc* Holocaust-Israel connection:.

◀ President Obama, addressing the whole world from Cairo on June 4, 2009:

> The aspiration for a Jewish homeland is rooted in a tragic history that cannot be denied. Around the world the Jewish people were persecuted for centuries, and anti-Semitism in Europe culminated in an unprecedented Holocaust. Tomorrow, I will visit Buchenwald.

◀ Ex-President Jimmy Carter (*Palestine: Peace Not Apartheid*, pp. 65-66):

> And then came the world's awareness of the horrors of the

Holocaust and the need to acknowledge the Zionist movement and an Israeli state.

The M.S.M., on its own, has occasionally subscribed to a Holocaust origin:

◀ *Inquirer*, Jerusalem Bureau Chief Matza (1/9/04):

> Born after World War II and the Holocaust in which millions of Jews were rounded up and killed, Israel was founded on the principle that Jews would never again be so weak.

◀ *A.P.* (9/10/07, *Inq.*):

> News of the arrests [of neo-Nazis in Israel] came as a shock in Israel, which was founded nearly 60 years ago as a refuge for Jews in the wake of the Holocaust.

# G

## <u>G</u>aza – Rockets, Responses and Rhetoric

The M.S.M. regularly reports rockets being launched from Gaza "at Israel," "into Israel," "into southern Israel." These rockets are not aimed at soldiers arrayed on a battlefield, but at civilian men, women and children in towns and cities in Israel. And not haphazardly, but in target shifts and volleys aimed at evading defenses protecting Israelis in cities. M.S.M. depiction of these relentlessly-launched rockets as launched "at Israel," "into Israel" impersonalizes the intentional targeting and intentional terror inflicted on people.

◀ *Haaretz* (8/23/11):

> The terror organizations in the Gaza Strip have changed their rocket-launch tactics in ***an attempt to evade*** the two Iron Dome anti-missile batteries deployed by the Israel Air Force in southern Israel, security sources say....
>
> After the Palestinian launch teams realized that the intercept systems deployed in the past two weeks around Ashkelon and Be'er Sheva provided near-perfect protection from rockets, they began targeting Ashdod and Okafim more frequently. And when they did aim at Be'er Sheva on Saturday, they did not fire one or two rockets, as in the past, but rather a volley of seven almost simultaneously.

Here are some typical M.S.M. articles in 2011 depicting rockets being launched impersonally "on southern Israel...on Israel...into southern Israel... into Israel...at Israel." And of the M.S.M. euphemizing the terrorists who relentlessly rocket civilians in towns and cities in Israel as "squads...factions... extremists...militants."

◀ *A.P.* (8/26/11. *Inq.*, A6):

> The [Gaza] *factions* had called a cease-fire late Sunday, but it dissolved almost immediately in a volley of rocket fire from Gaza **on southern Israel** and *retaliatory* Israeli air strikes.
>
> An Israeli air strike killed two Palestinian *extremists* in Gaza after a salvo of rocket attacks **on Israel**. Palestinian officials said the two were members of Islamic Jihad.

◀ An article (*A.P.*, 8/23/11, *Inq.*, A20) entitled "Gazans Renew Rocket Fire **On Israel**" employed this lede: "Palestinian *extremists* in the Hamas-ruled Gaza Strip launched rockets and mortar shells **into southern Israel** on Monday...." Paragraph 2: "Palestinians launched two rockets **into Israel**...."

What really happened here made paragraph 4: "Palestinians pummeled southern Israel with about 70 rockets Saturday night, killing an Israeli and wounding several others."

◀ *N.Y. Times* (Kershner, 8/22/11, *Inq.*, A6):

> A *retaliatory* Israeli strike in Gaza aimed at the *militant* group that Israel said carried out the attack [on passengers in cars and buses in Israel, killing six Israeli civilians] *led to* rocket fire from Gaza **into southern Israel**.

It's not easy for even a *N.Y. Times* to pack four slaps at Israel into one news article sentence, but this *N.Y. Times* news article managed it:

> A [1] *retaliatory* Israeli strike in Gaza aimed at the [2] *militant* group that Israel said carried out the attack [3] *led to* rocket fire from Gaza [4] *into southern Israel,*

◀ *A.P.* (4/30/11, *Inq.*): "Palestinian *squads* regularly launch rockets **at Israeli towns**" [closer to "at civilians in those towns"]

◀ *A.P.* (4/10/11, *Inq.*, A6):

> Palestinian *militants* fired more than 30 rockets **at southern Israel** on Saturday....
>
> Gaza *militants* fired more than 30 Grad-style Katyusha rockets and more than 10 mortar shells **into Israel** Saturday in what Israeli police said was the biggest single-day bombardment since the Gaza war.

The *Inquirer* headlined this "biggest single-day bombardment" of Israeli civilians from Gaza since the Gaza war, and Israel's response to it, as "Hamas *and Israeli* Attacks Escalate." Ah, the moral equivalence of Hamas firing rockets at Israeli civilians and Israel firing back at Hamas!

◄ *A.P.* (3/21/11, *Inq.*, A6): "Palestinian *militants* fired two rockets **into southern Israel** on Sunday ..."

◄ *A.P.* (3/20/11, *Inq.*), article lede:

> Palestinian extremists in Gaza fired more than 50 mortar shells **into Israel** on Saturday, **the heaviest barrage in two years**, Israeli officials said, *raising the prospect* of a Mideast flare-up.

This didn't begin, of course, in 2011. Here are two earlier instances illuminating the media's mindset.

◄ The *Washington Post* (9/21/07, *Inq.*, A15):

> U.S. Secretary of State] Rice's visit was somewhat overshadowed by the *Israeli government* decision Wednesday to declare the Gaza Strip, envisioned as a main component of a Palestinian state, a "hostile territory" because of *near-daily* rocket fire **into southern Israel.**

Some might think that what "overshadowed" the U.S. Secretary of State's visit *was* this "near-daily rocket fire" at Israeli civilians in southern Israel, not the "Israeli government" finally deciding, "Gee, this place is not friendly."

◄ The *L.A. Times*, 11/2/06 (*Inq.*, A6) used this lede: "Israeli troops backed by tanks and helicopter gunships killed eight Palestinians" in a Gaza clash with "extremists who have made it the *prime launching ground* for rockets **into Israel.**" Israel's intent was "to stop the *daily* firing of Kassam rockets **into southern Is rael.**" But "Hamas' *military* wing issued a statement saying it had *no intention* of halting the rocket attacks."

The M.S.M. fails to grasp the impact of this near-daily rocket file on people's lives in Israel. Ambassador Ron Prosor, Israel's Permanent U.N. Representative, asked "When It Comes to Israel, Why Is the World Silent?" in an op-ed in the *Chicago Tribune* (12/9/2011):

> Hamas deliberately fires rockets into the heart of Israel's major cities, which have exploded on playgrounds, near kindergarten classrooms and homes. Last month, a man was killed when a rocket stuck his car on his evening commute home. Many more people have been injured. In the last month alone, more than a *million* Israelis had to stay home from work and more than *200,000* students were unable to attend school. You don't read about this because if it's covered at all, it's buried in the back pages of newspapers.

The M.S.M. does find words – "fierce ... punishing ... devastating ... crippling ...inflicting collective punishment" –, related to this near-daily rocketing from Gaza of Israeli civilians in Israel. It heaps these harsh adjectives, not on the "militants" firing the rockets, but on Israel, its citizens driven to distraction by years of near-daily rocketing, going into Gaza to stop it.

◀ *A.P.* 6/1/10 (*Inq.*, A4): "Israel's **fierce** offensive against Gaza in the winter of 2008-09."

◀ *A.P.* (1/8/10, *Inq.*, A2): "After Israel unleashed a **punishing** offensive against Gaza a year ago to stop the *daily* barrages, rocket and mortar fire ebbed but did not stop."

◀ *A.P.* (12/28/09, *Inq.*, A3): "Israel's **devastating** offensive in Gaza"; "Israel launched its **punishing** three-week campaign of air strikes and ground incursions on Dec. 27, 2008, *saying* [as though this were in issue] the operation was meant to stop *years* of rocket attacks from Gaza."

◀ *A.P.* (12/22/09, *Inq.*, A3): "a **punishing** blockade…a **crippling** Israeli and Egyptian blockade of impoverished Gaza…an "embargo" that "has prevented the territory from rebuilding after Israel's **devastating** offensive a year ago to stop *daily* Palestinian rocket attacks."

◀ *A.P.* (12/15/09, *Inq.*, A12): "Israel's **devastating** military assault on Gaza a year ago." "Hamas has sharply curtailed rocket fire on Israeli border towns since last winter's Israeli offensive, which inflicted heavy losses on Hamas." "Since the end of the three-week war in mid-January, 242 rockets and mortars were fired, compared with 3,300 in 2008."

◀ *A.P.* (12/1/09, *Inq.*, A5): "the one-year anniversary of a **fierce** Israeli offensive in Gaza."

◀ *A.P.* (3/2/09, *Inq.*): "More than 110 rockets and mortar shells have exploded in Israel in the six weeks since it halted its air and ground onslaught against Gaza, which was meant to end the rocket threat….[PM Olmert promised] a severe response *if* the attacks didn't stop." [After another rocket landed shortly thereafter, the *Inq's* headline was "Israel's Leader Threatens Hamas."]

◀ *A.P.* (2/3/09, *Inq.*) quoting as a "**tough** statement" by PM candidate Livni her statement that Israel would "keep hitting Hamas *as long as* it attacks Israel."

◀ *L.A. Times* (1/21/08, *Inq.*, A8, "Israel Holds Back Fuel For Gaza Electric Plant"). The article stated UNRWA "joined human-rights organizations in condemning Israel for what they called **collective punishment.**"

◀ *Washington Post* (1/23/08, *Inq.*, A11) article headlined "Israel Eases Its Gaza Blockade, Allowing Shipments of Food, Fuel" noted [paragraph 7]: "Extremists launched 19 rockets at Israel *yesterday.*"

The *Washington Post* (12/6/05, *Inq.*, A6) inadvertently revealed its blindness to basic journalistic responsibility, when it reported that an Islamic Jihad "operative" was held responsible for a horrific shopping mall bombing in Netanya, Israel. Citing the duty of his organization to enforce its Road Map obligations

– to confront those engaged in terror and to dismantle terrorist capabilities and infrastructure – P.A. President Abbas [paragraph 8] solemnly swore: "Those who are responsible should be hunted-down by the Palestinian police." Yet, the very next sentence [paragraph 9] stated, with no apparent appreciation of its irony, that the Islamic Jihad was at that time conducting "a *news conference* in Gaza City."

# H

## Headlines – Not Always What Happened

Those who compose newspaper headlines are charged with the duty to give the readers a fair sense of the story they head. For wire-service as well as for in-house articles, the newspaper fashions the headlines. Given the deadline pressures under which daily newspapers operate, occasional inaccurate headlines are doubtlessly inevitable. But when a succession of misleading headlines damaging to one side of an international conflict repeatedly are generated over time in the same newspaper, imbalance may be at work. Here we examine some *Inquirer* headlines related to the Arab-Israeli conflict.

◄ On September 10, 2011, Cairo mobs rampaged unrestrained for hours through Israel's Egyptian embassy; ultimately, one barricaded door stood between the mobs and remaining Israelis. Frantic Israeli leaders, unable to get Egypt to act, telephoned U.S. Defense Secretary Panetta and then President Obama, whose intervention they credited for Egyptian rescue of the Israelis. The *Inquirer's* news article (*N.Y. Times*, 9/11/11, *Inq.*) called the Egyptian inaction "an extraordinary breach of Egypt's international commitments." The *Inquirer* headlined: **"Israel Evacuates Cairo Staff."**

◄ On August 18, 2011, infiltrators from Sinai killed six and wounded 30 civilians in cars and buses on Israel's Eilat-Beersheba road. The I.D.F. pursued the attackers back into Egypt, killing four. The *Inquirer's* news article (*N.Y. Times*, 8/19/11, *Inq.*) called the attack "the most serious on Israel from Egyptian territory in decades." The *Inquirer* headlined: **"Day of Killings On Israeli Border."**

◄ On April 7, 2011, Hamas claimed "responsibility" for striking a *school* bus in Israel with a *guided* anti-tank missile fired from Gaza, wounding a student, who later died; Israel responded against Hamas. The *Inquirer's* headline to this news article (*A.P*, 4/8/11, *Inq.*) omitted references to the targeted bus as a *school* bus and to the *guided* weapon Hamas had used, and down-graded Israel's response to tit-for-tat violence. The *Inquirer* headlined: **"Hamas Hit on Israeli**

**Bus Draws Retaliation."**

◄ On February 15, 2011, Israel protested Jordan's announcement that it might release from prison a Jordanian soldier who, in 1997, had shot fourteen eighth-grade Jewish schoolgirls on an outing on the Israeli-Jordanian border, murdering seven and wounding the others. The *Inquirer* could have headlined this news article (*A.P,* 2/16/11, *Inq.*) "Israel Rejects Call To Free Murderer of Seven Israeli Schoolgirls." The *Inquirer* did headline: **"Israel Rejects Call To Free Soldier."**

◄ An *Inquirer* article (*A.P.,* 1/11/11) began: "Three rockets fired from Gaza exploded Monday in an industrial section of the Israeli city of Ashkelon." The headline on *A.P.*'s website began "Rockets From Gaza Hit Israeli City...." The *Inquirer* headlined: **"Rockets Strike Gaza Town."** The next day the *Inquirer* ran a "Clearing the Record" note. Yet, given the clarity of the *A.P.*'s headline and lede, and the history of which side rockets the other's towns, what remains unexplained is how the *Inquirer* could have so confused what occurred.

◄ Unusually large, above-the-fold, emotional headlines make strong impressions on readers. On May 31, 2010, the I.D.F. killed nine pro-Hamas activists who had been fighting soldiers enforcing Israel's blockade against arming Gaza's Hamas rulers. The *Inquirer* ran a huge (greater than 12 sq. in.) headline and sub-headline beginning **"Outcry, Crisis After Deadly Raid By Israel"** (6/1/10). On August 7, 2010, the Taliban executed ten medical-aid workers, six of them Americans, in an Afghan forest. The *Inquirer* ran a far smaller, non-hysterical headline (8/8/10): "Aid Workers Shot Dead in Afghanistan," omitting who shot them.

◄ An article (*A.P.,* 3/2/09, *Inq.*) reported that "more than 110 rockets and mortar shells have exploded in Israel in the six weeks *since* it halted its air and ground onslaught against Gaza, which was meant to end the rocket threat...." It quoted P.M. Olmert promising "a severe response *if* the attacks didn't stop." Another rocket landed shortly thereafter. The *Inquirer* headlined: **"Israel's Leader Threatens Hamas."**

◄ An article (*A.P.,* 12/27/08, *Inq.*) reported that a rocket fired at Israelis from Gaza had fallen short, killing two Arab school girls. The *A.P.* used a headline, "Palestinian Rocket Misfires, Kills 2 Girls in Gaza." The *Inquirer* headlined: **"2 Palestinian Girls Killed in Attack."**

◄ An article (*A.P.,* 4/26/08, *Inq.*) reported that two Israeli factory guards had been *shot dead* by a Palestinian Arab whom "a spokesman for Islamic Jihad" said had snuck into Israel and reached the plant in a border industrial zone in which "Israeli factories employ Palestinians." The *Inquirer* headlined **"Two Israeli Factory Guards *Die.*"**

◄ An article (*A.P.,* 4/29/08, *Inq.*) reported that "The Israeli army shot four

40

Palestinian militants who were trying *to plant explosives* near the Gaza Strip border fence," and quoted Hamas calling them its members *"on a jihad mission."* The *Inquirer* headlined: **"Israeli Army Shoots Four *Palestinians*."**

◄ Using white phosphorus shells against civilians and in civilian areas is banned by the Geneva Convention. An article (10/23/06, *Inq.*) quoted an Israeli cabinet minister that "the Israeli army made use of phosphorous shells during the war against Hizbollah in attacks against military targets in open ground." But the *Inquirer* headlined this article: **"Israel *Says* It Used Banned Shells In War."** This too was followed by a "Clearing the Record" clarification.

◄ The *Inquirer's* article (4/21/04) quoted Sharon that Israel had not finished targeting "murderers" such as Hamas founder Yassin [who two months before had openly called for female "suicide" bombers because Israel was stopping the male ones] and his successor. The *Inquirer* headlined: **"Sharon: Hamas *Officials* Remain Potential Targets."**

◄ An 8/20/03 *Inquirer's* staff-writer article reported that a bombing of a packed Jewish-neighborhood Jerusalem bus had killed 20 and wounded 100, in what the article had termed "the worst since a cease-fire began nearly two months ago." Israel responded by targeting a Hamas leader. Three days after this truce-busting bombing (8/23/03), the *Inquirer* headlined its follow-up article: **"Hamas Leader Killed; Truce Off."**

◄ Arabs bombed Jerusalem buses *two days in a row*, murdering 25 and wounding 80 civilians, and threatened to *continue* such carnage. The *Inquirer's* headline (6/20/02) read **"Jerusalem Hit Again – And *Militants* Promise More...."**

◄ On July 12, 2001, the *Inquirer* ran an *A.P.* article leading: "A Palestinian woman in labor was barred from passing an Israeli military checkpoint for an hour and gave birth to a baby boy who died before reaching a medical clinic, *a doctor said* yesterday." The *Inquirer's* headline stated as fact: **"Birth—and Death—at Israeli Checkpoint; A Palestinian Newborn Died After an Hour-long Delay."** That evening, the *A.P.* corrected its initial version, which the *Inquirer* ran the next day, leading: "Israeli soldiers did *not* bar a Palestinian woman in labor from passing an Israeli checkpoint, her relatives said Thursday, contradicting initial claims by two Palestinian doctors who blamed a checkpoint delay for the newborn's death." The *A.P.*'s corrected headline was "Relatives of Woman who Gave Birth at Israeli Checkpoint Say They Were Not Held Up By Troops." The *Inquirer's* next day headline? **"Story Shifts on Baby Born at Checkpoint."**

# I

# Images: Doctored, Staged, Misleading, Mis-captioned

Even more than headlines, dramatic photos accompanying news articles grab readers' attention and rouse instant reactions. Israel has suffered great damage from their improper usage by the M.S.M., but less dramatic photos and captions have likewise damaged perceptions of Israel.

## Palestinian Youth Al-Dura Died "Under a Hail of Israeli Bullets"

Among the most infamous incidents is France 2's September 30, 2000, video of a 12-year-old Arab boy, shown crouching behind his father at the scene of fighting between Palestinian Arabs and the IDF in Gaza. The boy goes limp at the end and France 2 reported he died "**under a hail of Israeli bullets.**"

There is grave doubt about that. Here's what happened that day:

"One of the most worrying signs" for Israeli soldiers staring out from their military outpost in Gaza on the morning of September 30, 2000, wrote journalist Stephanie Gutmann in *The Other War: Israelis, Palestinians and the Struggle for Media Supremacy* (p. 45), was "the appearance of the flock of cameramen in the otherwise deserted square." Soon Gazans began to gather and attack the outpost with rocks and Molotov cocktails. The Israel Defense Forces responded with rubber bullets and tear gas. Around noon, the attacks and response escalated to gunfire.

Viral dissemination of France 2's TV news clip prompted reflex, unjustified condemnation of Israel, devastation of her image that has been carefully perpetuated regardless of subsequent revelations. Gutmann, who devoted a chapter of her book ("'Al-Dura' – A Case Study") to analyzing the reporting and its impact, explained (p. 41):

> The narrative was established for most of the world on the night of September 30, when France's powerful state-financed television channel, France 2, which was the exclusive owner of the videotape, reported that the twelve-year-old Palestinian had died "**under a hail of Israeli bullets.**" The incident rap-

idly became "'one of the most disastrous setbacks Israel has suffered in decades," in the words of Bob Simon, then bureau chief for CBS News in Jerusalem....Hussein Ibish, communications director of the American-Arab Anti-Discrimination Committee, called the film "one of the most damaging [images] in the history of Zionism."

The Committee for Accuracy in Middle East Reporting in America {"CAMERA"} has published two overviews: "'Backgrounder: Mohammed Al Dura; Anatomy of a French Media Scandal" and "The Al-Dura Cover-Up." These probes raised doubts that were amplified by re-enactment by the IDF: (1) The video does not show the shooter; (2) The Israelis were not positioned to have shot in the direction of al-Dura; (3) It is unclear whether al-Dura was shot; and (4) It is unclear whether al-Dura died.

A spokesperson quoted by Gutmann (p. 58) said Israel "took a while" to respond to the public relations aspect "because we don't understand that side of it as well as we should." Israel's adversaries understood, and filled the vacuum, memorializing him in rhetoric and deed. Bin-Laden and Daniel Pearl's murderers cited al-Dura; a street in Cairo and park in Morocco have been given his name, which is on websites, posters and T-shirts in Gaza; he's in textbooks and videos; he's honored in Europe in songs and performing arts; Arab countries and Belgium issued stamps with his picture (Gutmann, p. 42).

Philippe Karsenty, a French media watchdog, "claimed the footage was staged," citing similar scenes elsewhere in parts of the videotape that he saw. France 2 sued him for libel and won, but Karsenty successfully appealed. An interview published in the Middle East Quarterly {"M.E.Q."} quoted Karsenty (Fall 2008, pp. 57-65):

> "Yes, we won the case completely; the court decision was clear. The court, however, did not have to rule that the tapes were staged but, rather, said that I could publish what I wanted because I had evidence that it was staged. The written arguments say that I am right, yet all of what the court said intrinsically supported my statement that the incident was staged."

France's highest court has since ordered further proceedings, but the lesson for Israel and its supporters is clear: to counter media bias manifested as unwarranted blaming of Israel, delayed response exacerbates, not mitigates, the damage that's done.

## "Smoke and Mirrors" in the 2006 Lebanon War

*Reuters'* photographer Adnan Hajj photo-shopped a picture to show multiple columns of smoke rising from an Israeli-rocketed site in Beirut during the 2006 Israel-Hezbollah war. The doctored-photo (on the bottom) was intended "to show more intense smoke and destruction." *Reuters* admitted to the manipulation and apologized, fired Hajj, and removed the doctored photo from its archives. (Jewish Virtual Library)

Zombietime's analysis pointed out that, although the "actual significance" of the doctoring of this photograph is "not particularly great," it got the most M.S.M. attention because its doctoring was "the most clear-cut" of this *Reuters* photographer's photos of Beirut during that war.

Zombietime also analyzed "four types of photographic fraud perpetrated by *Reuters* photographers and editors" covering the Israeli-Hezbollah war:

(1) Digitally manipulating images after the photographs have been taken.

(2) Photographing scenes staged by Hezbollah and presenting the images as if they were of authentc spontaneous news events.

(3) Photographers themselves staging scenes or moving objects, and presenting photos of the set-ups as if they were naturally occurring.

(4) Giving false or misleading captions to otherwise real photos that were taken at a different time or place.

http://zombietime.com/*Reuters*_photo_fraud/;

http://www.jewishvirtuallibrary.org/jsource/History/doctoredphotos1.html.;
http://littlegreenfootballs.com/weblog/?entry=21956_Reuters_Doctoring_Photos_from_Beirut&only;

## Utterly Misleading Caption and Impression

The *N.Y. Times* jumped to a devastatingly incorrect interpretation of this *A.P.* photo it published also on September 30, 2000, captioned "An Israeli policeman and a Palestinian on the Temple Mount," as though the Israeli policeman, brandishing a club and shouting, had just beaten the Palestinian Arab youth bloody.

The "Palestinian's" father sent this e-mail to the Times:

Associated Press

An Israeli policeman and a Palestinian on the Temple Mount.

"Regarding your picture on page A5 (Sept 30) of the Israeli soldier and the Palestinian on the Temple Mount – that Palestinian is actualy my son, Tuvia Grossman, a Jewish student from Chicago. He and two of his friends were pulled from their taxicab while travelling in Jerusalem by a mob of Palestinian Arabs and were severely beaten and stabbed. That picture could not have been taken on the Temple Mount because there are no gas stations on the Temple Mount and certainly none with Hebrew lettering, like the one clearly seen behind the Israeli soldier attempting to protect my son from the mob."

(http://www.fraudfactor.com/ffmedia fraud9001.html)

## Misuse of Photos to Besmirch Israel – Depicting Jerusalem as Arab

◄ The *Inquirer* accompanied an *A.P.* article on Israel's authorizing new homes in Gilo (9/28/11, *Inq.*, A6) with a photo accurately described by this caption:

> A [Arab-attired] man walks past Damascus Gate, the main entrance to Jerusalem's **Old City**. Israel gave the go-ahead for the building of 1,100 Jewish housing units in **southeast** Jerusalem.

Honest Reporting noted that Gilo is a 40,000-resident Jewish community

**southwest** of the Old City that was started in 1971 on land purchased by Jews before World War II.  (http://honestreporting.com/gilo-in-perspective-2/)

◀ An article discussing Israel's having authorized new homes in Maale Adumim (8/18/04, *Inq.*) was accompanied by a photo of "**a Bedouin shepherd**" with goats.

Maale Adumim is a 36,000-resident Jewish community established in 1975 on land less than five miles from Jerusalem that was "uninhabited desert prior to 1975, much as the surrounding hills remain today." It was officially declared a "city" in 1991 and "was to be part of Israel" under President Clinton's plan. It is in "one of the largest industrial zones in the country" comprising "1.54 million square feet of industrial space," housing "over 120 factories."

http://www.jr.co.il/ma/history.htm;
http://www.govisitisrael.com/articlenav.php?id=140;
http://www.jr.co.il/ma/industry.htm

## Misuse of Photos to Besmirch Israel – Distracting from Focus on Terror

The impact of an article reporting an act of terrorism against Israeli civilians is diluted when the newspaper accompanies it with a photo depicting a scene other than the site which had been struck by terror.  Ponder the following *Inquirer* photo selections.

◀ The 12/6/05 *Inquirer* reported a "huge blast" made by a Netanya shopping mall bombing that "left bodies scattered outside" the site, its "glass and marble façade…shattered in places and stained with swirls of blood as far as 60 feet from the site of the explosion," with "body parts…found as far as 300 feet away." The photo was captioned accurately:

> A youth who says his brother blew himself up in the Israeli city of Netanya stands at the family house in the West Bank village of Illar.

◀ An article (*L.A. Times*, 4/20/08, *Inq.*, A2) stated Hamas had "claimed responsibility" for attacking the Kerem Shalom Israel-Gaza border crossing the prior day; it was headlined "Palestinian Militants Attack Key Israel-Gaza Border Crossing." The article quoted an Israeli general calling the attack "the largest militant operation since Israeli troops and settlers withdrew from the Gaza Strip in 2005." The accompanying photo did not show the "key" **Kerem Shalom** border crossing, but instead depicted Palestinian Arabs protesting at a **different** Gaza border-crossing with Israel:

> Palestinian women and children march near the **Erez** Crossing in a protest organized by the Islamic Group Hamas to

protest Israel's economic blockage of the Gaza Strip.

◄ The *Inquirer* accompanied an article (*A.P.* , 12/20/07, *Inq.*) headlined "Hit Hard *At a Festival*, Hamas Appeals for *Peace*" with a large photo of a small boy among a group of Muslims kneeling in prayer; it was captioned "A child stands amid worshippers…." But Israel did not strike those Muslims at prayer in a mosque "at a festival." During *the days of* that Festival of Abraham—during which rocketing of Sderot by Hamas had not abated—Israel struck back at the terrorist groups launching those rockets. And Hamas, which "said" that it was "working with other groups to stop the rocket-fire into Israel" (which Islamic Jihad denied) was appealing for a ceasefire, not "peace."

◄ An article (4/7/05, *Inq.*) shed light on an anguishing aspect of Israel's impending Gaza withdrawal; the "settlers" would have to dig-up and rebury their dead. The story was accompanied by a poignant photo of a woman gazing down at a grave. The caption explained that her husband had "**died** in January." The article text stated he had been "**killed** in January by a planted bomb [*i.e.*, by the **terrorists** who had planted the bomb] as he surveyed a fence."

◄ During the 2006 Israel-Hezbullah war, Hezbullah rained thousands of rockets down on the northern Israeli city of Haifa. The *A.P.* reported on August 10, 2006:

> Hizbullah Leader Urges Israeli Arabs to Leave Haifa
>
> BEIRUT — Hizbullah leader Sheik Hassan Nasrallah yesterday warned all Israeli Arabs to leave the port city of Haifa so the militant group could step up attacks without fear of shedding the blood of fellow Muslims.
>
> Haifa, Israel's third-largest city, has been the frequent target of Hezbollah's rocket attacks.
>
> "I have a special message to the Arabs of Haifa, to your martyrs and to your wounded. I call on you to leave this city. I hope you do this….Please leave so we don't shed your blood, which is our blood," Nasrallah said.

During this Nasrallah-directed Hezbollah bombing of Haifa, the *Inquirer* accompanied an editorial (7/21/06, *Inq.*, "When We Teach Our Children to Hate") with a pair of photos. One photo showed an Arab woman and her newborn child, whom she'd just named with the name of a Hezbollah missile. The other photo, titled "From Israel With Love," was of an Israeli girl pluckily inscribing "To Nasrallah" on the shell of a missile the Israeli army was about to launch back at Hezbollah. Both pictures, in the *Inquirer's* view, depicted Arabs and Jews "teaching their children to hate." (The *Inquirer* capped off its moral equivalence by admonishing Israel: "No child should be allowed anywhere near a shell." The *Inquirer* should have directed that piece of supercilious advice to sheller Nasrallah.)

# J

## Jewish State – Fundamental Part of Two-State Solution

The M.S.M. depicts Israel as the recalcitrant side on supporting "the two-state solution" proposed by the U.S. in the celebrated "Road Map." The M.S.M. quotes Palestinian Arab leaders chiding Israel for not supporting it. The reality is exactly the opposite. It is Israel that is in synch with America's "Two-States" definition as "two states for two peoples," and the Palestinian Arabs who are adamantly against it. [*See* Section 2 XII]

### America's Position on "Two-States": "Two States for Two Peoples"

◄ President Bush, the Road Map's promulgator, made clear at the Road Map's 2003 introduction at Aqaba that "two states" included a Jewish state:

> America is strongly committed and I am strongly committed to Israel's security as a vibrant **Jewish** state.

◄ U.S. Special Envoy George Mitchell, who repeatedly met with Israeli and Palestinian Arab leaders, reiterated that American view of "two states." (*A.P.*, 4/17/09, *Inq.*):

> "U.S. policy favors…a **two-state solution**, which would have a Palestinian state living in peace alongside the **Jewish** state of Israel," Mitchell said.

Excerpts from U.S. State Department "On-The-Record Briefing" by United States Special Envoy Mitchell, Sharm el-Sheik, Egypt September 14, 2010:

> All of us reaffirmed our commitment to reaching a shared goal of a just, lasting and secure peace. Our common goal remains **two states for two peoples**….
>
> We have said many times that our vision is for a **two-state solution** that includes a **Jewish** democratic state of Israel.

◄ "Two states for two peoples" was reiterated by U.S. Permanent Representative to the U.N. Susan E. Rice in her address to the Conference of Presidents of Major American Jewish Organizations on December 14, 2011:

> There is no substitute for direct, face-to-face negotiations. The goal remains a lasting peace: **two states for two peoples**, Israel as **a Jewish state and the homeland for the Jewish people**, and the state of Palestine as the homeland of the Palestinian people, each state enjoying self-determination,

mutual recognition, and peace. That is the only path to Israel's decades-long quest for security and the only path to fulfilling the Palestinian people's legitimate aspirations.

## Israel's Position on "Two-States": "Two-States for Two Peoples"

◄ Israeli P.M. Netanyahu's statement to the Cabinet meeting on April 20, 2009:

> We insist that the Palestinians – in any diplomatic settlement with us – will recognize the State of Israel as the national state of the Jewish people. The entire international community demands that we recognize the principle of **two states for two peoples** and we are discovering that this is two states but not for two peoples but two states for one people, or two states for a people-and-a-half.

◄ Excerpts from Israeli Ambassador Ron Prosor's address to the U.N. Security Council, July 26, 2011, (Israel Ministry of Foreign Affairs):

> Our nation seeks a lasting peace in which the Palestinians will have their own state, alongside – but not instead of – the Jewish state of Israel....

> Mr. President, on the issue of the Jewish state, we must have clarity as well. For lasting peace to take hold, Israel's recognition of a future Palestinian state *must be met* with an equal acknowledgement that Israel is the Jewish state.

> Israeli Prime Minister Netanyahu has stated *openly and repeatedly* that *we will accept a Palestinian state,* alongside a Jewish state. Yet, the Palestinian leadership has not done the same. They will not tell their own people that they accept a Jewish State....

## Media Misportrayal of Palestinian Arab and Israeli Positions on "Two-States"

The M.S.M. quotes Palestinian Arabs as professing support for "the two-state solution" and chiding Israel for not supporting it:

◄ *Jerusalem Post* (1/10/10) quoting "top Palestinian negotiator Saab Erekat":

> "**We want** a clear recognition of **the two-state solution** and the 1967 borders," Erekat said.

◄ *L.A. Times* (4/22/09, *Inq.*), (but see Israel Prime Minister's Office release, 4/20/09, two days earlier, quoted above):

> The newly installed Israeli government of Prime Minister

Benjamin Netanyahu has **not** endorsed the two-state goal endorsed by the United States.

◀ *A.P.* (4/13/09, *Inq.*):

Abbas has said there was no reason to negotiate **if Netanyahu did not support** a "two-state solution."

◀ *A.P.* (2/13/09, *Inq.*):

Yesterday evening, Palestinian Authority President Mahmoud Abbas urged Israel's incoming leaders to press ahead with peace efforts....**Israel should "accept** the two-state solution–Palestine and Israel living side by side in security and peace," Abbas said.


## What Palestinian Arabs Actually Mean by "Two States"

What do Palestinian Arabs really mean by "two states," and is this in synch with what the U.S. and Israel mean by it? Palestinian Arabs *don't* mean "two states for two peoples," one state for Arabs and the other for Jews.

◀ On the very day, September 23, 2011, that Abbas addressed the United Nations, seeking U.N. recognition of a western Palestine Arab state, YNetNews.com quoted Abbas:

Abbas: No to Jewish state

On Friday afternoon [9/23/11], Abbas said he was adamant about not recognizing Israel as the Jewish state.

"They talk to us about the Jewish state, but I respond to them with a final answer: **We shall not recognize a Jewish state**," **Abbas said** in a meeting with some 200 senior representatives of the Palestinian community in the US, shortly before taking the podium and delivering a speech at the United Nations General Assembly.

◀ Caroline Glick's *Jerusalem Post* column (Townhall.com, 8/5/11) quoted a senior P.A. negotiator's statement showing clearly that Palestinian Arabs understand exactly what the U.S. and Israel mean by "two states for two peoples," and that they expressly reject it.

Glick:

Israel has no one to negotiate with because the Palestinians reject Israel's right to exist. This much was made clear yet again last month when senior PA "negotiator" Nabil Sha'ath said in an interview with Arabic News Broadcast, "The story of '**two states for two peoples**' means that there will be a Jewish people over there and a Palestinian people here. *We* *will never accept this.*"

◄ One news service that reported on the resolutions that Fatah adopted at is 2009 General Assembly was TomGrossMedia.com (8/11/09), "As Fatah Radicalizes, Peace Prospects Dim":

> A further resolution explicitly said Fatah would **oppose** recognizing Israel as a Jewish state.

◄ *Jerusalem Post* columnist Caroline Glick (JPost.com, 8/13/09, "Column One: Fatah's Message") likewise reported on resolutions on which both Fatah's "old guard" and "young guard" were in substantial agreement:

> Both demanded that all Jews be expelled from Judea, Samaria and Jerusalem ahead of the establishment of a Jew-free Palestinian state.

> Both claimed that any settlement with Israel be preceded by an Israeli withdrawal to the indefensible 1949 armistice lines and by Israel's destruction as a Jewish state through its acceptance of millions of foreign-born, hostile Arabs as immigrants within its truncated borders.

◄ On September 21, 2010, Deputy Israeli Foreign Minister Ayalon met with Palestinian Authority Prime Minister Fayyad at the U.N. in New York. The article the next day (*A.P.*, 9/22/10, *Inq.*, A7, "Diplomats Press Israel to Extend Moratorium") alluded obliquely to that Ayalon-Fayyad meeting, stating "Israel disagreed that construction was a major impediment to the talks," and quoting Ayalon: "Let's concentrate on the real issues and not just put the obstacle in the settlements."

The *A.P.* didn't elaborate on what the Israeli official said those real issues were. But a Zionist Organization of America News Release that day did.

> More Proof Palestinians Don't Want Peace

> P.A. Prime Minister Fayyad Freaks Out, Walks Out: Won't Accept Two States for Two Peoples

> Palestinian Prime Minister Salaam Fayyad, wrongly called a 'moderate,' angrily left a U.N. meeting and cancelled a scheduled press conference with Deputy Foreign Minister Danny Ayalon in New York on Tuesday. Fayyad became hysterical and ran out of the room when Ayalon refused to approve a joint press release of the meeting which **referred only to "two states" but did not include the words "two states for two peoples."**

> ...Deputy Foreign Minister Ayalon said, "...I was very surprised that there was apparently no acceptance of the idea of two states for two peoples. I also said that I don't need the

Palestinians to say Israel is a Jewish state in Hebrew. I need them to say it in Arabic to their own people. **If the Palestinians think that they can create one Palestinian state and one dual-nationality state, this will not happen....**"

◄ Liberal *Haaretz's* Ari Shavit (4/23/09), after stating that Israel had come to recognize Palestinian Arabs' right to a state:

> However, in no case – neither at Oslo, Camp David or Annapolis – did the Palestinians go a parallel distance. They shattered no taboo and shed no fundamental refusal. To this day they **do not recognize** the Jewish people rights or its nation-state.

◄ The *Jerusalem Post's* review (4/23/09) of historian Benny Morris' book, *One State, Two States: Resolving the Israel/Palestine Conflict,* after stating that "Morris concludes that a majority of Jews during the Mandate and Israelis in the years since have come to accept the notion of two states for two peoples," continued:

> However, the Arabs have **not**. The historian takes the reader through the various covenants and declarations of the PLO, Fatah and Hamas and illustrates that even when claims of moderation are made by an Arab, they do not reflect reality.

◄ The *A.P.* (4/17/09, *Inq.*):

> [Netanyahu has] demanded that the Palestinians recognize Israel as a Jewish state, [which is a step] they have **refused to take**.

Despite M.S.M. depiction of Palestinian Arab leaders calling on Israel to accept a Two-State solution – as though they themselves accept it – it is only Israel and the U.S. which together accept "the Two-State Solution" in the only sense that it has any meaning: one state for Arabs and the other for Jews (*i.e.*, two states for two peoples).

## The Jewish People's Commitment to a Jewish State

Despite a recent M.S.M. suggestion [*see* "Killing the Peace Process" below] that Netanyahu's insistence on Israel as "a Jewish state" may be just a "tactical ploy," the Jewish people's commitment to the land of Israel as the Jewish state runs very deep.

In 1947, British Foreign Secretary Ernest Bevin recognized that "the creation of a sovereign Jewish state" was "the essential point of principle" for the Jews:

> There are in Palestine about 1,200,000 Arabs and 600,000 Jews. **For the Jews, the essential point of principle is the**

**creation of a sovereign Jewish state.** For the Arabs the essential point of principle is to resist to the last the establishment of Jewish sovereignty in any part of Palestine." (Great Britain, Parliamentary Debates, Commons, vol. 433, col. 988, quoted in Bell, *Terror Out of Zion*, New York, St. Martin's Press, 1977, p. 188)

Indeed, dividing Palestine into an "Arab state," not a "Palestinian" state, and a "Jewish state" is what the 1947 U.N. General Assembly Resolution 181, the Partition resolution, was all about. It mentions "the Arab state" and "the Jewish state" over and over, and "Palestinian state" not at all.

The Jews' Jewish-state commitment didn't begin in 1947 either, or with the late 19th century modern Zionist movement. It's a commitment that reaches back 3,000 years. [See Section 2 III]

Nor is Palestinian Arab rejection of the Jewish state new. Following failure of the 2000 Camp David negotiations, then Israeli P.M. Ehud Barak stated why in his opinion Arafat had rejected what this liberal Israeli administration had considered its "extremely generous" peace offer: "At the deepest level, Arafat does not accept the…right of the State of Israel to exist as a Jewish state" (Myre & Griffin, *This Burning Land*, p. 20).

# K
# "Killing the Peace Process" – Media Label for Israeli Action/Inaction

To Israel's supporters, the M.S.M. misportrays whatever Israel does as a ploy to block peace process progress. Ten Israeli "ploys" are listed here. There are others, like the M.S.M. telling readers that a particular Israeli minister's very appointment to Israel's cabinet "effectively ruled out" peace talks. [*See* "Land Swaps."]

### (1) Israeli Insistence on "Jewish state" Recognition is "A New Stumbling Block"

The centrality to Jewish peoplehood of the land of Israel as the Jewish people's homeland dates back three thousand years and continues through those three millennia to today; this long centrality cannot be summarily dismissed as having started when the modern Zionist movement started in the late-19th century, nor can it be minimized by claiming it suddenly arose in the mid-20th century. Israel's insistence that she be recognized as the Jewish state is rooted in ancient and modern history; it didn't begin with P.M. Netanyahu. [*See* "Jewish

State."]

◄ The *L.A. Times* (10/24/10, *Inq.*, A3) suggested, using the media ventriloquism dummy "some see," that Israeli P.M. Netanyahu's insistence that Palestinian Arabs recognize Israel as a Jewish state served only as a distraction from the need to deal with "settlements":

> Some see Netanyahu's actions as **a tactical move** designed to put Palestinians on the defensive, paint them as rejectionists and **divert attention** from Israel's controversial settlement construction in the West Bank, which has thrown peace talks into crisis.

The *Inquirer's* headline left off the figleaf qualifier "some see":

> A *New Stumbling Block* to Mideast Peace Talks; Israel Presses Palestinians to Recognize "Jewish" State.

Israel's demand to be recognized as a Jewish state is fundamental, neither "a tactical move" intended to "divert attention," nor "a new stumbling block."


## (2) Israel Rejecting Impossible Palestinian Arab Demands "Lessens" Peace Chances

Apparently, Arab demands can never become so outrageously impossible for Israel to accept that the M.S.M. can assign the Arab side's making of those demands – not Israel rejecting them – as the action lessening peace chances.

A 1/17/01 *A.P.* article (*Inq.*, A3), headlined in the *Inquirer* as "Israeli Leader Rejects 2 Palestinian Demands," carried this lede: "Israeli Prime Minister Ehud Barak dismissed two main Palestinian demands yesterday – lessening the chances of achieving a peace deal."

Those two "main Palestinian demands" – the rejection of which by Israel, not their initial issuance by the Arabs, was claimed by the M.S.M. to lessen the chance to achieve a peace deal – were for Israel's demographic and Jewish extinction:

> (1) "that all Palestinian refugees and their descendants, about four million people, be given the right of return to their former homes in Israel," and
>
> (2) "[Palestinian Arab sovereignty] over a disputed Jerusalem holy site – Haram as Sharif, known to Jews as Temple Mount."


## (3) Israel Continuing to Build Homes for Jews in Jerusalem Is "Latest Setback" for Peace

Israel builds homes for Jews in Jerusalem, Israel's united eternal capital; the current (conservative) government *continues* to do what all prior (conservative and liberal) governments have done since 1967, including *during* peace talks. Israel will retain Jewish Jerusalem neighborhoods in any peace deal. Contrary to how the M.S.M. presents this continued activity to readers, it's the P.A. now demanding that Israel cease building homes for Jews in its capital as a pre-condition to resuming peace talks that's "the latest setback" and "kink."

◄ *A.P.* (12/30/09, *Inq.*, A3): "In **the latest setback** for peace efforts, Israel said Monday that it planned to build nearly 700 homes in East Jerusalem."

◄ *Inquirer* editorial, "Unsettled Dispute" (3/11/10): "Plans to expand a housing settlement in Jerusalem have **put a kink in efforts** to forge peace in the Mideast."

◄ *Inquirer* op-ed essay, "Worldview" (3/18/10) by in-house foreign affairs columnist Trudy Rubin: "Continued building in and around *Arab East* Jerusalem makes it **impossible** for this part of the city to become – as it must in any peace settlement – the capital of a Palestinian state."

◄ *A.P.* (3/28/10, *Inq.*, A10): "Senior Israeli cabinet ministers plan to meet today to draw up a response to President Obama's demand for [Israeli] peace gestures toward the Palestinians....Washington has demanded the gestures to try to jump-start U.S.-brokered peace talks, which were **derailed** by Israeli plans to **continue** building in contested East Jerusalem."

◄ *A.P.* (5/2/10, *Inq.*, A4): "A first attempt [by the Arab League] to get ["long-stalled"] indirect [peace] talks going **collapsed** in March when Israel announced a new housing project in East Jerusalem."

◄ *A.P.* (5/9/10, *Inq.*, A20): "Negotiations are being **overshadowed** by Israel's refusal to halt settlement construction on war-won land."

## (4) Israel Restating "Longstanding" Positions "Undermines" Peace Efforts

An Israeli leader merely *restating* longstanding Israeli positions is enough to prompt the M.S.M. to blame Israel for "clouding" a new U.S. peace mission, "threatening to undermine" U.S. efforts to restart peace talks due to the "timing" of the restatement.

The lede of an article (*A.P.*, 4/23/10, *Inq.*, A13) claimed:

> Israeli Prime Minister Benjamin Netanyahu on Thursday rejected U.S. calls to halt construction in disputed East Jerusalem, **clouding** a new peace mission by Washington's Mideast envoy.

Acknowledged in paragraph 4, however, was that this so-called "rejection" was not new: "Netanyahu was repeating his longstanding position." But the *A.P.* reported as fact its judgment that it was "the **timing** of the statement" by

Netanyahu – his reiteration of his longstanding position "shortly after envoy George Mitchell had arrived" – that **threatened to undermine** Mitchell's latest efforts to restart peace talks."

But Netanyahu did not "blindside" Mitchell. During the preceding day's U.S. State Department Daily Press Briefing, spokesperson Crowley had admitted as much; referring to Netanyahu's comments on building homes for Jews across the "Green Line' in Jerusalem, he said: "I don't think that they necessarily are new" because "we understand that the Israelis have a longstanding position." He added: "We have some indication that both sides are willing to engage seriously on the issues that are on the table," and that "we felt it was fruitful for George to travel." Israel did nothing new that "threatened to undermine" Mitchell's mission.


### (5) Israel Making a "Move" (that Wasn't a Move), Not Making a Move, Hurts Peace Talks

The M.S.M. has portrayed Israel's repeated voicing of a longstanding position as Israel "yesterday" having "rejected" a U.S. request, a "move" that put an upcoming "summit" in question, and a week later portrayed that *same* Israeli position as Israel "holds firm" and "won't bend," which "could signal trouble" for that upcoming summit. Either way, Israel makes a "move" or Israel "holds firm" and "won't bend," Israel's to blame.

◀ An article (*A.P.*, 9/15/09, *Inq.*, A4) carried a headline ("Netanyahu Rejects Calls for Freeze") and sub-headline ("His *move* angered Palestinians and put in question a N.Y. summit next week") that stretched across five columns of newsprint; the lede mirrored this portrayal of Israeli intransigence...

> Prime Minister Benjamin Netanyahu **yesterday rejected** U.S. calls to freeze all settlement construction in the West Bank and east Jerusalem, angering Palestinians and **putting** a New York summit in question.

...although the fact that "Netanyahu has *repeatedly* voiced these positions," and wasn't born a rejectionist "yesterday," was registered later in the article.

◀ A follow-up article (9/22/09, *Inq.*, A12) carried a headline ("Netanyahu Holds Firm On Settlements") which reflected the content of the lede:

> Israeli Prime Minister **won't bend** on his opposition to a settlement freeze...[T]he *tough* Israeli line could **signal trouble** for today's summit [at the U.N. in New York].

Actually, it was Israel that *did* make a move, bent, didn't hold firm, to induce the Palestinian Arab side just to return to the table. She instituted a 10-month Judea/Samaria building freeze. After frittering away 9 of those 10 months, the

Palestinian Arabs finally sat down to negotiate, only to jump-up less than a month later, when that 10-month Israeli moratorium expired.

◄ Here's the "credit" afforded Israel (*A.P.*, 6/17/11, *Inq.*, A22) for that accommodation:

> The latest round of peace talks broke down in September, just three weeks after their launch, with the *expiration* of an Israeli moratorium on settlement construction in the West Bank.

### (6) Israel's Willingness for Talks with No "Pre-Conditions" Blocks "Imminent Breakthrough" While Palestinian Arab-Demanded "Pre-Conditions" are Ignored

The M.S.M. takes a dimmer view of Israeli than of Palestinian Arab peace talk "conditions," even though Israel has not demanded any pre-talks' conditions.

◄ *A.P.* (5/19/09, *Inq.*): After Israeli P.M. Netanyahu emerged from a White House meeting with President Obama, he was quoted as having stated Israel had agreed

> to restart the Palestinian peace process "immediately," but with **conditions** that indicated that no breakthrough was imminent.

Those **conditions** were tethered to the Road-Map, namely, Israeli security concerns and Palestinian Arab recognition of one of the Two-State Solution's two states as the Jewish state. Later in that article, "the chief Palestinian negotiator" was quoted as demanding...

> an immediate and complete freeze on all settlement activity, including natural growth, lifting of all restrictions on Palestinian movement, and an immediate end to Israel's siege on Gaza

...but those Palestinian Arab **preconditions** were not perceived by the reporter as having torpedoed the imminence of any breakthrough. In any case, confirmation of which side truly harbors peace talk resumption *pre*-conditions emerged in at least four articles:

◄ *A.P.* (6/17/11, *Inq.*, A2, "Palestinians Stick to Demand for Construction Freeze"): "The **Palestinians have refused to negotiate** without a new moratorium that also includes East Jerusalem. **Israel is demanding talks without preconditions**, and it says that settlements should be one of the topics discussed."

◄ *Jerusalem Post* (4/23/10): "*Since coming into office*, Netanyahu has insisted that the two sides talk directly **without preconditions**."

◄ *A.P.* (9/25/11, *Inq.*, A8): Abbas included in his peace talk **pre-conditions** both "a halt to Israeli settlement construction" and that they be "based on borders [actually ceasefire lines] before the 1967 Six-Day War."

◄ *A.P.* (9/27/11, *Inq.*, A9): The Quartet called for "a resumption of peace talks without **pre-conditions**," but "Abbas said he would return to the negotiating table only if Israel halts settlement construction and accepts the pre-1967 war lines as the basis for talks."

The P.A. had negotiated with Israel during the Oslo talks without a "settlements"-freeze pre-condition. It became a P.A.-demanded pre-condition after President Obama had made it an issue.


## (7) Israel's Military "Offensive" in Gaza Caused Peace Talks "Breakdown"

◄ *A.P.* (5/2/10, *Inq.*, A4): Prior to peace talks breaking down over Israel building "a new housing project in East Jerusalem," "**peace efforts broke down** over Israel's military offensive on Hamas-ruled Gaza."

That Israeli "military offensive" in Gaza had constituted a response to *years* of *near-daily* rocketing of Israeli civilians from Gaza. The M.S.M. should have blamed that relentless Arab rocketing of civilians in Israel – not Israel finally, inevitably acting to stop it – for disrupting peace efforts.

◄ Between February 28 and March 6, 2008, the *Inquirer* ran a series of headlines on Israeli action in Gaza. Those headlines did not mention that Hamas had escalated the scope and potency of its relentless rocket attacks from targeting Negev towns like Sderot with short-range Qassams to launching more powerful, longer-range Grad-class Katyusha rockets at the major Israeli coastal city of Ashkelon. These unprecedented attacks placed a great many more Israelis in range of sustaining great harm. Turning a blind eye to this, *Inquirer* headlines included:

> Mideast Peace Talks Off; Palestinians Suspend Discussions; Israel Vows to Keep Up Gaza Attacks (*Inq.*, 3/3/08)

> Abbas Declines to Set Time For Resuming Talks; He Met With Rice, Who Pushed for the Resumption of Negotiations Broken Off Over Israel's Incursion into Gaza (*Inq.*, 3/5/08)

> Mideast Talks Back on Track, Rice Says in Visit to Region; Abbas Had Halted Them After Israel's Incursion into Gaza; No Date for a Restart was Announced (*Inq.*, 3/6/08)

The Inquirer's shockingly imbalanced omissions of "escalation," "Grad" or "Katyusha rockets," "Ashkelon" and even "Hamas" from this series of headlines is detailed in "Violence" below.

### (8) Israeli *Announcement* It would *Monitor* "Incitement" Caused "Further Strain"

The *Inquirer* headlined its article (*A.P.*, 11/4/10, *Inq.*, A2): "Israel To Monitor Palestinian 'Incitement'," with "Incitement" in quotation-marks to portray it as merely an Israeli claim, and sub-headlined it: "Palestinians Accused Netanyahu of *Trying To Divert Attention* from the Impasse in Talks."

The text portrayed Israel's "announcement" that it planned *to monitor* the incitement (which it neglected to state that the Road-Map called on Palestinian Arabs *to cease*), and *not* the incitement itself, as having "**further strained**" the "increasingly tense" atmosphere following breakdown of peace talks.

### (9) Media Blames *Israel* as Side that "Has Long Refused To Budge" On Key Issues

◄ A 1/9/10 *A.P.* article ( *Inq.*, A3) reported on a possible "bold shift" in American Mideast policy, a change from seeking "incremental Mideast progress" to jumping directly to "negotiations on the toughest issues," borders and Jerusalem, which it called "two defining and difficult issues that *Israel has long refused to budge on.*"

Israel *has* "budged" on both, the Palestinian Arabs on neither, on multiple occasions. Israel had agreed to divide western Palestine [*i.e.*, the portion of the original League of Nations Palestine Mandate remaining after the excision of the 80% east of the Jordan River as all-Arab Transjordan (today Jordan)] into Jewish and Arab states, two states for two peoples. Also, previous Israeli Prime Ministers (Barak at Camp David and more recently Olmert) had proposed peace plans that had included re-dividing Jerusalem, but those offers had been rejected by the P.A., "moderate" Abbas' Fatah, and Hamas. Meanwhile, the P.A. has never "budged" on not recognizing a Jewish state, or on borders, or on Palestinian Arab refugees.

A smattering of media reports have recognized that it is Abbas who won't budge. He was quoted on 9/7/10 in the *Jerusalem Post* and on 9/8/2010 in the *New York Daily News*: "I cannot allow myself to make even one concession.... if [Israelis] demand concessions on the rights of the refugees or the 1967 borders, I will quit." An accompanying *New York Daily News* editorial concluded:

> Faster than you can say "two-state solution," the direct Israeli-Palestinian peace talks begun with such fanfare have hit their first huge obstacle: an *utter unwillingness to budge* on the part of Palestinian Authority President Mahmoud Abbas.

Quoting that "I will quit" threat by Abbas, that editorial asked: "How do you negotiate with someone who proclaims his intransigence?" Recognizing that rejecting the "right of return" demand is existential for Israel, the *New York Daily News* rightly concluded: "Though there might technically be a nation of that name ["Israel"], its primary defining characteristic–being a Jewish homeland–would be lost."

### (10)  Israel Electing a "Right-Wing" Prime Minister Renders Talks' Chances "Slim"

◄  *A.P.* (3/8/09, *Inq.*):

> Abbas is the leading Palestinian proponent of a peace deal with Israel, but with a right-wing government [Netanyahu] poised to take power there, chances of new talks are slim."

[*See* "Land Swaps," in which the M.S.M. reported that Israel's mere appointment of Minister Lieberman to its cabinet destroyed all chance of new peace talks.]

# L

# Land Swaps are Kosher Unless an Israeli's Proposal

Few issues expose the M.S.M.'s Arab-Israel double-standard as clearly as "land swaps." Proposed territorial exchanges between Israel and Palestinian Arabs were reported matter-of-factly when made by Ambassador George Mitchell and Mahmoud Abbas. But when comparable land swaps were proposed by Israeli Foreign Minister Lieberman, the M.S.M. reacted angrily. The issue gained added importance after President Obama expressed his belief, in May 2011, that the final borders between Israel and a Palestinian Arab state should be "the 1967 lines with agreed swaps."

### Israeli Proposing the Same Land Swaps as Palestinian Arabs "Rules-Out" Peace Talks

◄  An article (*A.P.*, 10/31/06, *Inq.* A10, "Israeli Cabinet Adds Hawkish Partner") portrayed appointment of Yisrael Beiteinu party leader Avigdor Lieberman to the Israeli cabinet as having "effectively ***ruled out*** any serious moves to revive Middle East peace negotiations." This conclusion stemmed from his alleged advocacy for "trading Arab towns inside Israel for Jewish settlements in the West Bank" because this "would effectively strip Israeli Arabs of citizenship by shifting them to a Palestinian state." Curiously, that article's final paragraph noted that Hamas – which had "won Palestinian parliamentary elections in January and formed a government" – calls "for Israel's destruction";

yet, *that* posture apparently hadn't "effectively ruled out" peace talks.

◄ An *Inquirer* article (10/29/06) by staff-writer Warwick called Lieberman's Yisrael Beitenu party a

> **far right-wing** party, led by the **polarizing** Avigdor Lieber-man, who bluntly believes Arabs and Jews can't live together,

a man who is an

> **ultra-nationalist** who his critics say is a **racist** for his atti-tudes toward Arabs.

◄ *Inquirer* columnist Trudy Rubin opined (3/15/09) that Lieberman is

> **notorious** for calling on Israel to **rid itself** of **most** of its Arab citizens and **relocate** them to a future Palestinian Arab entity.

Ms. Rubin warned that Lieberman's "**inflammatory** views may **undercut** any new peace moves in the region."

◄ *A.P.* (6/30/10, *Inq.*, A8): "Lieberman is a *contentious* figure because he supports redrawing Israel's borders to *push* areas with heavy concentrations of Arabs into Palestinian jurisdiction."

◄ In contrast to these heated characterizations, many of them in news articles, of this Israeli minister as far-rightwing, polarizing, ultra-nationalist, racist, no-torious, inflammatory, contentious, because of his plans "to rid Israel of most of its Arab citizens by relocating them," is Lieberman's dispassionate, reasoned op-ed in the *Jerusalem Post* (6/24/10) explaining his proposal in peace-pro-moting, diplomatically-recognized terms:

> There needs to be an exchange of populated territories to create two largely homogenous states, one Jewish Israeli and the other Arab Palestinian. Of course, this is not to preclude that minorities will remain in either state where they will re-ceive full civil rights.

Lieberman cited a U.N. General Assembly resolution (55/153 of 2001) recog-nizing territorial exchanges and specifying nationality changes in such cases.

◄ The M.S.M. likewise misstated Lieberman's "loyalty oath" legislation at-tempt. (*A.P.*, 6/30/10, *Inq.*, A8): "He [Lieberman] also undertook a failed effort to force Israeli *Arabs* to take a loyalty oath or lose their citizenship." Not exactly. Here's how the *Washington Post's* Lally Weymouth phrased what Lieberman advocated when she interviewed him on March 1, 2009: "One of the reasons you are so popular is because you called for a loyalty oath for *all* citizens of Israel...."

## Media's Inconsistent Calmer Portrayal of Palestinian Arabs' and Ameri-can Land Swap Proposals

◄ *A.P.* (10/11/07): "The Palestinians are ready to yield parts of the West Bank to Israel if compensated with an equal amount of Israeli territory, the lead Palestinian negotiator [Qureia] told the Associated Press yesterday."

◄ *A.P.* (5/23/10, headlined by the *Inquirer* as "Abbas *Sheds Light* on Mideast Talks"): "The Palestinians are ready to swap land with Israel, although differences remain over the amount of territory to be traded....In previous negotiations, the two sides agreed that Israel would swap some of its territory to compensate the Palestinians, but gaps remained on the amount of land to be traded."

◄ *Arutz Sheva* reported (6/10/09): "U.S. Middle East envoy George Mitchell sounded out the Palestinian Authority on a land swap that would allow Israel to retain large population centers in Judea and Samaria in return for the PA's receiving land that includes Arab cities....The land swap idea originally was proposed by Foreign Minister Avigdor Lieberman, chairman of the Yisrael Beitenu party."

# M

## "Moderate" Abbas and Fatah vs. "Hard-Line" Israelis

There are multiple contexts in which the M.S.M. misportrays P.A. President Abbas and his Fatah movement as "moderate," and Israeli P.M. Netanyahu and other Israelis as "tough" and "hard-line." Some specific misportrayals (*e.g.*, on "killing the peace process" and the "two-state solution") are detailed elsewhere herein; here we cover blanket media misportrayal of Palestinian Arab leaders as "moderate" and Israeli leaders as "hard-line."

### Fatah Is Not "Moderate"

Resolutions adopted by "moderate" Fatah at its August 2009 Bethlehem General Assembly reveal not moderation but extremism on all principal issues.

On Jerusalem:

*Jerusalem Post* (8/8/09):

> *Return* [they never held any of it] of both **east and west Jerusalem** to Palestinian control was a "red line" which was nonnegotiable, and would need to be fulfilled before any peace talks could renew, Israel Radio reported....The document went on to state that **all** of Jerusalem, including the surrounding villages, belonged to the Palestinians, and lands conquered following the Six-Day war shared the **same status**

as those located within the green line....A document adopted by the delegates of the assembly declared that Fatah would "continue to sacrifice victims until residents of Jerusalem are **free of settlements and settlers.**"

*Christian Science Monitor* (8/11/09):

The congress adopted a resolution that *all* **of Jerusalem** be *returned* to the Palestinians.

TomGrossMedia.Com (8/14/09, Conf. of Presidents' "Daily Alert"):

Another resolution decreed that placing **both east and west Jerusalem** under Palestinian control is a 'red line' that is non-negotiable.


On Arab Refugees:

TomGrossMedia.com (8/14/09, "Daily Alert"):

A resolution approved by the assembly stated that Fatah will not give up the armed struggle until all the descendants of those claiming to be of Palestinian Arab origin can live **inside Israel.**


On Fatah's Official Armed-Wing:

*Jerusalem Post* (8/8/09, Khaled Abu Toameh, JPost.com)

The conference also endorsed the Aksa Martyrs Brigades as Fatah's *official* armed wing....The Aksa Martyrs Brigades, which was established shortly after the beginning of the second intifada in September 2000, has been responsible for many terrorist attacks – including suicide bombings – that killed and wounded **hundreds of people.**


On Israel as the Jewish State:

TomGrossMedia.com (8/11/09):

A further resolution explicitly said Fatah would **oppose recognizing Israel as a Jewish state.** In other words, in spite of misreports by apologists for Fatah in the Western media, Fatah made it clear it is still not willing to accept the principle of *two states for two peoples*: a predominantly Jewish state and a predominantly Palestinian state living side-by-side in peace.

On Jews and Arabs in Each Other's Territory:

*Jerusalem Post* (8/13/09, Caroline Glick, "Column One"):

> At the conference, Fatah's supposedly feuding old guard and young guard were united in their refusal to reach an accommodation with Israel....
>
> Both demanded that **all Jews be expelled** from Judea, Samaria and Jerusalem ahead of the establishment of a Jew-free Palestinian state.

Both demanded that any settlement with Israel be preceded by an Israeli withdrawal to the indefensible **1949 armistice lines** and by Israel's destruction as a Jewish state through its acceptance of **millions of foreign-born, hostile Arabs** as immigrants within its truncated borders.

## Abbas is Not "Moderate"

◄ On the day, September 23, 2011, Abbas addressed the U. N., seeking U.N. recognition of a western Palestine Arab state, YNetNews.com quoted Abbas:

> They talk to us about the Jewish state, but I respond to them with a final answer: **"We shall not recognize a Jewish state,"** Abbas said in a meeting with some 200 senior representatives of the Palestinian community in the US, shortly before taking the podium and delivering a speech at the United Nations General Assembly.

◄ *Jerusalem Post* (9/7/10), directly quoting Abbas: "'If they demand concessions on the rights of the refugees or the 1967 borders, I will quit. I cannot allow myself to make **even one** concession,' he said."

◄ CAMERA, Eric Rozenman, "Abbas the Relative Moderate," 3/18/09, on what Abbas briefed the Jordanian daily Al-Dustour on the 2007 Annapolis summit: "Abbas stressed that he is **opposed to the so-called 'Jewish State.'** "

◄ *Jerusalem Post* (1/11/07): "The issue of the refugees is **'non-negotiable,'** Abbas said. 'We will **not give up one inch** of land in Jerusalem . . . '"

◄ A 2007 Ami Isseroff article, http://www.zionism-israel.com/hdoc/Abbas _ROR.htm, quoted Abbas as having said of Jerusalem: "Jerusalem must *return* to our sovereignty." The article pointed out that "Jerusalem in fact was never under the sovereignty of Palestinian Arabs in all of recorded history."


## Media Portrayal of Fatah and Abbas as "Moderate"

◄ *A.P.* (11/12/09, *Inq.*, A10): "Abbas' **moderate** Fatah faction."

◄ *A.P.* (8/4/09, *Inq.*, A3): "the Palestinians' **moderate** Fatah party."

◄ *A.P.* (3/8/09, *Inq.*): "...unity talks between the Islamic **militant** Hamas and the Fatah movement of **moderate** Palestinian Authority President Mahmoud Abbas."

◄ *A.P.* (2/10/09, *Inq.*, A3): "the **moderate** Palestinian government in the West Bank."

◄ *A.P.* (2/4/09, *Inq.*, A9): "peace talks between Israel and Palestinian Authority President Mahmoud Abbas' **moderate** West Bank-based administration."

## Media Portrayal of Israeli Prime Ministers as "Hard-Line"

### Netanyahu

◄ *A.P.* (3/8/09. *Inq.*): "Abbas is the leading Palestinian proponent of a peace deal with Israel, but with a right-wing government [Netanyahu] poised to take power there, chances of new talks are slim."

◄ *Inquirer* headline (2/28/09, A2): "Israeli **Hard-Liner** Fails To Get Support" (*i.e.*, from "his chief moderate rival [Livni].")

◄ *Inquirer* sub-headline (2/24/09): "…**hard-liner** Netanyahu."

◄ *A.P.*, (2/13/09, *Inq.*, A3): "**hawkish**," "**hard-line**," "**hawkish bloc** headed by Likud," "**hawkish**," "Netanyahu's own opposition to peace-treaty talks with the Palestinians."

◄ *A.P.* (2/12/09, *Inq.*, A2): "**hard-line**," "**tough line**," "**hawks** who would stall peace-making with the Palestinians," "**hard line**," "**hawk camp**," "Netanyahu's fellow **hard-liners**."

◄ McClatchy (2/11/09, *Inq.*, A2): "**hawkish**," "national camp," "right-wing."

◄ *A.P.* (2/10/09, *Inq.*, A3): "**hawkish** candidates who would not pursue a peace deal with the Palestinians," "**hard-liners**," "**nationalist right wing**," "**hard-line**."

◄ *A.P.* (2/9/09, *Inq.*, A3): "**hawkish**," "right wing," "**hawkish**."

### Barak

◄ *A.P.* (1/17/01, *Inq.*) article led that then Israeli Prime Minister Barak
> dismissed two main Palestinian demands yesterday – lessening the chances of achieving a peace deal.

Those two demands? A "right of return" for about "four million Arabs" and Palestinian Arab sovereignty over the Temple Mount.

### Olmert

◄ 3/2/09 (*Inq.*, A3) *A.P.* article noted that "more than 110 rockets and mortar shells have exploded in Israel in the six weeks *since* it halted its air and ground onslaught against Gaza, which was meant to end the rocket threat…." The *A.P.*

quoted Olmert as promising "a severe response *if the attacks didn't stop.*" It said there was "no comment from Hamas or other Gaza militant groups," but that "several hours after Olmert spoke, a rocket exploded in southern Israel." The *Inquirer* headlined: "Israel's Leader Threatens Hamas."

# N

## "Nakba" – The "Catastrophe" of Israel's Survival

The historical event that occurred in Palestine in the 1948 period was Arab rejection of its partition into Arab and Jewish states, followed by Israel's declaration of independence at the Mandate's expiration, followed instantly by a multi-nation Arab invasion for Israel's destruction. A greater number of Middle Eastern Jews, most of whom fled to Israel where they were absorbed, were displaced from vast Muslim lands in that period than Arabs left tiny Israel. The Arab refugees' plight was, as Efraim Karsh titled his final chapter of *Palestine Betrayed,* "A Self-Inflicted Catastrophe."

Instead of telling Western readers annually that "Nakba"-commemorating Arabs are bewailing the injustice to them of Israel's "establishment…creation…founding," the M.S.M. should relate the "Nakba" to Arab partition rejection and the failure of the Arab invasion for Israel's destruction, neither of which garners more than rare M.S.M. mention.

◀ *N.Y. Times* (6/6/11, Kershner, *Inq.* A6):

> May 15, the day Palestinians mark as the "**Nakba**," or catastrophe, of *Israel's establishment* in 1948.

◀ *A.P.* (9/9/09, *Inq.*, A4):

> Palestinians say Israel refuses to recognize their hardship, including the *expulsion and exile* of hundreds of thousands during the war that followed *Israel's creation* in 1948, which Palestinians refer to as the **Nakba** or "catastrophe."

◀ Photo caption (5/16/05, *Inq.*, A6)

> To mark the 57th anniversary of **Al-Nakba**, which is Arabic for "the catastrophe." Palestinians in the West Bank and Gaza Strip held rallies to lament *Israel's founding,*

This *A.P.* article described in lead paragraph 1 "angry protesters" marching as "Palestinians mournfully commemorated the day Israel was *created.*"

# O

## "Occupied Territories" – Really, Disputed

Among the M.S.M.'s descriptions of areas captured by Israel in the 1967 war is "occupied territories." The term "occupation" is a legal concept in international law. Arguments swirl around the Geneva Conventions (which Israel claims is not applicable to Judea/Samaria), the League of Nations' Palestine Mandate (which calls for "close settlement by Jews on the land"), and other international documents. [*See* generally, *e.g.*, CAMERA "Backgrounder: Jewish Settlements and the Media"; Jewish Virtual Library, "Myths & Facts On-Line: The Settlements," and Section 2 hereof.] Israel has a strong case it is not "occupying Palestinian territory," based on its claims to its homeland. The M.S.M. engages in partisan bias in describing Judea/Samaria as "occupied."

◀ *A.P.* (4/5/11, *Inq.* A14):

> Palestinians have refused to negotiate as long as Israel builds housing for Jews in East Jerusalem and the West Bank, **occupied territory** the Palestinians claim for a future state.

◀ *L.A. Times* (3/13/11, *Inq.*, A4), on Palestinian Arabs slitting a "settler" family's throats while they slept: "… worry that violence will be renewed in **the Palestinian territories.**"

◀ *L.A. Times* (12/10/10, *Inq.*, A21):

> Palestinian officials have insisted they won't hold talks with the Israelis unless settlements in areas **occupied** in 1967 are frozen.

◀ *A.P.*, 11/11/10 (*Inq.*, A17):

> Palestinians have said they will not resume the talks unless Israel halts construction of new housing in Jewish settlements in **Israeli-occupied** West Bank and in East Jerusalem. They have demanded that Israel renew a 10-month West Bank settlement slowdown that expired in late September, and add Jerusalem to it."

◀ *A.P.*, 8/16/10 (*Inq.*, A7):

> The Palestinians want to set up a state in the lands **occupied** in 1967 – the West Bank, East Jerusalem and the Gaza Strip.

◀ *A.P.*, 7/9/10 (*Inq.*, A6):

> The Palestinians, however, are demanding that Israel indefi-

nitely freeze its settlement construction in **occupied** territories, including in East Jerusalem, before direct talks can proceed.

◄ The U.N. Secretary General has himself said that the world regards "East Jerusalem" and "the West Bank" as "**occupied** lands." *A.P.*, 3/21/10 (*Inq.*, A6), directly quoting the U.N.'s Ban Ki-Moon:

> The world has condemned Israel's settlement plans in East Jerusalem. ...Let us be clear. All settlement activity is illegal anywhere in **occupied** territory and must be stopped.

The *A.P.* on its own, in that article, added:

> Yesterday, Ban rejected Israel's distinction between East Jerusalem and the West Bank, *noting* that both are **occupied** lands.

### "Seized by Israel in 1967"

The M.S.M. sometimes likewise distorts the manner in which Israel came into possession of these "occupied lands."

Diaspora Jews old enough to remember May 1967 cannot forget the chilling, encompassing fear that we felt – and could only imagine how Israelis felt – as Arab armies massed on Israel's narrow boundaries, Jordan signed a military pact with Egypt, Egypt closed the Straits of Tiran, the U.N. folded its tents, and Nasser issued blood-curdling cries for Israel's annihilation: "We intend to open a general assault. This will be total war. Our basic aim is the destruction of Israel." And then, as it seemed a second Holocaust loomed, tiny Israel, hopelessly outclassed in every war-waging criterion – land, population, armaments –, miraculously, it seemed to us, overcame those impossible odds. The M.S.M. has repeatedly mocked Israel's gains in that defensive war for survival as lands Israel "seized" in 1967.

◄ CNN (10/2/11): "Israel on Sunday defended its decision to build 1,100 new homes in the southern Jerusalem neighborhood of Gilo, **which Israel seized** following the war in 1967."

Gilo is a south*west* Jerusalem Jewish neighborhood of about 40,000 built on ground bought by Jews *before World War II* – HonestReporting.com. It was invading Jordan that had done the seizing.

◄ *NPR* (9/16/11, "All Things Considered"): "Abbas said U.N. recognition of a state on territory **seized by Israel** in the 1967 Six-Day War will allow the Palestinians to negotiate with Israel as equals."

◄ *Washington Post* (11/2/10, Glenn Kessler): "the Golan Heights, which was **seized by Israel** in the 1967 Six-Day War."

◄ *L.A. Times* (9/17/10, *Inq.* A2): "land it [Israel] **seized** in the 1967 war."

◄ *L.A. Times* (3/10/10, *Inq.*, A1, 16): "an Orthodox neighborhood on land **seized** by Israel after the 1967 war."

◄ *A.P.* (11/27/07, (*Inq.*, A14): "Arab lands [Israel] **seized** in 1967."

◄ *A.P.* (11/23/07, *Inq.*, A3): "land [Israel] **seized** in the 1967 war."

◄ *A.P.* (3/19/05, *Inq.*, A2): "land **seized** in the 1967 war."

◄ *A.P.* (10/21/04, *Inq.*): "Palestinians claim the West Bank and Gaza - **seized** by Israel in the 1967 war - for a future state."

◄ *N.Y. Times*, 8/14/04 (*Inq.*): "[Golan Heights] **seized** from Syria"

◄ *A.P.*, 7/26/04 (*Inq.*, A2): "territories **seized** from Jordan, Egypt and Syria in the 1967 Mideast war."

◄ *Knight-Ridder*, 5/7/04 (*Inq.*): "territory it [Israel] **seized** in the 1967 Arab-Israeli war"

◄ *A.P.*, 2/7/04 (*Inq.*, A3): "territory it [Israel] **seized** in the 1967 Middle East war"

◄ *L.A. Times*, 9/15/03 (*Inq.*): "land **seized** from Syria during the 1967 Middle East War"

◄ *Inquirer* staff-writers, 2/27/02 (A2): "[Saudi offer to normalize relations] in return for Israel's withdrawal from the territories it **seized** in the 1967 Six-Day War."

◄ *A.P.* (1/28/01, *Inq.*, A4): "[areas of Jerusalem] **seized** by Israel in 1967"

Reflect on the scope of this "Seized By Israel" club's membership: the *Washington Post*, *N.Y Times*, *L.A. Times*, *A.P.*, *NPR*, CNN, *Knight-Ridder* [RIP], *Inquirer* staff-writers.

# P
# "The Palestinians" – Really, the Jews

No single term is so determinative of Western public perception of right-and-wrong in the Arab-Israeli conflict as is reference to Palestinian Arabs as "*the* Palestinians." Even Israeli and Diaspora Jews join in this usage, and recoil from suggestion they stop. But, as shown below [Section 2, IV], "Palestinian" *used to mean* primarily Palestine's Jews, and not that long ago. In December 2011, the term "Palestinian" was reopened for discussion by a comment made by a contender for the GOP's U.S. presidential nomination. Pro-Israel commentators came out of the closet in support. Given the devastating impact of the M.S.M.'s entire lexicon on what readers glean from Mideast news articles, supporters of Israel and balanced reporting should seize this opening to reeval-

uate their own usage of all its Israel-delegitimizing terms, not least our gratu-
itous bestowing upon Arabs in Palestine the mantle of "The Palestinians."

Palestine's Arabs not only deny the historicity of the Jewish people's historical connection to Israel [*See* "Denial of Ancient Jewish History."], but claim
that *they* are the aboriginal inhabitants of the land. In response to Gingrich,
P.A. Prime Minister Salam Fayyad told CNN, "The Palestinian people inhabited the land since the dawn of history," and Fatah Revolutionary Council
member Dmitri Dilani added that "the Palestinian people" are "descended from
the Canaanite tribe of the Jebusites that inhabited the ancient site of Jerusalem
as early as 3200 B.C.E." (Caroline Glick, *Jerusalem Post*, 12/12/11).

But where were these "Palestinian Jebusites" when Jewish Jerusalemites
were defending Judah and its Jerusalem capital against the Assyrian and Babylonian empires; when Maccabees were wresting Jerusalem and the land back
from Alexander's Seleucid successors; when Jewish soldiers of the Jewish
kingdom Judaea were defending Jerusalem against the Roman Empire in 63
and 37 B.C.E. and 66-70 and 132-135 C.E.?   Palestinian Arabs weren't there
at that time. Foreign Arabs conquered Palestine from its Byzantine rulers in
the year 638. Today's Palestinian Arabs are mostly descended from Arab and
other Muslim immigrants who arrived long thereafter. [*See* Section 2, IV]

The U.N. General Assembly's 1947 partition resolution repeatedly referred
to "the Jewish state" and "the *Arab* state," never using the term "Palestinian"
instead of "Arab," but the M.S.M. has anachronistically replaced "Arab" with
"*Palestinian*." This is an M.S.M. historical revisionism *smoking gun*, a demon-
strable misstatement no less than the M.S.M.'s misstatement of the Road Map
as calling upon the P.A. "to rein in *militants*," when the document uses forms
of "terror" over and over, and the M.S.M.'s mathematically monstrously wrong
misstatement for years of "*millions* of Palestinian refugees and their descendants."

◄ "1948" entry in McClatchy timeline, May 8, 2008 (*Inq.*):

> 1948: U.N. proposed separate **Jewish** and **Palestinian** states;
> Britain left on May 14…fighting between **Jews** and **Pales-
> tinians** caused two-thirds of Palestinian population to flee.

◄ *A.P.* (2/28/09, *Inq.*) referenced the UN 1947 partition plan as calling for
"…separate **Jewish** and **Palestinian** states." The *Inq.* headlined: "…separate
states for **Palestinians** and **Jews**"

◄ *A.P.* (3/16/08, *Inq.*): "…the U.N. partition plan of 1947, which envisioned
**Jewish** and **Palestinian** states living side by side in peace."

◄The M.S.M. has pressed its divestiture of Jews from equity in the term
"Palestinian" to the *reductio ad absurdum*. Jerusalem has again had a Jewish
majority since the late *1800's*. But that didn't prevent the *A.P.*, in the very
course of a rare acknowledgement of Jerusalem's Jewish majority, from ap-

portioning the population of this most important of cities between "Jews" and "Palestinians." *A.P.* (3/10/08, *Inq.*): "...about two-thirds of Jerusalem's 700,000 residents are **Jews**, and the rest are **Palestinians**." The *Inquirer's* accompanying photo caption: "...**Jews** and **Palestinians** share the waiting room at (Jewish) Shaare Zedek hospital in Jerusalem."

# Q

## "Al-Quds"– Not Your Forefathers' Jerusalem

"Naming things" is a large part of what fighting anti-Israel media bias is all about: "Judea and Samaria" vs. "West Bank," "settlements" vs. "communities," "terrorists" vs. "militants," "ceasefire lines" vs. "borders," etc. Not least in the name used to refer to it, "the core of the core is Jerusalem," as Netanyahu told a Jerusalem conference in a somewhat different context in 2010.

An article generated by Arabs (10/15/11, www.onislam.net) entitled "U.N. Warns Israel Over Al-Quds Settlements" used this appellation in its lede:

> A new Israeli plan to build a new settlement in Al-Quds (occupied East Jerusalem) is inviting huge condemnations....

An article generated by Israelis (12/15/11, *Arutz Sheva*) reported on a meeting of what is viewed as a "very popular" subcommittee dealing with the naming of cities on highway signs in Hebrew, English and Arabic, the Subcommittee for the Authorization of Place Names of the Knesset Names Committee. *Arutz Sheva* wrote:

> Of most concern is Jerusalem–Yerushalayim in Hebrew– which is called "Ursalim" in Arabic. Most of the highway signs on Road 1, in fact, currently use Ursalim, adding in parentheses the term "al-Quds," a transliteration of the Hebrew "Ir Hakodesh," or Holy City. In traditional Jewish literature, Jerusalem is usually termed "Yerushalayim Ir Hakodesh," but the latter part of the term is not commonly used today by secular Jews. Meanwhile, the Arabic term "al-Quds"–really a copy of the Jewish term–has come to be used by anti-Israel groups, signifying an "Arabized" term for the city, and indicating Arab "ownership" of Jerusalem's history.

The Western media doesn't literally call Jerusalem "al-Quds" in its "Arabized" sense. But it has on occasion come close by displacing the name of the Jewish people's holiest site in Jerusalem with the name used by Muslims who came there a millennium and a half later, calling it "Haram as Sharif, known to

Jews as Temple Mount" (*A.P.*, 1/17/01, *Inq.*, A3).

Netanyahu correctly calls Jerusalem "the core of the core" of the Jewish people's homeland connection to *Eretz Yisrael*, the land of Israel. The core of that core is the Old City and City of David, with their incalculably precious archeological remains of formative Judaism and ancient Israel. These and nearby historic Jewish neighborhoods are not some satellite "East" Jerusalem the M.S.M. calls "traditionally Arab," and in which Jews, of all peoples, are alien "settlers." They are an integral part of the Jerusalem that in the past 3,000 years has been the capital city of three native states – all of them Jewish – and which has again had a Jewish majority since the 1800's.

Jerusalem has *never* been ruled by Palestinian Arabs. The land's *next* native state following Jewish Judaea's final fall in 135 C.E. is modern Israel in 1948. The Jews' tenacious physical presence in Jerusalem from ancient times through the long post-Biblical foreign-rule centuries is summarized in Section 2 V.

# R

## Refugees – "Palestinians and Their Descendants" vs. Jews

### "Millions of Palestinian Refugees and Their Descendants"

Among journalism's more monumental misstatements was its reporting, re-iterated for years, of "millions of Palestinian refugees and their descendants from the war that followed Israel's creation," sometimes from just "Israel's creation," of which this January 4, 2001, *Knight-Ridder* sentence published, *inter alia*, on page 1 of the *Inquirer* is a classic example:

> [Under President Clinton's plan,] Palestinians would have to scale back demands that nearly *four million Palestinian refugees and their descendants* be able to exercise a right of return to land they fled or were forced to leave in 1948 during the creation of Israel. In exchange, Palestinians would gain
> ....

That single sentence contains many imbalances, but focus here on the M.S.M.'s fantastically exaggerated, reckless recitation for *years* of "*millions* of Palestinian refugees and their descendants," of which more instances are cited below.

British Foreign Secretary Ernest Bevin stated to Parliament on February 14,

1947 (Great Britain, Parliamentary Debates, Commons, vol. 433, col. 988, quoted in Bell, *Terror Out of Zion*, p. 188):

There are in Palestine about 1,200,000 Arabs and 600,000 Jews.

Samuel Katz wrote in his classic work *Battleground: Fact & Fantasy in Palestine* (paperback edition rev. 1985, p. 23):

In 1947, there were approximately one million Arabs in the whole of western Palestine. (British figures, certainly inflated, put the number at 1,200,000; independent calculations claim 800,000-900,000). Of these, the total number actually living in that part of Palestine which became Israel was, *according to the British figure* [emphasis in the original], 561,000 [footnote citing sources]. Not all of them left. After the end of hostilities in 1949, there were 140,000 Arabs in Israel. The total number who left could not mathematically have been more than some 420,000.

Media watchers' efforts eventually halted repeated media recitation of "millions of Palestinian refugees and their descendants," but the misstatement's sheer magnitude misshaped, even poisoned, many, many readers' perception of Palestine equities. Consider the frequency, and lasting impact of that frequency, with which the *Inquirer,* for one M.S.M. news purveyor, pounded "millions of Palestinian refugees and their descendants" into readers' perceptions during one particularly egregious month, January 2001:

◄ JANUARY 4, 2001: "…Palestinians would have to scale back demands that **nearly four million Palestinian refugees and their descendants** be able to exercise a right of return to land they fled or were forced to leave in 1948 during the creation of Israel. In exchange, Palestinians would gain…." (*Inq.*, 1/4/01, A1, 16, *Knight-Ridder*)

◄ JANUARY 9, 2001: "Thousands of Palestinians…were especially upset [yesterday] over Clinton's urging that Arafat relax his demand that **four million Palestinian refugees and the descendants of those who fled their homes in 1948** be allowed to reclaim them inside what is now Israel." (*Inq.*, 1/9/01, A2, *Knight-Ridder*)

◄ JANUARY 10, 2001: "Clinton's peace proposal also would give the Palestinians sovereignty over East Jerusalem and the holy site in exchange for Palestinians dropping their claim that **millions of refugees and their families** have the right to return to homes in what is now Israel." (*Inq.*, 1/11/01, A2, *A.P.*)

◄ JANUARY 12, 2001: "In return, the Palestinians would

scale back their claim of right of return to Israel for **millions of refugees and their families**." (*Inq.*, 1/12/01, A2, *A.P.*)

◄ JANUARY 13, 2001: "Israel, backed by Clinton, rejects the Palestinians' demand that it grant **nearly four million refugees and their descendants** the right to return to their former homes in Israel." (*Inq.*, 1/13/01, A4, *A.P.*)

◄ JANUARY 14, 2001: "Clinton's proposal envisions a Palestinian state in all of the Gaza Strip and almost all of the West Bank, including Arab areas and key Christian and Muslim holy sites in Jerusalem; however, the Palestinians would have to give up their demand that **millions of refugees** be allowed to return to Israel proper." (*Inq.*, 1/14/01, A2, *A.P.*)

◄ JANUARY 21, 2001: "[Israeli Premier Barak] has flatly rejected Palestinian demands that **millions of Palestinian refugees and their descendants** be allowed to return to their former homes in Israel." (*Inq.*, 1/21/01, A2, *A.P.*)

Usually at lower intensity, such M.S.M. references to "millions of Palestinian refugees and their descendants" continued for years. Unlike other M.S.M. mischaracterizations of 1948 (e.g., distortion of Palestine's attempted partition as "Israel's 1948 creation" or "founding," and of the Arab invasion as "the war that followed Israel's creation" without the invading Arab states even named), "millions" was a *mathematical* misstatement. It should not have endured as long as it did.

And in addition to the literally incorrect "millions of Palestinian refugees and *their* descendants," ambiguous phrases like "millions of refugees and descendants," sometimes combined with suggestive expressions, left open to reader interpretation that "millions" had left. For example, the *Washington Post* (4/16/04) referred to "Mohammed Dhahir and **millions of other Palestinian refugees** who have long claimed rights to the land **they** left behind."

Contesting the *Inquirer's* persistent "millions of Palestinian refugees and their descendants" became the first campaign of the weekly "Brith Sholom Media Watch," of which this book's co-author Verlin has been the writer. After considerable correspondence in 2002 and 2003, then-*Inquirer* Foreign Editor Ned Warwick sent Verlin an *Inquirer* foreign staff research memo Warwick had commissioned, followed by an *Inquirer* "clearing the record" the next time "millions" appeared. The writer of that foreign staff memo wrote in part:

> Mr. Verlin is right in saying there are not millions of refugees from the 1948 war....I believe the *Inquirer* has at times been too inexact in its use of language to state the number of people involved....

But in the M.S.M.'s leading lights, "millions" endured.

◀ The *Washington Post* stated on 4/16/04 that, in endorsing P.M. Sharon's disengagement plan, President Bush may have lowered the hopes of one

> Mohammed Dhahir and **millions of other Palestinian refugees** who have long claimed rights to the land **they** left behind.

◀ The *N.Y Times* wrote on 4/14/04 of

> American rejection of the right of **millions of Palestinian refugees** from the Arab-Israeli war of 1948 **and their descendants** to return to their lands in what is now Israel.

The media watchdog group CAMERA garnered corrections from both groups.

*Washington Post* (4/19/04):

> An April 16 report from Jordan that referred to millions of Palestinian refugees should have noted that this includes the descendants of the refugees who fled in 1948 from lands that are now Israel.

*N.Y. Times* (4/17/04):

> A news analysis article on Thursday about President Bush's endorsement of Prime Minister Ariel Sharon's plan to withdraw the Israelis from Gaza referred *imprecisely* to the number of Palestinian refugees for whom Arabs have demanded the "right of return." The reference to millions encompassed not just Palestinian refugees from the Arab-Israeli war of 1948 but also their descendants.

Ah, "imprecisely," indeed.

That same week, the *A.P.* appeared to have gotten the message. It began the week (*A.P. Inq.*, 4/12/04):

> Israel also wants assurances that **millions of Palestinian refugees and their descendants** will be barred from returning to Israel

but ended it (*A.P. in Inq.*, 4/16/04):

> Arafat said in a televised speech that he would never give up the right of return of the **hundreds of thousands of Palestinians** who fled or were forced from their homes in the war that created Israel, as well as their descendants. [We wonder if the *A.P.* ever told Arafat what he'd said.]

CAMERA also garnered a correction from *NPR*, which had reported on April 15, 2004:

> **millions** of Palestinians *who fled* during the Arab-Israeli War of 1948.

Los Angeles area media watcher David Frankenthal elicited a correction from the *L.A. Times*, which had reported on April 24, 2004, p. 10:

> **millions** of Palestinian refugees who fled or were driven out during Israel's war of independence.

The breathtaking scope of this multi-magnitude misstatement of "***millions of Palestinian refugees and their descendants***" by the pillars of American journalism – the *N.Y. Times*, the *Washington Post*, the *A.P.*, the *L.A. Times*, *NPR* – inevitably affected public perception in a fashion that could only have been extremely devastating to Israel.

But as horror-movie sequels have shown, stakes don't always stick in vampires' hearts.

*N.Y. Times*, July 24, **2007** (Kershner, *Inq.*, A2):

> the fate of **millions of Palestinian refugees** who fled after the 1948 war **and their descendants.**

And even, *Jerusalem Post* editorial, March 4, **2009**:

> [U.S. Secretary of State Hillary] Clinton needs to tell Abbas to abandon his outrageous demand for the "right" of "return" for **millions of Palestinian refugees and their descendants** to Israel proper.

(Brith Sholom Media Watch engaged in a successfully-concluded exchange of correspondence with the *Jerusalem Post's* editorial page editor regarding that statement.)

But, vampire watchers, keep your mallets and wooden stakes at the ready.

> Alan Dershowitz, May 25, **2011**,
>
> (http://www.hudson-ny.org/2151/obama-explains-and-makes-it-worse)

> The Palestinian leadership must recognize, as I believe they do, that there will be no "right of return" of **millions of Palestinian refugees and their descendants** to Israel. Compensation can be negotiated both for those Palestinians who left Israel as a result of the 1948 wars and for those Jews who left Arab countries during and after that same period.

Prof. Dershowitz is among the Good Guys, but here he explained and made it still worse.

## Jewish Refugees From Muslim Lands

The M.S.M. invariably distorts the Arab-Israeli conflict's "refugee" issue as pertaining solely to "Palestinians who fled or were forced from their homes during Israel's creation," as seen in the examples above of just the times it said "millions."

Over and over in describing the 1948 Arab-Israeli war's Arab refugees, the M.S.M. employs graphic terms – "uprooting...expulsion and exile...forced from their homes...forced to leave...forced out...expelled...driven from... forced from their lands...forced from lands...driven out...driven from their homes...fled their homes" – to describe their displacement from Israel. In contrast, during the first years of Brith Sholom Media Watch, the *Inquirer*-Israel-coverage-focused weekly media watch written by co-author Verlin, BSMW found two lonely articles on the Jewish refugees from Muslim lands in that era.

◄ One traced the history of the Jews of Iraq (*A.P.*, 4/18/03, *Inq.*), depicted as a community stretching back millennia to the "Babylonian captivity" of 10,000 Jews seized from the conquered kingdom of Judah in 597 B.C.E.:

> [M]any remained here on the Tigris and Euphrates rivers, down the generations, and by the mid-20th-century they numbered about 250,000....For centuries under the Turkish Ottoman Empire, Muslims and Jews lived peacefully together here [not exactly the case]. By the 1940's, however, Nazi-inspired pogroms terrorized the Jewish community and, after Israel's founding in 1948, about two-thirds **left** for new beginnings there. Thousands more **left** through the years, amid discrimination and persecution that ebbed and flowed.

◄ A second, authored by S. S. Nelson (*Knight-Ridder*, 1/8/04, *Inq.*, A13), noted that a possible thaw in Libyan-Israeli relations had prompted Libyan leader Gadhafi to signal

> willingness to allow Libyan Jews to **emigrate** to Israel. He also proposed compensating Jews who had already **emigrated** for property confiscated from them.

So, in contrast during those years to the 1948 Arab-Israeli war's Arab refugees, whom *Inquirer* readers were told had been uprooted, expelled, exiled, forced from the homes, forced to leave, forced out, driven from their homes, *Inquirer* readers were told this about that war's Arab lands' Jewish refugees – they emigrated, they left.

More recently, occasional pieces have started to employ some of the images of wrenching displacement the M.S.M. has applied to Arab refugees all along:

◄ *A.P.* (2/22/09, *Inq.*, A4):

> Hundreds of thousands [of Middle Eastern Jews] **fled** or were **expelled** from Arab lands around the time of Israel's 1948 creation, and today, only several tens of thousands remain.

◄ *A.P.* (9/14/08, *Inq.*, A21, paragraphs 14-15, of 18):

> The 1950's, according to the Jewish Agency, which handles immigration, saw the arrival of 765,000 Jews from North

Africa and the Middle East, **driven out** by the Arab backlash that followed Israel's creation....

Starting in the early 1980's, Israel clandestinely airlifted 80,000 members of Ethiopia's ancient Jewish community, nearly 15,000 of them in just two days in 1991.

Displacements of Christian and even Muslim Mideast minorities have likewise received but little journalistic notice of the M.S.M. Consider how little known is the ethnic cleansing of Iraqi Kurds upon which a little light was shed in this (*Knight-Ridder*, 3/15/03, *Inq.*, A4) article:

**Tens of thousands** of Kurds, Turkmen, and other minorities have been living in the northern [Kurdish controlled, "no-fly" zone] enclave since being **expelled** from the Kirkuk region by Hussein's Baath Party in waves of **ethnic cleansing**. Thousands have been killed or have disappeared, their property given to Arabs from elsewhere in Iraq. The "**Arabization**" program is aimed at consolidating Baghdad's grip on oil-rich areas dominated by minorities.

...and its final three (17th - 19th) paragraphs...

New York-based Human Rights Watch charged in a report yesterday that the "**Arabization**'" campaign has **continued unabated** since the 1991 uprising.

The group said it "believes that the Iraqi government's systematic and continuing forced transfer" of some 120,000 minority-group members is a crime against humanity.

If U.S. troops invade, the report said, they must prevent displaced people from wreaking vengeance on those who expelled them and those who occupied their properties.

[*See* Section 2, XVIII, XIX].

# S

# "<u>S</u>ettlements" if Jewish, "Neighborhoods, Villages" if Arab

"Settlements" is a dirty word, connoting intrusion into a place of people who have no roots there. The *Inquirer*, for one, instantly retracted it when it applied it to Arabs. *Inquirer* (3/16/02, A4):

Clearing the Record:    In an *Inquirer* article Thursday [3/14/02] on President Bush's news conference, the words **"Palestinian settlements"** were used in reference to attacks by the Israeli military in the West Bank and Gaza Strip.  The attacks were directed at Palestinian towns and refugee camps.

Actually, Israel's "attacks" were directed "at" terrorists *in* those "Palestinian towns" and Arab "refugee camps" from the *1948* war.  And at least once the media called Jews living in Israel "settlers": A 12/30/08 *Inquirer* editorial referred to "Hamas rocket attacks on Jewish settlements in southern Israel."

## "Jewish Settlements" versus "Palestinian Towns, Villages, Neighborhoods"

The M.S.M. contrasts "Jewish settlements" with "Palestinian neighborhoods," "towns" and "villages."  Many of the news as well as opinion articles cited herein use these terms, but the contrast is most pointed when "settlements" and these contrasting terms are used close together.  For example:

◄   An editorial (3/11/10, *Inq.*) contrasted a **"Jewish settlement** in East Jerusalem" against a **"Palestinian neighborhood"** nearby.

◄   An article (*L.A. Times*, 3/13/11, *Inq.*, A4) contrasted "Jewish *settlers*" living in "a West Bank Jewish **settlement**" in "*the Palestinian territories*" near an Arab "**village**" with "*residents.*"

## Even Jews *Re*-establishing  What Had Been Jewish Jerusalem Neighborhoods are "Settlers"

◄   *Knight-Ridder* (3/15/04, *Inq.*).  *Ten times* in an article on Jews attempting
>    to **reestablish** a Jewish presence in what **had been** a Yemenite Jewish village in the Silwan neighborhood [of Jerusalem] until Arab riots in the 1920's and '30's *drove the Jewish residents out,*

that article denigrated those Jews as "settlers."

## There Is No "East" Jerusalem and Jews are Not Jerusalem "Settlers"

Jerusalem has been one single, undivided city from before its capture by King David (c. 1000 B.C.E.) until the present day, with one brief nineteen-year exception (1948-1967).  During that interval, part of the city was invaded and illegally seized by Transjordan (renamed Jordan in 1951) until its ouster from west of the Jordan River by Israel.

Yet today's M.S.M., almost a half-century after that brief division of Jerusalem ended, insistently incessantly refers to the part of Jerusalem that invading Transjordan had held as though it were a separate city of "East"

Jerusalem; indeed, it labels Jews "settlers" if they choose to continue to live in that part of this city that has had a Jewish majority since the 1800's. Jerusalem's political and demographic history [*see* Section 2 V], shows that Jews are the *last* of all peoples whose relation to Jerusalem is that of alien settlers.

### The Media Acknowledges Jews Reject Being Called Jerusalem "Settlers"

*A.P.* (12/28/09):

> Israel insists that Jewish neighborhoods in East Jerusalem are not settlements, but rather part of its own capital.

The *A.P.* is right about Israel's insistence. Netanyahu told a Jerusalem conference on February 17, 2010:

> [T]he core of the core is Jerusalem. Jerusalem is the capital of Israel; Jerusalem is the capital of the Jewish people; Jerusalem is unified, it is indivisible and it will stay that way.

Netanyahu told AIPAC (American Israel Public Affairs Committee) in March 2010:

> The Jewish people were building Jerusalem 3,000 years ago and the Jewish people are building Jerusalem today. Jerusalem is not a settlement. It's our capital.

This view is held also by the majority of Diaspora Jewry, regardless of political persuasion and religious movement. In that same month of March, 2010, the then-leader of the liberal Union of Reform Judaism, which represents America's one million Reform Jews, Rabbi Eric Yoffie, told an assembly of U.R.J. leaders:

> The Union of Reform Judaism, like most American Jewish organizations, supports a united Jerusalem under Israeli sovereignty.

> This means that we believe housing units constructed in Jerusalem by Israel are not settlements and they are not illegal [he added, advocating a "temporary moratorium," that "a great many things that are legal are not prudent or wise."]

The liberal Israeli paper *Haaretz* reported:

> Yoffie asserted that Israel should not renounce the claim to all of Jerusalem as Israel's eternal capital, or Israel's right to build anywhere within Jerusalem's borders.

## 2010 – Just One Year's Worth of Media Denigrating Jews as "East" Jerusalem "Settlers"

The M.S.M. incessantly hammers-home an image of upper-case "E" "East" Jerusalem's distinct existence and the "settler"-status of Jews residing therein. The intensity of this blanket-rhetoric can be gleaned from noting the media's repetitious use of these terms in the course of a year:

◀ *A.P.*, 1/23/10 (*Inq.*): "Abbas has said repeatedly that he will not resume negotiations without a complete Israeli **settlement** freeze in the West Bank and **East** Jerusalem."

◀ An *Inquirer* editorial (3/11/10) used "**settlement**" eight times, contrasting a "Jewish settlement in **East** Jerusalem" [Ramat Shlomo] with a nearby "Palestinian **neighborhood**."

◀ *L.A. Times* (3/11/10, *Inq.*, A8): "[Israel plans] new housing units in **East** Jerusalem."

◀ *N.Y. Times* (3/12/10, *Inq.*, A4): "housing units for Jews in **East** Jerusalem."

◀ *A.P.* (3/13/10, *Inq.*, A2): "new Jewish housing in **East** Jerusalem….housing for Jews in **East** Jerusalem."

◀ *A.P.* (3/14/10, *Inq.*, A11): "…a new Jewish housing project in **East** Jerusalem."

◀ *A.P.* (3/15/10, *Inq.*, A2): "…plans to expand a Jewish neighborhood in **East** Jerusalem….1600 [planned] homes for Israelis in **East** Jerusalem….the fate of **East** Jerusalem is the most explosive issue."

◀ *L.A. Times* (3/16/10, *Inq.*, A4):

> A day after calling for calm, Israeli Prime Minister Benjamin Netanyahu *pushed* Israel further toward confrontation with the United States yesterday by declaring that housing construction in Jerusalem would *continue unchanged*. "Construction in Jerusalem will continue in any part of the city, as it has during the last 42 years," he told a meeting of his Likud Party, referring to the Jewish expansion in **East** Jerusalem that began after Israel captured the territory in 1967.

(Note how, to the *L.A. Times*, Israel saying it would "continue" to do "unchanged" what it had been doing for 42 years "*pushed*" Israel toward confrontation with the U.S.)

◀ *N.Y. Times* (3/17/10, *Inq.*, A3): "Jewish building in **East** Jerusalem….scattered disturbances by Palestinians in **East** Jerusalem….Israeli control and construction in **East** Jerusalem….the Palestinians want **East** Jerusalem for their future capital…Israel has annexed **East** Jerusalem….plans for 1,600 new Jewish housing units for **East** Jerusalem….**East** Jerusalem housing plans… .proposing to remake an entire Palestinian neighborhood in **East** Jerusalem."

◄ *N.Y. Times* (3/18/10, *Inq.*, A6): "a diplomatic crisis over building in contested **East** Jerusalem....in and around **East** Jerusalem....plans for 1,600 new housing units for a Jewish neighborhood in **East** Jerusalem....Israel annexed **East** Jerusalem....the Palestinians claim **East** Jerusalem....new building projects in **East** Jerusalem....Israeli building in Jewish neighborhoods of **East** Jerusalem....The Palestinians oppose all Israeli building in **East** Jerusalem. Palestinian leader Mahmoud Abbas said Israel had to stop all **settlement** activity before any talks could start."

◄ *A.P.* (3/18/10, *Inq.*, A6): "Israeli construction in **East** Jerusalem....every new housing project in **East** Jerusalem....**East** Jerusalem **settlements**....While Israelis consider the **neighborhoods** to be like any other in the city, in the eyes of the Palestinians, Washington officials, most governments in the world, and the United Nations, they are **settlements** like those Israel has built in the West Bank."

◄ *A.P.* (3/19/10, *Inq.*, A3): "disputed **East** Jerusalem," "Israel's plans to build 1,600 apartments for Jewish residents in **East** Jerusalem," "the Ramat Shlomo neighborhood in **East** Jerusalem," "Palestinians claim **East** Jerusalem as their land."

◄ *L.A. Times* (3/20/10, *Inq.*, A2): "Israel's plan to build 1,600 housing units in **East** Jerusalem."

◄ *A.P.*, (3/21/10, *Inq.*, A6): "Israel has agreed to curb **settlement** construction in the West Bank, but not in **East** Jerusalem."

◄ A 4/15/10 *N.Y. Times* photo caption referred to the Jewish Jerusalem neighborhood of Ramat Shlomo as "a Jewish settlement in the West Bank." On 4/18/10, *Arutz Sheva* reported that, following receipt of a complaint from CAMERA, the *Times* issued this correction:  "It is a **neighborhood** in **East** Jerusalem, not a settlement in the West Bank." ["Neighborhood" is good, but *Arutz Sheva* went on to call "East Jerusalem" and "West Bank" misleading.]

◄ *N.Y. Times* (5/4/10, *Inq.*, A8): "...a complete **settlement** construction freeze by Israel, including any additional Jewish housing in **East** Jerusalem."

◄ *A.P.* (5/8/10, *Inq.*): "The Palestinians refuse to enter into direct negotiations unless Israel halts all **settlement** construction in the West Bank and **East** Jerusalem, which the Palestinians claim as a future capital."

◄ *A.P.* (5/23/10, *Inq.*, A4): "Israel wants to annex major Jewish **settlements** in the war-won West Bank and **East** Jerusalem."

◄ *A.P.* (5/28/10, *Inq.*, A5): "The Palestinians have insisted that Israel impose a full freeze on **settlement** construction in the West Bank and **East** Jerusalem, captured areas they claim for their future state – in order to hold direct talks."

◄ *A.P.* (6/1/10, *Inq.*, A4): "...plans for additional **settlements** in a part of Jerusalem that Palestinians consider the likely capital of a new Palestinian state."

◄ *N.Y. Times* (6/1/10, *Inq.*) called Israel and the U.S. as being "at odds" over "**settlements** in **East** Jerusalem."

◄ *A.P.*, 7/9/10 (*Inq.*, A6): "The Palestinians, however, are demanding that Israel indefinitely freeze its **settlement** construction in occupied territories, including in **East** Jerusalem, before direct talks can proceed."

◄ *A.P.* (7/17/10, *Inq.*, A2):

The Palestinians have warned White House envoy George J. Mitchell that it will be difficult to revive peace talks if Washington cannot stop Israel from demolishing Arab homes or building for Jews in **East** Jerusalem.

Abbas has said he won't return to the negotiating table unless Israel freezes all **settlement** construction in the West Bank and **East** Jerusalem.

◄ *A.P.* (8/11/10, *Inq.*, A3):

[Abbas wants] Israel's acceptance of a Palestinian state that would include the West Bank, **East** Jerusalem, and Gaza Strip, with minor adjustments. Abbas also wants a freeze on Israeli **settlement** construction in **those** territories, which were occupied by Israel in the 1967 Mideast War.

◄ *A.P.* (8/16/10, *Inq.*, A7): "The Palestinians want to set up a state in the lands occupied in 1967 – the West Bank, **East** Jerusalem and the Gaza Strip."

◄ *N.Y. Times* (9/2/10, *Inq.*, A16): "[Abbas wants] an end to Israeli **settlement** building in the West Bank and **East** Jerusalem and the right of Palestinian refugees to return to their homes in what is today Israel."

◄ *N.Y. Times* (9/15/10, *Inq.*, A3): "The United States has long opposed Israel's **settling** of Jews in **East** Jerusalem."

◄ *A.P.* (10/9/10, *Inq.*, A3): "Foreign ministers from the 22-member Arab League warned Israel of the consequences of continuing **settlement** construction in the Palestinian territories and **East** Jerusalem."

◄ *A.P.* (10/12/10, *Inq.*, A6): "Some 300,000 Jewish settlers live in the West Bank, in addition to nearly 200,000 Israelis living in Jewish **neighborhoods** in **East** Jerusalem." [Note contrasting depictions of Jewish communities across the "Green Line": "neighborhoods" are in "East" Jerusalem, but "settlers" inhabit the West Bank.]

◀ *A.P.* (10/26/10, *Inq.*, A2): "[Palestinian negotiator Saeb Erekat said] Israel was acting unilaterally through **settlement** construction in the West Bank and **East** Jerusalem."

◀ *A.P.* (11/9/10, *Inq.*, A4): "… **settlement** activity–including the **East** Jerusalem projects."

◀ *A.P.* (11/11/10, *Inq.*, A17): "Palestinians have said they will not resume the talks unless Israel halts construction of new housing in Jewish **settlements** in **Israeli-occupied** West Bank and in **East** Jerusalem. They have demanded that Israel renew a 10-month West Bank **settlement** slowdown that expired in late September, and add **Jerusalem** to it."

◀ *A.P.* (11/22/10, *Inq.*, A2): "Mahmoud Abbas said a proposed 90-day freeze on Israeli **settlement** construction would not get him back to the negotiating table unless it includes **East** Jerusalem, a condition Israel staunchly opposes."

◀ *N.Y. Times*, Bronner (12/14/10, *Inq.*, A12): "the proposed [90-day building] freeze excluded **East** Jerusalem."


## When Just "East" Isn't Deemed Clear Enough, There's "Traditionally Arab East"

The M.S.M. on occasion feels the need to be more pointed about "East" Jerusalem meaning "*Arab* East":

◀ *A.P.* (3/21/10, *Inq.*, A6): "**traditionally Arab Eas**t Jerusalem."

◀ *Inquirer* foreign affairs columnist Trudy Rubin (*Inq.*, 3/18/10): "Continued building [by Israel] in and around **ARAB EAST** JERUSALEM makes it impossible for this part of the city to become – as it must in any peace settlement – the capital of a Palestinian state."

◀ *A.P.* (1/21/10, *Inq.*, A6): "the **traditionally Arab eastern sector** of the city"

◀ *A.P.* (7/20/09, *Inq.*, A1): "**traditionally Arab East** Jerusalem"

◀ *A.P.* (3/24/05, *Inq.*, A3), quoting unidentified "Israeli lawmakers": "Sharon's government has revived a plan to build 3500 new housing units around the settlement to encircle **Arab east Jerusalem** with Jewish neighborhoods."

◀ *N.Y. Times* (3/22/05, *Inq.*, A3): "Palestinians criticized the [Maale Adumim] expansion plan as an attempt to expand the Jewish presence in and round **the traditionally Arab eastern parts of Jerusalem.**"

◀ *Knight-Ridder* (9/5/04, *Inq.*, A5): "**ARAB EAST** Jerusalem, which both Palestinians and Israelis claim as their own." (Rather begs the question, doesn't it?)

## But How "Arab" was "Arab East Jerusalem" – Really?

What the M.S.M. calls "East Jerusalem" is the historical heart of Jerusalem; it includes the Old City with its Temple Mount, Western Wall, and Jewish, Christian and Armenian as well as Muslim (not just "Arab") Quarters, plus residential neighborhoods held by Jordan between 1948 and 1967. This "East" Jerusalem is not even really "East" of Jerusalem; for example, the over-the-Green-Line Jewish neighborhood of Gilo is southwest of the Old City and west of some Jerusalem areas on the Israeli side of the "Green Line." Nor is "East" Jerusalem a satellite city offset in that direction from a main city in the sense that "East Chicago" (which is in Indiana) is offset from Chicago and "East St. Louis" (which is in Illinois) is offset from St. Louis.

Nor was Jerusalem "traditionally Arab," either historically or demographically. Palestinian Arabs have never ruled any part of the city. Before Transjordan invaded in 1948, the last foreign Arabs to have ruled Jerusalem were foreign dynasties that ruled it – much of the time under control of the Turks – between the Arab conquest in 638 and the Crusade in 1099.

◄ As for demographics, Martin Gilbert in *Jerusalem, Rebirth of a City*, p. 44, quoted an 1847 British visitor:

> Dr. Kitto commented on the inhabitants. "Although," he wrote, "We are much in the habit of regarding Jerusalem as a Moslem city, the Moslems do not actually constitute more than ***one-third*** of the entire population."

◄ British Consul James Finn, 1858:

> The Mohammedans of Jerusalem are less fanatical than in many other places, owing to the circumstances of their numbers scarcely exceeding ***one-quarter*** of the whole population– and of their being surpassed in wealth (except among the Effendi class) in trade and manufactures by both Jews and Christians. ["British Consul James Finn to Earl of Clarendon, Jerusalem, 1 January 1858, FO 78/1383 (Political No. 1), in Hyamson, Consulate, 1, p. 257," quoted in Peters, *From Time Immemorial*, p. 198 and n.27.]

Note that both of these mid-19th century references refer to *all* Muslims, not just Arabs, as constituting just "one-third" or "one-quarter" of Jerusalem's population.

◄ *Boston Globe* columnist Jeff Jacoby (7/22/09):

> Palestinian irredentists claim that eastern Jerusalem is historically Arab territory and should be the capital of a future Palestinian state. In reality, Jews always lived in eastern Jerusalem – it is the location of the Old City and its famous

Jewish Quarter, after all, not to mention Hebrew University, which was founded in 1916. The apartment complex that Obama opposes is going up in what was once *Shimon Hatzadik*, a Jewish neighborhood established in 1891. Only from 1948 to 1967– during the Jordanian occupation – was the eastern part of Israel's capital "Arab territory." Palestinians have no more claim to sovereignty there than Russia does in formerly-occupied eastern Berlin.

◄ Zionist Organization of America News Release (6/6/11), "ZOA Refutes Propaganda Lies About Jerusalem By the Arab/Muslim World":

> [M]edia reports routinely refer to the parts of the city that Israel won in the 1967 war as "historically Arab East Jerusalem." In fact, the accurate description would be "historically Jewish East Jerusalem."
>
> There has been a Jewish majority throughout Jerusalem since the 1800's. The Jewish majority in "eastern Jerusalem" was interrupted only by the 1948 Arab war against newborn Israel, when the Jewish residents of that part of the city were forced to flee for their lives....
>
> Dr. Ben-Arieh's research reveals the historical irrelevance of many of the phrases and clichés that are in vogue today. The label "Quarters," – referring to the Jewish Quarter, Muslim Quarter, Christian Quarter, and Armenian Quarter in the Old City – was imported to the Holy Land by European visitors during the 1800's....there were many Jews living in the Christian, Muslim and Armenian "Quarters" throughout the 1800s, right up until they were driven out by Arab pogromists in the 1930's....Ben-Arieh also mentions that some contemporary Arab neighborhoods in eastern Jerusalem, such as Silwan, were originally Jewish neighborhoods whose residents were murdered or expelled by Arab pogromists, who then occupied their homes and made these neighborhoods de facto Arab villages.

## Even "Moderate" Fatah Demands "ALL" of Jerusalem

The subsection on "Moderate Abbas and Fatah" references the resolutions, not widely reported by the M.S.M., which Fatah adopted at its 2009 General Assembly in Bethlehem. If there is an Arabic word for *chutzpah*, it applies to the resolution adopted on Jerusalem, which the *Jerusalem Post* (8/8/09) and *Christian Science Monitor* (8/11/09) reported as demanding "the **return** of both east and west Jerusalem to Palestinian control."

# T

## "Terrorists" – What Media's "Militants" Actually Are

The M.S.M.'s propensity to mislabel murderers of Israeli civilians merely as "militants" has become so deeply engrained in Mideast reporting that railing against such euphemizing of terrorism may seem futile. But there are several contexts in which such media misusage of the plain meaning of English words has to be fought. These include:

(1) Where the intended carnage is so heinous no term but "terror" suffices;

(2) Where the perpetrating group openly flaunts attacking civilians;

(3) M.S.M. exclusion of Israel from worldwide war against terror;

(4) Replacing "terror" with "militants" in media's indirect quotes;

(5) Media violation of its own 'usage of terrorist' guidelines;

(6) Media calling incontrovertible murderers "suspected militants."

But note, first, that media euphemizing of mass-murderers of Israeli civilians is not universal. The *Dallas Morning News*, for one paper, announced in July 2005 that it had stopped labeling people who "strap bombs to their chests and detonate them in an Israeli café" as "insurgents." It said: "They are terrorists."

### (1) Intended Carnage So Heinous No Term But "Terror" Suffices

◄ In March 2011, a Palestinian Arab snuck into the house of a Jewish family asleep at night and stabbed to death the father, mother, children aged 11 and 3, and an infant. The 3/13/11 *Los Angeles Times* article (*Inq.*) reported:

> **Palestinian militants** have *defended previous such attacks* against Jewish settlers in the West Bank, describing the settlers as combatants in the conflict rather than civilians.

Sleeping children are not "combatants,"and defending slitting their throats is not "militancy."

### (2) Perpetrating Group Openly Flaunting Attacking Civilians

Even Palestinian Arab groups openly flaunting their intention to keep attacking Israeli civilians doesn't drive the M.S.M. to abandon its euphemizing of them as "militants."

◄ The 6/20/02 *Inquirer's* Israel article reported on dispatchers of "suicide" bombers who'd exploded and incinerated Jerusalem city buses two days in a row vowing to continue such carnage. The Inquirer headlined: "Jerusalem Hit Again – And *Militants* Promise More …."

◄ A 4/24/11 *McClatchy* article (*Inq.*, A6), reporting on explosion in Jerusalem of a bomb "packed with small ball bearings" that killed one and wounded dozens at a bus station included this vow of one group's "armed wing":

> [T]he al-Quds Brigade, the *armed wing* of the Palestinian Islamic Jihad, **welcomed** the attack and vowed to **continue** targeting **cities** deep inside Israel.

Hamas, for one group, revels in flaunting its attacks on Israeli civilians.

◄ An *L.A. Times*, 11/2/06 (*Inq.*, A6) article used this lede: "Israeli troops backed by tanks and helicopter gunships killed eight Palestinians" in a Gaza clash with "extremists who have made it the *prime launching ground* for rockets into Israel." Israel's intent was "to stop the *daily* firing of Kassam rockets into southern Israel." But "Hamas' *military* wing issued a statement saying it had *no intention* of halting the rocket attacks."

◄ Midway down, the *A.P.'s* 1/20/04 (*Inq.*, A8) article rather matter-of-factly quoted Hamas founder Yassin that "the Islamic group would *increasingly recruit* female suicide bombers" because "male bombers were increasingly being held back by Israeli security measures":

> Also yesterday, the founder of Hamas said *the Islamic group* **would increasingly recruit female suicide bombers.** Last week, Hamas sent its first female assailant, a 22-year-old woman who blew herself up at the Gaza-Israel crossing and killed four Israeli border guards. Sheikh Ahmed Yassin said in Gaza that there had not before been a need for women to carry out bombings. Now, he said, women must step up to fulfill their obligations. He suggested that male bombers were increasingly being held back by Israeli security measures.

Yet the *A.P.* called this a statement of an "Islamic group," not of a "terrorist" group.

In a targeted-attack two months later, Israel killed this terrorist leader who had been brazenly advertising for female mass-murder bombers. The *Inquirer* reacted on successive days by ignoring this fact: On 3/23/2004, the op-ed page headlined "Did Peace Die Along With Sheikh Yassin?" [Brith Sholom Media Watch asked (rhetorically), "Did Medical Ethics Die With Mengele?"] and on 3/24/2004, the editorial cartoon by in-house cartoonist Tony Auth depicted Israel as strangling the peace dove.

◄ A *Bloomberg News* article (12/14/11), "Hamas Marks 24th Anniversary, Says It Killed 1,365 Israelis," quoted a Hamas leader: "The armed resistance and the armed struggle are our only choice to liberate the land, to liberate all of Palestine from the sea to the river and expel the invaders," Ismail Haniyeh, the top Hamas leader in Gaza, told the crowd. The article summarized Hamas' accomplishments:

> Hamas *militants* have carried out 1117 attacks against Israel, including 87 suicide bombings, and have launched 11,093 rockets at Israeli targets, according to the e-mailed statement.

*Bloomberg News* headed the section of its article including these terrorism statistics a recap of Hamas' "*Military* Operations."

◄ In 2001, Israel target-killed a Hamas terrorist, whom the *Jerusalem Post* (11/25/2001) described thusly:

> [He was wanted] for masterminding the 1997 terrorist attacks in Jerusalem's **Mahaneh Yehuda** shuk and **Rehov Ben-Yehuda** pedestrian mall, which killed 21 people. Security sources said he also had a hand in most of the major suicide bombings this past year, including the June 1 attack at the **Dolphin disco** in Tel Aviv and on August 9 at the **Sbarro pizza parlor** in Jerusalem, which claimed the lives of 36 people and over 200 wounded. He was also behind the 1999 suicide bombings in Haifa and Tiberias in which there were no casualties. Abu Hanuod's expertise was the ability to link bomb makers with suicide bombers. Security officials said that Abu Hanuod had recently dispatched suicide bombers from Tulkarm, but those attacks were foiled at the last minute. He was in the midst of preparing more suicide attacks inside the Green Line, security sources said last night.

On this topic on this same day, the lede of a Knight-Ridder article (*Inq.*, A2, "Israel Defends Assassination") portrayed him militarily…

> An unrepentant Israel yesterday defended the assassination of the radical Hamas movement's *military* leader, with Foreign Minister Shimon Peres calling Mahmoud Abu Hanuod "a professional terrorist" who was planning more attacks.

…and it wasn't until paragraph 15 (of 19) that the battlefield record of this "military leader," which paragraph 15 acknowledged had been his involvement "in a long string of terror attacks," was elucidated:

> The prime minister's office released a statement late Friday saying Abu Hanuod had been involved in a long string of terror attacks, including this year's bombings of a Sbarro pizzeria in Jerusalem and a discotheque near Tel Aviv. It noted that Abu Hanuod had been jailed for a time by Palestinian security officials, but had been set free.

The M.S.M. doesn't write that Palestinian Arabs and their supporters "*consider*" the parts of Jerusalem, Judea and Samaria that Jordan had seized and held from 1948 to 1967 to be places now called "East Jerusalem" and "the West Bank," or that they "*consider*" Jews living there to be alien "Jewish settlers." The M.S.M. writes that these places *are* "East Jerusalem" and "the West Bank," and that Jews there *are* "Jewish settlers." But with all this *flaunted* involvement in terrorism, the M.S.M. doesn't write that Hamas *is* a terrorist organization. It writes that Hamas is "deemed," "labeled," "considered," "classified as" a terrorist organization. But the cold fact is that mass murderers of civilian bus passengers and restaurant patrons *are* terrorists. This is far clearer and more certain than that "East" Jerusalem and "the West Bank" are place-names known to history, and that Jews, of all peoples, living there are alien "settlers."

◀ *A.P.* (10/11/11, *Inq.*, A9): "The militant Islamic group [Hamas] is **considered** a terrorist organization by the United States and the European Union, among others."

*A.P.* (*next day*, 10/12/11, *Inq.*, A6): "Hamas has sent *dozens* of suicide bombers into Israel, killing *hundreds*."

◀ *A.P.* (8/17/11, *Inq.*, A6): "Hamas, which Israel, the United States, and the European Union have **labeled** a terrorist group."

◀ *A.P.* (4/3/11, *Inq.*, A12): "The Iranian-backed group [Hamas] has killed *hundreds* of Israelis in rocket attacks and suicide bombings."

But *A.P.* three days later, (4/6/11, *Inq.*, A6): "Hamas is **deemed** a terror group by the United States."

◀ *A.P.* (6/4/10, *Inq.*, A4): "**Most** Western countries **classify** Hamas, which has killed *hundreds* of Israelis in suicide bombings and other attacks, as a terrorist group."

◀ *A.P.* (11/24/09, *Inq.*, A1, 8): "Israel, the United States, and the European Union **label**" Hamas, "the Iranian-backed group that controls Gaza," to be "a terrorist group for sending suicide bombers into Israel, killing *hundreds*."

◀ *N.Y. Times* (Isabel Kershner) reported (8/10/07, *Inq.*) that "Israel refuses to deal with Hamas, which Israel **considers**" to be "a terrorist organization."

◀ *A.P.* (1/19/07, *Inq.*): "Israel said it could not feed money [the $100 million in tax funds it released that week to Abbas] to a Hamas-led government, **labeling** Hamas a terror group because of its history of *dozens* of suicide bombings that killed *hundreds* of Israelis over the last decade."

◀ *L.A. Times* (3/19/06, *Inq.*): "Israel, the United States, and the European Union **consider**" Hamas to be "a terrorist organization" for having "carried out dozens of suicide attacks" against Israelis.

◀ *A.P.* (2/13/06, *Inq.*, A3): "[Hamas] has killed *hundreds* of Israelis in suicide bombings....[Hamas] has been **branded** a terrorist organization by the United States"

◄ *Inquirer*, 1/28/03: "Israel and the United States **consider** them [Hamas and its ilk] terrorist organizations."

◄ *Inquirer* (Jerusalem Bureau Chief Matza), 6/11/03: "Many attacks on Israelis have been suicide bombings carried out by Hamas, an Islamic resistance group the United States **considers** a terrorist organization."

### (3) M.S.M. Excluding Israel From Worldwide War Against Terror

◄ The *Baltimore Sun* ran a December 1, 2002 (*Inq.*, A2, "Israel Tries To Link Itself With U.S. War On Terror") article that led:

> Since the Sept. 11 attacks, Israel has been trying to link its battles against Palestinians to the Bush administration's global war against terrorism. But...Israel has been unable to convince the world that it is fighting the same war as the United States.

The article explicitly distinguished "Palestinian militant groups" from terrorists:

> While the differences might be lost on Israelis – who say they are the targets regardless of who is doing the targeting – the distinctions are crucial to the Palestinians. They believe their fight for a state is legitimate and to some extent justifies the use of violence.

◄ Not just "Palestinian militants," but *Al-Qaeda-linked* groups have targeted Israel, as reflected in the headline ("Qaeda-Linked Group Threatens Israelis, in Hebrew") and text of a Yahoo News article (11/18/10):

> DUBAI (*Reuters*)–An **al-Qaeda-linked** group issued a Hebrew threat on Thursday to avenge Israel's killing of two Gaza **militants**, in what an expert said was the first use of the language for such propaganda.
>
> In the half-minute-long recording posted on a website used by declared al Qaeda affiliates, a hoarse male voice tells the "aggressor Jews" they will not be safe from rockets and other attacks until they "leave the land of Palestine."

◄ An article (*A.P.*, 12/30/07, *Inq.*, A2) quoted bin Laden himself:

> "We intend to liberate Palestine, the whole of Palestine from the [Jordan] river to the sea....We will not recognize even one inch for Jews in the land of Palestine..." **bin Laden** said.

◄ That was not the first time al-Qaeda itself had expressly threatened Israel.

A *Reuters* report (9/11/06), headlined on its website "Al Qaeda Warns of Attacks in Gulf, Israel," led that al Qaeda had

> warned in a video aired on the fifth anniversary of the September 11 attacks that U.S. allies Israel and the Gulf Arab states would be its next target in a campaign that would seal the West's economic doom.

The *Reuters* report directly quoted deputy Al-Qaeda head al-Zawahiri warning the West:

> You have to bolster your defenses in two areas....[T]he first is the Gulf... and the next [target] is Israel. The current of holy war is closing on it and your end there will put an end of the Zionist-crusader supremacy.

On the other hand, examples are legion of the M.S.M. freely using "terror" to describe terrorism directed at *non*-Israelis.

◄ The *Inquirer's* 4/30/04 front-page headlined

> Battlefields *Around the World* were in the Thick of the Counter**terror** Fight Yesterday

above a set of references under the heading "*Many Fronts* in the War On **Terror**" to articles on Uzbekistan, Britain, the Philippines, Spain and the U.S.

◄ Terror can strike right next-door to Israel, and be reported as such by the same *Inquirer* reporter who called the eleven Israeli athletes murdered at the Munich Olympics "killed" by "Palestinian guerrillas"(*Inq.*, 3/13/04, Matza). The October 29, 2002, *Inquirer* ran a front-page staff-writer article on the murder of a U.S. diplomat in Jordan, in which Jerusalem Bureau Chief Matza raised the issues "as to whether it was a result of **terrorism**," "the work of a **terror** group," and whether "it appeared to be an act of **terrorism**."

There may be room for debate in distinguishing "militancy" from "terrorism," but the dividing line must not be the ethnicity of the victim. In the summer of 2002, one of this book's co-authors (J.V.) spoke at a grassroots Jewish community protest on the *Philadelphia Inquirer*'s sidewalk. He began:

> We're here today because *mass murderers* who pack bombs with nails, screws, rat poison and hate, to murder and maim as many men, women and children as they possibly can, in buses, restaurants, shopping malls, discos, pool halls, parks and a Bat Mitzvah and a Passover seder, aren't *militants*, anytime, anywhere. They're *terrorists*, every time, everywhere.

## (4) M.S.M. Replacing of "Terror" with "Militants" in Indirect Quotes

"Indirect" quotation, paraphrasing what an official, spokesperson or document literally said, is common and accepted in news articles, but grants no license to alter meaning or nuance. A clear breach of that fidelity obligation occurs when a news article indirectly quotes an Israeli or other leader or spokesperson as having referred to attackers of Israeli civilians as "militants," when the speaker had not used that term. Israeli leaders and spokespersons are so unlikely to euphemize murderers and those bent on murdering Israeli civilians as "militants" that the media should directly quote any Israelis so using that term.

### "Israel" "Saying Militants"

◀ *A.P.* (9/4/11, *Inq.*, A6):

> **Israel** *says* that Gaza's Hamas rulers get weapons, ammunition, and rockets through the tunnels and smuggle **militants** out.

> …**Israel** *says* Gaza **militants** entered Sinai through the tunnels and crossed back into Israel, attacking vehicles and killing eight Israelis [six of them civilians].

◀ Note this lede of this news article (*A.P.*, 4/29/07, *Inq.*):

> The Israeli army shot four Palestinian **militants** who were trying to *plant explosives* near the Gaza Strip border fence yesterday, killing three and seriously wounding one, an Israeli army spokeswoman *said*.

### Bibi "Saying Militants"

◀ On August 21, 2005, *Knight-Ridder* reporter Nissenbaum, writing as an *Inquirer* staff-writer, wrote that Netanyahu had "warned" in his pre-Gaza withdrawal cabinet resignation letter protesting Israel's impending Gaza withdrawal…

> that Israel's move would create a fertile environment for **militants**,

…perhaps not recalling or caring that just a fortnight earlier, August 9, 2005, she had co-authored with *Inquirer* Jerusalem Bureau Chief Matza an *Inquirer* article that had quoted Netanyahu's cabinet resignation letter directly:

> "I am not willing to be part of a process that ignores reality and proceeds to establish an Islamic **terror** base that will threaten the entire country," Netanyahu wrote in his resignation letter.

◀ See also (*A.P.*, 12/20/05, *Inq.*):

> Netanyahu has condemned Sharon's Gaza pullout, *saying* the

unilateral move encouraged Palestinian **militants** to wage more attacks against Israel.

Sharon "Saying Militants"

◄ *A.P.* (5/9/05, *Inq.*):

> Prime Minister Ariel Sharon *said* yesterday that Israel would not release more Palestinian prisoners until the Palestinian Authority took tougher action against **militant** groups – the latest sign of trouble for a strained cease-fire.

But *Haaretz,* not the most militant of Israeli newspapers, had published on the preceding day, 5/8/05, a "*Haaretz* Service and The Associated Press" article, which *Haaretz* headlined:

> PM: No Further Prisoner Releases Until PA Acts Against **Terror**

Its lede:

> Prime Minister Ariel Sharon **said** Sunday that Israel will not release any more Palestinian prisoners until the Palestinian Authority 'fulfills its commitment to crack down on the **terror** organizations."

The *N.Y. Times* (5/9/05, Erlanger) had him say both (which he didn't):

> Mr. Sharon *said* the prisoners would remain behind bars until the Palestinian Authority moved harder against **terrorism and militancy**, telling his cabinet, "Let it be clear, there will be no prisoner release before steps are taken against **terror**," said an official who briefed reporters.

◄ An article (*A.P.*, 4/21/04) directly quoted Sharon that, in Israel's ongoing fight against "terror," it had targeted two successive "murderers" at the head of Hamas:

> "We will fight **terror** and we will not let up on them," Sharon said. "In that way, we got rid of the first **murderer**, and that way a few days ago we got rid of the second **murderer**, and that is not the end."

The *Inquirer* headlined this article: "Sharon: Hamas **Officials** Remain Potential Targets."

Olmert "Saying Militants"

◄ Less "right-wing" Israeli P.M. Olmert got the M.S.M.'s terror-paraphrase treatment, via this headline (*A.P.*, 12/31/07, *Inq.*):

> Israel Calls For Crackdown; The peace process can't move forward, Olmert *said*, until Palestinians rein in **extremists**.

But the *A.P.*'s paragraph 5 said what he'd said:

> "As long as the Palestinian Authority doesn't take the necessary vigor against **terror** organizations, Israel won't be able to carry out any change that would expose it to any jeopardy or endanger Israel's security," he *said*.

## "Settlers" Saying "Militants"

◀ *Inquirer* Jerusalem Bureau Chief Matza (2/3/04, A2) directly quoted a "settler" leader:

> I have no doubt that the current government will not survive if Sharon carries out this [Gaza withdrawal] plan, especially since **terrorism** is still calling the shots.

The article summarized settlers' contention as

> Settlers contend their presence, along with army units assigned to protect them, keep Palestinian **militants** bottled up.

## "Mickey and Me"

One of this book's co-authors had an e-mail exchange with Michael Matza, then the *Inquirer*'s Jerusalem Bureau Chief, regarding whether a Matza-quoted Israeli spokesperson had actually used the term "militants."

In June, 2002, a Matza *Inquirer* article directly quoted Israeli government spokesperson Ranaan Gissin:

> Given the fact that the Palestinian Authority is doing nothing…we have to deploy our forces in such a way that **[militants]** won't be able to leave their launching pad.

Co-author Verlin e-mailed Mr. Matza, asking him what was the term Mr. Gissin had actually used for which the *Inquirer* had substituted "militants" in brackets. Mr. Matza replied:

> Dear Mr. Verlin:
>
> The word Mr. Gissin used in his quote was "they." Because the word "they" would have been unclear, we substituted the word "militants" and placed it in brackets to accurately convey Mr. Gissin's meaning.
>
> Sincerely, Michael Matza.

To which co-author Verlin replied:

> Dear Mr. Matza:
>
> Thanks very much for your e-mail supplying the word ["they"] actually used by Mr. Gissin. To be perfectly frank,

I'd suspected he'd used a different word, also beginning with 'T'. To that extent, I did you injustice.

However, still to be perfectly frank, I do not think that your putting the word "militants" in brackets did in fact "accurately convey Mr. Gissin's meaning."...What you did, Mr. Matza, was to...stuff the media's word "militants" into a direct quote of an Israeli official, as though he'd have used it. Would Sharon's spokesman really have used it? If not, it was not Mr. Gissin's meaning that you accurately conveyed to your readers. Am I wrong?

Jerry Verlin

That ended the e-mail exchange, but that's how Michael Matza, chief of the *Inquirer*'s only-such-place-in-the-world Jerusalem Bureau, came by the *nom de guerre* "Mickey Militant."


## Media Paralleling Direct "Terrorists" Quote with Indirect "Militants" Quotes

Some news articles place a direct quote of an Israeli spokesperson saying "terror" in parallel with a paraphrase using "militants." Consider:

◀ *A.P.* (8/23/03, *Inq.*):

> Israel vowed to hunt down and kill **militant** leaders unless Palestinian authorities rein in the armed groups.... "Israel hasn't closed the door on the road map," spokesman Dore Gold said. "But there are really two possibilities: Either the Palestinian Authority will begin to dismantle the **terrorist** infrastructure – or Israel will."

Perhaps, through paralleling a speaker's directly quoted use of "terrorists" with a paraphrase saying "militants," the M.S.M. is signaling to readers that "militants" is the accepted term for the group the speaker called "terrorists" [like telling readers that an Israeli who'd called Judea and Samaria "Judea and Samaria" had used "the biblical name" for "the West Bank"].


## Media on Americans and Europeans Calling Terrorists "Militants"

◀ The 8/25/01 *Inquirer* directly quoted President Bush:

> If the Palestinians are interested in a dialogue, then I strongly urge Mr. Arafat to put 100 percent effort into solving **terrorist** activity, into stopping the **terrorist** activity....The Israelis have made it very clear that they will not negotiate under **terrorist** threat.

The *Inquirer* introduced this *three-times*-using-"terrorist" direct quote with:

President Bush, speaking at a news conference in Crawford, Texas, said yesterday that Arafat "can do a better job" of reining in **militants**.

◄ *Inquirer* article (3/30/02):

Powell called on countries around the world to condemn Palestinian attacks...."Let's be clear about what brought it all [Gen. Zinni's efforts] to a halt: **terrorism**....That's what has caused this crisis to come upon us – not the absence of a political way forward, but **terrorism** in its rawest form," Powell said.

The *Inquirer* article added:

Powell's call for others to join him in urging Arafat to crack down on Palestinian **militant** groups went unheeded.

◄ Near the end of a news article (12/11/01, *Inq.*) appeared:

In Brussels, the 15-nation European Union called on Arafat to dismantle "the **terrorist** networks Hamas and Islamic Jihad....

The article characterized the EU foreign ministers as having issued a statement

calling on Arafat to dismantle **militant** Palestinian groups and declare an end to the violent uprising against Israel. European countries traditionally have tilted toward the Palestinians, and the move reflected the increasing international pressure on Arafat to crack down on **militants.**

Media on *Arafat* Calling Terrorists "Terrorists"

On February 3, 2002, PLO leader *Arafat* wrote a celebrated Sunday *N.Y. Times* op-ed in which he referred to some of the M.S.M.'s "militant" Palestinian Arab groups in these terms:

They are **terrorist** organizations, and I am determined to put an end to their activities.

Arafat was characterized (*A.P.*, 2/4/02, *Inq.*) as having used

some of the strongest language he has ever used to denounce Palestinian **militants** who carry out bombings and shootings against Israeli civilians.

The *A.P.* proceeded to observe...

Israel has dismissed Arafat's efforts to actually rein in the Palestinian **militant** groups as superficial at best,

...and quoted Colin Powell:

"I'm pleased [Arafat] condemns **terrorism**, and that's good.

Now what we need is action against **terrorism**,"
whose directly-quoted statement was prefaced with

the United States has demanded that the Palestinian leader do
more to crack down on **militants**.

What was all this really about? The *A.P.* explained:

Arafat did not cite any "terrorist groups" [*A.P.*'s quotation
marks] by name, and several recent shootings and a bomb attack have been carried out by the Al Aqsa Brigades, which is
part of Arafat's Fatah movement. Most of the suicide bombings that have killed dozens of Israelis were carried out by the
Hamas and Islamic Jihad groups. Arafat has been reluctant
to confront Palestinian **militants**, and some of his own followers expressed skepticism that it would be any different this
time. A West Bank leader of the Al Aqsa Brigades, who gave
his name as Abu Mujahed, said Arafat "is under great pressure, especially from the Americans, and because of that, he
describes us as **terrorists**."

### Road Map Calling On P.A. "To Rein In Militants"

In 2003, U.S. President Bush promulgated the "Road Map" plan for phased-
implementation of Arab-Israeli peace. Phase I expressly required the Palestinian Authority to end "violence and *terrorism*," to confront "all those engaged
in *terror*," to undertake "dismantlement of *terrorist* capabilities and infrastructure," to "declare an unequivocal end to violence and *terrorism*." [*See* Section
2, I] But the M.S.M. substitutes "militants," a term that does not appear in the
Road Map.

As with the M.S.M.'s mischaracterizing of the U.N. partition resolution as
having called for Jewish and "Palestinian" states, the M.S.M.'s misstating of
the Road Map in this terrorists-to-militants euphemizing way is a brazen bias
*smoking gun*.

◀ *A.P.* 9/18/03: "...disarm the **militants**, as required by the road map."

◀ *Inquirer* sub-headline 9/28/03, A16: "The road map to peace calls for **militants to be reined in**...."

◀ Knight-Ridder (S.S. Nelson) 11/13/03: "[a "key" road map provision is]
the disarming and dismantling of **Palestinian militant groups**."

◀ *A.P.* (12/18/03): "[the road map] calls on the Palestinians to dismantle
**militant** groups."

◀ *A.P.* (2/7/04, *Inq.*, A3): "... road map calls for Palestinians to **rein in militants**."

◀ *A.P.*, (4/2/04, *Inq.*, A2), describing the Palestinians' Road Map obligation: [T]he U.S. diplomats made it clear they expected the Palestinians to honor their road map obligations – particularly the requirement to **dismantle violent groups.**

◀ *A.P.*(7/2/05): "Israel and the United States [not to mention the Road Map] have demanded that Abbas disarm **militant** groups, including Hamas and Islamic Jihad."

◀ *Washington Post* (12/6/05): "Israeli Prime Minister **Sharon has demanded** that Abbas disarm the Palestinian groups **as a prerequisite for progress** on the U.S.-backed road map to peace." [This is a *requisite* of the road map, not a "Sharon-demanded *pre*requisite.]

◀ The *A.P.* reported (5/18/09) that Netanyahu has "*tried to persuade* the Americans" that Hamas "must be reined in before peacemaking with the Palestinians can progress," but that "the Americans have not been persuaded." [Actually, it's the Americans who've *been doing* the persuading.]

## (5) Media Violation of Its Own "Usage of Terrorist" Guidelines

The *Philadelphia Inquirer* has had a style manual (rev. Dec. 2002) covering usage of "terrorist" and "terrorism." It began by cautioning: "[G]roups and factions often wish The *Inquirer* to characterize their foes as terrorists in order to make them appear as enemies of the United States and its people." It listed five contexts in which use of "terror" is appropriate: "In direct quotations" (the only context not requiring editor approval); in indirect quotes of government officials using the term; "to describe an individual or group that has credibly claimed responsibility for terrorist acts"; to describe someone convicted of "an act of terrorism"; and

> In *rare* cases where the question of terrorism is not in dispute, such as the attacks of Sept. 11, 2001, or at **the Munich Olympics**, or historical events such as the attack on the Archduke Francis Ferdinand in Sarajevo.

It admonished: "Militant is not to be used in an attempt to avoid saying terrorist."

> To describe a group, use words that describe what it has done or what it is accused of doing. An example: The group Hamas, which has admitted involvement in many suicide bombings, claimed responsibility [*Inq.*-speak for "credit"] for the attack.

◀ Contradicting the *Inquirer's* own guidelines' specific citing of "the Munich Olympics" as one of three examples it gave of "rare cases where the question of terrorism is not in dispute," that newspaper's Jerusalem Bureau Chief stated in a 3/14/04 (*Inq.*, A2) article that the eleven Israeli athletes murdered by terrorists there had been "killed" by **"Palestinian guerrillas."**

## (6) M.S.M. Mis-describing Incontrovertible Murderers as "Suspected Militants"

The extremes to which the M.S.M. has gone to bestow presumption of innocence – *"suspected* militants" – upon attackers of Israeli civilians would be comical if these "suspects'" actions were harmless.

◄ *Inquirer* (8/17/02): "Israeli soldiers destroyed two houses belonging to *suspected* West Bank militants yesterday," [but neither was there to protest because earlier in the year each **suspect** "**blew himself up**," as the article put it, one killing 17 Israelis and the other wounding two.]

◄ *Inquirer* (11/8/02):

Also yesterday, a *suspected* Palestinian suicide bomber and an apparent accomplice were killed in an explosion at a military checkpoint near the Jewish settlement of Kedumim, near the West Bank city of Nablus, the army said.

The *suspected* bomber, one of three Palestinians in a taxi stopped at the checkpoint, was **wearing an explosive belt and yelled** "**Allahu Akbar**" ("God is great") as he ran at the troops, who fired at the man, the army said. The belt exploded, killing the second man and injuring the third. It was not clear whether the bomber detonated the explosives or whether the shooting caused the blast.

◄ The *A.P.* reported on 2/11/03 (*Inq.*, A13) that "Israeli troops killed two *suspected* Palestinian militants." One, killed while trying to escape soldiers who called on him to surrender, was a "senior fugitive" of the Popular Front for the Liberation of Palestine, "a radical PLO faction." The other, killed "near the Jewish settlement of Netzarim," was "carrying an assault rifle and hand grenades, the army said."

◄ An article (*A.P.*, 8/23/03, *Inq.*, A2) started thusly: "Israeli troops killed a Palestinian bombing **suspect**" the previous day. The article identified him as "a follower of the Al Aqsa Martyrs Brigade," and quoted the Israeli military that he had been "involved in an Aug. 12 suicide bombing that killed an Israeli man in a supermarket in central Israel, a charge **confirmed** by Al Aqsa members."

◄ *Washington Post* (8/30/03, *Inq.*):

An Israeli man was killed when a *suspected* Palestinian assailant fired at his car....Shalom Harmelech was killed when a *suspected* Palestinian gunman shot at his car....Israeli officials said. The Al Aqsa Martyrs Brigade, associated with Palestinian leader Yasser Arafat's Fatah faction, **claimed responsibility** for the attack.

◀ An article (*A.P.*, 5/4/05, *Inq.*, A3) reported that for "the first time a *suspected* member of a Hamas rocket squad was taken into custody [by Abbas' P.A.] since the group promised Abbas in March that it would halt attacks on Israel." He was arrested with a rocket launcher in his car "minutes after insurgents had fired two rockets toward an Israeli town." The article noted that he was shortly released by the P.A. under Hamas and Egyptian pressure.

◀ *A.P.* (11/5/08, *Inq.*, A7):

> Hamas then fired mortars across the Gaza border into southern Israel, and Israel answered with the air strike, killing five *suspected* Palestinian extremists, Israeli **and Palestinian** officials said. The army said the air strike aimed at the mortar launchers and him them.

# U

## United Nations – Even Worse In The Press

### Misreporting The "Goldstone" Commission's Commission

Even in dealing with the United States, Israel has had troublesome first-hand experience with whether express written assurances of current presidents survive their presidency. [*See*, e.g., Eliott Abrams' 6/26/09 *Wall Street Journal* article on President Bush's written agreements with Israel on construction in Judea/Samaria made in connection with Israel's Gaza withdrawal.] It is understandable, therefore, why Israel might not cooperate with a United Nations inquiry where the U.N. agency's then-president's assurances were oral, not written, and to the effect that what was "implied" in an investigating panel's commission – investigating both sides' "alleged" international law violations – overrode its express written commission to investigate "Israel's" already-determined-to-have-occurred violations. That is exactly why Israel didn't articipate in the U.N.'s investigation of "Cast Lead" Israel-Hamas fighting in Gaza.

*A.P.* (7/16/09, *Inq,.* A4):

> The United Nations has launched a probe, headed by a respected war-crimes prosecutor [a Jewish South African judge named Goldstone], into the actions of *both* Israel and Hamas.

"… both Israel and Hamas"? *Jerusalem Post* article on that same day quoted the U.N.'s exact written words (paragraph 14) in the Goldstone Commission's commission:

> "...investigat[ing] all violations of international human rights law and international humanitarian law *by the occupying power, Israel, against* the Palestinian people throughout the Occupied Palestinian Territory, particularly in the occupied Gaza Strip, *due to the current aggression* (Cast Lead).

It was a kangaroo court, as commissioned. So where did the *A.P.*'s "both" come from? That *Jerusalem Post* article quoted Judge Goldstone as having "indicated" to the "then-president of the [U.N.'s] Human Rights Council" Goldstone's view that the commission should examine "*alleged* war crimes and human rights violations on all sides," and that the then-president told him that "this was already *implied* in the resolution."

The *Jerusalem Post* article then quoted an Israeli Foreign Ministry spokesperson that the language of the Goldstone panel's written commission was NEVER CHANGED. "'There is no formal expansion of the mandate. The only relevant mandate is the one which includes operational paragraph 14 [quoted above]....That's the only legal basis of this mission,' said [spokesperson] Levy."

### Burying the Palmer Report on Israel's Legal Gaza Blockade

The *Inquirer* obsessed on "Israel's deadly raid on an aid flotilla bound for Gaza" for over a year. The *Inquirer*'s coverage began on June 1, 2010, with a huge (greater than 12 sq. in.) headline and sub-head at the top of its front page "Outcry, Crisis After Deadly Raid By Israel...." Every day for a week, the *Inquirer* ran an article on Israel's "aid flotilla raid"on its front page or A2, and many more articles through the summer and fall, and some in 2011, with "raid" appearing in headline and text over and over, down to August 18, 2011 (*Inq.*, A6), which the *Inquirer* headlined "No Israel Apology To Turkey Over Raid."

On September 2, 2011, the *Inquirer* ran a *N.Y. Times* article which it headlined: "U.N.: Israeli Blockade of Gaza Legal," which reported

> the [U.N. Report's] conclusion that Israel's naval blockade is in keeping with international law and that its forces have the right to stop Gaza-bound ships in international waters.

The *Inquirer* ran this bomb-shell U.N. report on page *18.*

But the *very next day*, the *Inquirer* (9/3/11) ran above-the-fold on front page A1, and article it headlined:

> Turks Oust Top Israeli Diplomat; They Want an Apology for a Raid Last Year

# Delegitimizing the Jews of Hebron as "Ultranationalist Jewish Settlers"

In the context of reporting the U.N.'s objections to Israel declaring the Cave of the Patriarchs and Rachel's Tomb national heritage sites, the *A.P.* delegitimized Hebron's Jews as "ultranationalist Jewish settlers" in "the West Bank."

◄ On February 23, 2010 (*Inq.*, A8, "Clashes Erupt in West Bank City"), the *A.P.* reported that "the Palestinians," who "claim all of the West Bank as part of a future state," were "enraged" that Israel had added "a disputed Hebron shrine," the Cave of the Patriarchs, along with "a second **West Bank shrine**," Rachel's Tomb, to its list of national heritage sites. The article, which called Hebron Jews "**ultranationalist Jewish settlers**," reported that the U.N.'s representative "*noted* the sites were holy to Jews, Christians, and Muslims alike."

◄ Three days later (*A.P.*, 2/26/10, *Inq.*, A17, "Netanyahu Tries To Calm Tension on Shrines"), Netanyahu was quoted as saying that designating the shrines as heritage sites wasn't "a political decision," just "concerned with preserving heritage." The article continued: "The move angered Palestinians, who want Israel out of the territory. The United States, United Nations, and some European nations have expressed opposition [to Israel's action]." For the second time that week, the *A.P.* labeled Jews in Hebron, one of the Yishuv's historic four holy cities with Jewish connections going back to Israelite origins, "**ultranationalist Jewish settlers.**"

The M.S.M.'s term "ultranationalist Jewish settlers" conveys that Jews have no historical connection to this "West Bank" city, Hebron. The U.N.'s "noting" that the Cave of the [Jewish] Patriarchs, and the Tomb of [Jewish matriarch] Rachel, are "holy to Jews, Christians, and Muslims alike" is an attack on the Jewishness of every Jewish shrine which Transjordan managed to grab in 1948-1967. And the U.N. can no more "note" that Rachel's Tomb, what the media calls "a West Bank shrine," and the Patriarchs' Cave are "holy to Jews, Christians, and Muslims alike," than it can "note" that Rachel's Tomb is "a mosque." [*See* Shragai, *Jerusalem Post*, November 8, 2010: "Until 1996, Nobody Called Rachel's Tomb a Mosque; Analysis: UNESCO's recent designation flies in the face of Jewish history, Islamic tradition and Ottoman confirmation."]

There is insufficient space here to recount the historical connection of M.S.M.-labeled "ultranationalist Jewish settlers" with Hebron. But it includes Abraham, the Biblically-detailed terms of whose purchase of the Cave "authentically reflect the social customs of the second millennium [B.C.E.]." (Dr. John Bright, *A History of Israel,* p. 72); David, who was crowned King there; its defense by King Hezekiah of Judah against the Assyrians; and its recovery for Judaea by the Maccabees from the Seleucids; the building there of "an ancient Jewish shrine, which was also venerated by Christians," of which "the Muslim sanctuary is largely of crusading or earlier Jewish construction" (Dr. James Parkes, *Whose Land? A History of the Peoples of Palestine,*" pp. 168-

169); and Hebron's status as one of the Yishuv's four Holy Cities. There may not be a city on earth which has longer links to a people than this "West Bank" city of Hebron has to these "ultranationalist Jewish settlers."

# V

## Violence – Israeli Responses Are Not "Offensives" and "Retaliation"

We look at three levels of media misportrayal of Palestinian Arab-Israeli violence: Who started it? Are Israel's responses against perpetrators of attacks on Israeli civilians fairly labeled Israeli "retaliation"? When Israel is driven by incessant, even escalated, rocketing of Israeli civilians from Gaza to go into Gaza to stop it, are such actions Israeli "offensives," and does the M.S.M. fairly portray the rocketing escalation that forced Israel into such action?

### Israel's Response as "Starting" the Violence

In M.S.M. cause-and-effect physics, it's often not Arabs attacking Israelis, but Israel *responding* to Arab attacks, that starts violence.

◀ A classic instance occurred on 8/23/01 (A3); the *Inquirer* told readers:

> [T]he day's **violence began** in the early hours when an **Israeli** antiguerrilla unit **shot and killed** a Palestinian, Ahed Haniya, *who was setting a bomb* on a roadside close to a Jewish settlement, Palestinian and Israeli sources said.

◀ *A.P.* (12/22/10, *Inq.*, A10):

> Israel on Tuesday launched heavy air strikes on Gaza in *retaliation* for Palestinian rocket attacks, **raising the prospect** of a new round of bloody fighting after a two-year lull.

◀ Can Palestinian Arabs' actions, as opposed to Israeli responses, raise prospects of flare-up? Yes, but the Arabs really have to work at it. The *A.P.*'s March 20, 2011 (*Inq.*), article led:

> Palestinian extremists in Gaza fired *more than 50* mortar shells into Israel on Saturday, **the heaviest barrage in two years**, Israeli officials said, **raising the prospect** of a Mideast flare-up.

Elsewhere than in Israel, "the heaviest barrage in two years" *would be* a "flare-up." (The *Inquirer* headlined this "heaviest barrage in two years" as, ho-hum, "Shells Fired From Gaza Into Israel.")

◄ An article (*L.A. Times*, 3/13/11, *Inq.*, A4) on a Palestinian Arab breaking into a Jewish "settler" family's home at night and murdering the parents and three children raised

> worry that violence *will be renewed* in the Palestinian territories and heightened fear of retaliation by settlers or the Israel Defense Forces.

Apart from whether Israeli response against perpetrators of such attacks on civilians sinks to "retaliation" [*see* immediately below], slitting a sleeping family's throats while they slept *was* a "renewal of violence."

## **"Retaliation" – Media-Speak for Israel Shooting Back at the Terrorists**

Webster defines "retaliate" as "to return like for like, esp. injury for injury," derived from "re" + "talio," meaning "punishment in kind." Is that what Israel does – "retaliate" – when it targets, not Arab civilians, but the *very* terrorists who attack Israeli civilians with rockets, mortars and "suicide" bombs? The M.S.M.'s repeated labeling of Israel's responses against attackers of Israeli civilians as Israel "retaliating" denigrates the legitimacy of Israel's inescapable response against terrorists preying on its civilians into the mud of terrorists attacking civilians. It is the mirror-image of the M.S.M.'s labeling those terrorists "militants."

◄ *A.P.* (8/26/11, *Inq.*, A6), "Gaza Extremists Call 2d Cease-fire":

> The factions had called a cease-fire late Sunday, but it dissolved almost immediately in a volley of rocket fire from Gaza on southern Israel and **retaliatory** Israeli air strikes.

◄ An article (*McClatchy*, 8/21/11, *Inq.*, A2) on terrorists who had crossed into Israel from Sinai and murdered six Israeli civilians in cars and buses, and two soldiers, on Israel's Eilat-Beersheba road, and then fled back into Egypt with the I.D.F. on their heels, called "the **ensuing** fighting between Israeli forces and suspected assailants" in Egypt part of "Israel's **retaliation**" for the "ambush that killed eight Israelis."

◄ *N.Y. Times* (8/22/11, *Inq.*, A6) reported "a **retaliatory** Israeli strike in Gaza aimed **at** the *militant* group that Israel said *carried out the attack* led to rocket fire from Gaza into southern Israel."

◄ In April 2011, Hamas claimed "responsibility" for launching a *guided anti-tank* missile at a *school* bus in Israel, mortally wounding a schoolboy. Without mentioning either that the bus Hamas claimed credit for targeting was a *school* bus, or that Hamas had fired a battlefield missile meant for a tank to target it, the *Inquirer* headlined its 4/8/11 (*Inq.*, A11) *A.P.* article, "Hamas Hit on Israeli Bus Draws **Retaliation**." The *A.P.'s* lede mentioned both of these facts:

An anti-*tank* missile fired from the Gaza Strip struck a *school* bus Thursday in southern Israel, wounding the two people on board, one of them critically, and prompting fierce Israeli **retaliation** that killed five Palestinians.

Some might regard as "fierce" the targeting of a school bus with a guided missile meant for a tank, but doubt was cast on the propriety of the *A.P.* lede's reference to Israel "retaliating" by reference to what Israel targeted [not Gaza school buses] in paragraph 2, and on the propriety of the A.P. lede's identification of those killed as "five Palestinians" by reference to the non-civilian status of at least four in paragraph 3.

Paragraph 2 acknowledged that the airstrikes and tank fire that Israel "unleashed" in its "heaviest assault" on Gaza since its "broad military offensive" two years ago was directed "*against Hamas targets.*" Paragraph 3 identified those "five Palestinians" left unidentified in the lead. One was claimed by an Arab official to be a civilian. "Three others were extremists," and the fifth "a *Hamas* policeman."

The article two days later (*A.P.*, 4/10/11, *Inq.*, A6) reported: "Hamas says Israel used excessive force in its **retaliation.**"

◀ A 4/24/11 *McClatchy* article (*Inq.*, A6), reporting on explosion in Jerusalem of a bomb "packed with small ball bearings" that killed one and wounded dozens at a bus station, included:

> [T]he al-Quds Brigade, the armed wing of the Palestinian Islamic Jihad, **welcomed** the attack and vowed to **continue** targeting **cities** deep inside Israel.

The article directly quoted an Israeli official on what the article called his call "for swift Israeli **retaliation.**" Here's the "retaliation" it quoted the Israeli as vowing: "With these **murderers**, these **terror** organizations...we must act, or we will lose our deterrence."

Turning to "the violence along the Gaza border," the article reported on "extremist groups firing more than *60 rockets* into Israel [*i.e.*, at civilians in Israel] over the last week, injuring several Israelis," and that "Israel has responded with *targeted* airstrikes," but called this the two sides having "engaged in **tit-for-tat** violence."

◀ Also in March 2011, Palestinian Arabs stabbed to death a father, mother, children (11 & 3 and an infant) in the dead of night as they slept in their beds. The *L.A. Times* (3/13/11, *Inq.*, A4) article cited

> worry that violence *will be* renewed in *the Palestinian territories* and heightened fear of *retaliation* by *settlers* or the Israel Defense Forces.

◀ A 4/22/10 *A.P.*, article (*Inq.*, A10) similarly blamed Israeli "retaliation" for

Gaza rocket attacks, not the attack for which Israel was "retaliating," as "raising the prospect" of a new round of fighting. It led:

> Israel on Tuesday launched heavy air strikes on Gaza in **retaliation** for Palestinian rocket attacks, **raising the prospect** of a new round of bloody fighting after a two-year lull.

◄ Israel's "retaliation" doesn't even have to be military. In a 10/25/07 *A.P.* (*Inq.*) article, Israel threatening to cut electric power to Gaza "each time rockets hit Israeli territory" made the "**retaliation**" cut.

◄ Israelis themselves don't call their military response against terrorists who target Israeli civilians "retaliation." But the M.S.M. has said that they do. The *Inquirer* headlined its article (*A.P.*, *Inq.*, A3) article on Israel's internal report on its Cast Lead operation:

> Israel Defends its Actions in Winter Gaza Offensive; A Report *Said* Hamas Rocket Attacks Justified **Retaliation**

A search of the I.D.F.'s 100-plus-page PDF report document for the word fragment "**retal**" returned no hits. What the report did stress is that Israel was *defending* Israeli citizens from Arab rocket attacks on Israeli civilians.

◄ This article (*A.P.*, 9/4/07, *Inq.*, A4) captures how the M.S.M. views Palestinian Arab attacks on Israeli civilians and Israel's response:

> A Palestinian rocket exploded yesterday in southern Israel next to a day-care center crowded with toddlers, sparking anger and panic in the *frequently* targeted town of Sderot and bringing **warnings of retribution** from Israeli leaders.
>
> No one was hurt. Terrified mothers rushed to comfort their screaming babies, schoolchildren ran for cover, and angry parents said they wouldn't send their children back to school until they got classrooms outside town.
>
> Prime Minister Ehud Olmert pledged to provide "better security for the residents," indicating he would step up the Israeli *offensive* against Palestinian **militants** who fire rockets into Israel from the Gaza Strip. Islamic Jihad claimed **responsibility** for launching seven rockets *at Sderot*.

Folks who claim *credit*, not "*responsibility*," for firing rockets not "*into Israel*," but, as here, at "a *day-care center* crowded with toddlers" in "the *frequently targeted town* of Sderot," aren't "*militants*," and Israel's response against them isn't an "*Israeli offensive*." And an Israeli prime minister telling "terrified mothers" who "rushed to comfort their screaming babies" that Israel would "step up" its response against those "who fire rockets" at Israeli civilians is issuing promises to terrified mothers that Israel would interdict that rocket fire, not issuing "warnings of *retribution* from Israeli leaders."

## "Offensives" – Media-Speak for Israeli Responses Against Terrorists

When Israel responds to an attack on Israeli civilians by targeting its perpetrators, the M.S.M. besmirches that targeted response as Israeli "retaliation." On occasion, however, Israel sees the need – as the only way to stop relentless near-daily rocketing of Israeli towns and cities from Gaza – for military action in Gaza. The M.S.M. calls such action an "Israeli offensive." The most intense was December 2008's "Cast Lead." But in March 2008, Israel conducted a smaller such operation, following a grave Hamas escalation in rocketing. One major Western newspaper's miscoverage of that responsive Israeli action furnishes a case study in imbalanced portrayal of Israel defending her civilians from indiscriminate rocketing.

## The "Israeli Offensive" of March 2008

The following is an excerpt from the *Inquirer*-focused Brith Sholom Media Watch's Alert #375 for the week ending March 9, 2008. It chronicles, without benefit of hindsight (including awareness of "Cast Lead"), that this major American daily consistently failed to headline that Israel's "offensive" constituted a ***response*** to Hamas's grave escalation in rocket-potency and targeting from small Qassams at Negev towns like Sderot, to large Grads at major cities like Ashkelon:

> This Week in the *Inq.*: Hamas Rocketing of Ashkelon Utterly Ignored In *Inq.* One-Sided Headlining of "Israeli Incursions In Gaza"
>
> = = = = = = = = = = = = = = = = = = = = = = = = = = = = = =
>
> You WOULDN'T KNOW from reading the headlines in the last ten days' *Inq.*'s that Hamas has ESCALATED from launching media-monikered "homemade" rockets each day at Sderot to launching full scale military class Iranian-made Grad (Katyusha) rockets at Ashkelon and Ashdod. Look and see for yourself the *Inq.* headlines oozing moral equivalence between Arabs rocketing Jewish civilians and Israel's "retaliatory" striking back at the rocketeers, with the *Inq.*'s focus every day upon Gaza and not even once mentioning Ashkelon and Sderot.
>
> *Inq.* headline (Thursday, 2/28/08, A16, *A.P.*): "ISRAELIS, GAZANS SWAP FIRE; DEATH ON BOTH SIDES"; sub-head: "The Bloodshed Heightened Fears of a New Wave of Violence. Rice to Visit the Region Next Week."
>
> *Inq.* headline (Friday, 2/29/08, A16, *A.P.*): "VIOLENCE

ESCALATES; ISRAELI SAYS GAZA ACTION IS OP-TION"; sub-head: "The Defense Chief Hinted at an Invasion as Rocket Attacks and Air Strikes Intensified"

*Inq.* Headline (Saturday, 3/1/08, A3, *N.Y. Times*): "LESS VIOLENCE IN ISRAELI, GAZA CLASHES"

*Inq.* headline (Sunday, 3/2/08, A1, *L.A. Times*): "DOZENS KILLED IN ISRAELI TROOP ACTION IN GAZA"; inset sub-head: "Civilians Also Killed in Hunt for Militants Firing Rockets."

*Inq.* Headline (Monday, 3/3/08, A1, *A.P.*): "MIDEAST PEACE TALKS OFF"; sub-head: "Palestinians Suspend Discussions; Israel Vows to Keep Up Gaza Attacks. Condoleeza Rice is Due in the Region This Week."

*Inq.* headline, Tuesday, 3/4/08, A1, *N.Y. Times*: "ISRAELIS EXIT GAZA; HAMAS SEES GAIN'; sub-head: 'Amid the Losses, It Claimed a Hezbollah Resistance Model."

*Inq.* Headline (Wednesday, 3/5/08, A3, *N.Y. Times*): "ABBAS DECLINES TO SET TIME FOR RESUMING TALKS"; sub-head: "He Met With Rice, Who Pushed for the Resumption of Negotiations **Broken Off Over Israel's Incursion into Gaza.**"

*Inq.* Headline (Thursday, 3/6/08, A2, *L.A. Times*): "MIDEAST TALKS BACK ON TRACK, RICE SAYS IN VISIT TO REGION; **Abbas Had Halted Them After Israel's Incursion Into Gaza.** No Date For a Restart was Announced."

*Inq.* Headline (Friday, 3/7/08, A1, *N.Y. Times*): Caption above photo: "Carnage At a Jerusalem Seminary", headline: "GUNMAN OPENS FIRE, KILLS EIGHT STUDENTS."

As Dr. Bruce Epstein correctly diagnosed a similar headline in the *St. Petersburg* (Florida) *Times*: "Murderer not identified as a Palestinian, Victims not identified as Israeli."

*Inq.* Headline (Saturday, 3/8/08, A1, *A.P.*): "ISRAEL EYES PEACE TALKS DESPITE ATTACK"

Now, let's look at the place names mentioned in these Israeli-Gazans' action headlines.

Did you see the place name ASHKELON mentioned ONCE as an attacked place in these headlines?

Did you see SDEROT mentioned once as a place constantly being attacked?

Did you ANY PLACE IN ISRAEL, even just "ISRAEL," mentioned as a place where Israeli-"Gazan" action is taking place?

OR DID YOU JUST SEE

\*\*\* "ISRAELI Says GAZA Action is Option; The Defense Chief Hinted at an Invasion" (Friday, 2/29)

\*\*\* "Dozens Killed in ISRAELI Troop Action IN GAZA" (Sunday, 3/2)

\*\*\* "ISRAEL Vows To Keep Up GAZA Attacks" (Monday, 3/3)

\*\*\* "ISRAELIS Exit GAZA" (Tuesday, 3/4)

\*\*\* "Negotiations Broken Off Over ISRAEL'S Incursion into GAZA" (Wednesday, 3/5)

\*\*\* "Abbas Had Halted [Talks] After ISRAEL's Incursion into GAZA" (Thursday, 3/6)

Did ASHKELON and SDEROT deserve to be mentioned, along with Gaza, Gaza, Gaza, Gaza, Gaza, Gaza, in these *Inquirer* headlines? Over these same ten days, I printed out 12 PAGES of news article squibs about Arab rocketing of Ashkelon and Sderot from the Conference of Presidents' "Daily Alerts." Here are a few samples:

Thursday, 2/28: "Fifty Palestinian Rockets Bombard Israel, Israeli Killed at Sapir College, Ashkelon Hospital Targeted."

Thursday, 2/28: "Ashkelon Residents Realize: We're Just Like Sderot."

Thursday, 2/28: Editorial in *Ha-aretz*: "The dozens of rockets that were fired Wednesday from Gaza – one of which killed Roni Yihye – have placed the I.D.F. on the threshold of a major raid into the Palestinian territory. Responsibility for the escalation lies entirely with the Palestinian side: the Hamas government."

Friday, 2/29 (*A.P.*/International Herald Tribune): "The Israeli city of Ashkelon (pop. 120,000), located 17 kilometers (11 miles) from Gaza, was hit by several Iranian-made Grad (Katyusha) rockets on Thursday, fired by Hamas militants in Gaza. One hit an apartment building, slicing through the roof and three floors below, and another landed near a school, wounding a 17-year-old girl."

Friday, 2/29: "Ten Palestinian Rockets Hit Ashkelon"

Monday, 3/3: Israel Ministry of Foreign Affairs: "The 122 mm. Grad rockets (also known as Katyushas) fired from Hamas-controlled Gaza against the Israeli city of Ashkelon are a standard military artillery weapon, equipped with a weapons-grade high explosive fragmentation warhead. The range of the rockets fired against Ashkelon is over 20 km., an upgraded capability which places about a quarter of a million Israeli civilians in constant danger of Hamas attack."

NONE of this, not the continued daily Arab bombarding of Sderot, not the NEWLY LAUNCHED Arab bombarding of Ashkelon, a civilian city, by standard military artillery shells equipped with weapons-grade high explosive fragmentation warheads, was Headline News to the *Inq.*, just Israel launching Gaza "attacks" and "incursions."

By 2011, Israel had deployed an "Iron Dome" rocket interception system to protect her cities located within the range of escalated rocketing capability from Gaza. The Gaza rocketeers have taken steps to evade and overwhelm it. But, by any standards of honest reporting, intentional on-going rocketing of civilians in cities warrants newspaper headlines. The absence of such headlining has contributed to the "mission creep" that has played-out in Gaza Arabs' rocketing of civilians in Israel, first in desert towns, and now in major cities, leading to larger Israeli military actions to stop it. Nowhere else in the world would such relentless rocketing of civilians in towns and cities be accepted so casually by the media.

# W

## "The West Bank" – Not Its Name for 3,000 Years

### Media Uses "West Bank" to Denigrate Jewish Connection to Judea and Samaria

The M.S.M. uses the term "the West Bank" to refer to the portions of Judea/Samaria that invading Jordan had seized in 1948 and held until ousted by Israel in 1967. Such occurrences are legion, and almost exclusive.

◄ On 10/3/10, the *Inquirer* captioned a photo (not relevant to the news article, but quite picturesque):

A Palestinian shepherd walks near the Jewish settlement of

Revava, near **the West Bank** village of Salfit...."

◀ *N.Y Times* (10/3/10, Bronner, *Inq.*, A15) quoted an Israeli official quoting Israeli P.M. Netanyahu:

> "Everyone knows that restrained and moderate building in **Judea and Samaria** in the coming year will not affect the peace map at all," he [Netanyahu] said, according to the [Israeli] official, using **the biblical term for the West Bank.**

◀ An article (*L.A. Times*, 3/13/11, *Inq.*, A4) dealing with the murder of a Jewish family as they slept in their beds in a **"West Bank** settlement," used the expression **"West Bank"** five times, including in contrasting "Jewish *settlers* in the tightly guarded *compound* of Itamar" against Arab "*residents* of the **West Bank** *village* of Awarta."

◀ *USA Today* (9/20/11) noted that "Jews have lived in '**Judea and Samaria,' the biblical name for the West Bank,** for thousands of years."

## Where the term "West Bank" Came From, When, and Why

An explanation of M.S.M. misuse of "West Bank" appeared in the Jewish newspaper *Forward*, "This Side of the River Jordan" (www.forward.com/articles/131482), in October 2010.

Citing mid-September 2010 articles by Jackson Diehl in the *Washington Post* and Roger Cohen in the *N.Y. Times* which called "Judea and Samaria" the "Israeli nationalist term" and a "biblical reference," respectively, the *Forward* columnist, "Philologos," wrote that when he sees this, "I want to scream." Philologos went on:

> One would like to ask the Diehls, the Cohens and all the others a simple question: In the long centuries after the final redaction of the Hebrew Bible, which took place sometime in the second or first century BCE, what, in their humble opinion, was the hill country south and north of Jerusalem called?

"It certainly wasn't 'the West Bank,'" he wrote, "a term that is barely 60 years old" and was "introduced in the early 1950's to denote the area of Palestine west of the Jordan River that was annexed by [the invading Hashemite Arab kingdom of] Transjordan" in the 1948 war.

Jordan's government website states its name-change from Transjordan occurred when it officially assumed responsibility for representing the Palestinian Arabs, a position that does not fit neatly into the current P.A. narrative rejecting any refugee resolution that would involve the Hashemite kingdom. Jordan: "On April 11, 1950, elections were held for a new Jordanian parliament in which the Palestinian Arabs of the West Bank were equally represented. Thirteen days later, Parliament unanimously approved a motion to unite the two banks of the Jordan River, constitutionally expanding the Hashemite Kingdom of Jordan in order to safeguard what was left of the Arab territory of Palestine from further Zionist expansion." [*See* http://www.kinghussein.gov.jo/his_palest ine.html.]

Philologos cited references to the hill country south and north of Jerusalem as "Judea" and "Samaria" all through the post-Judaea Hadrian-to-Hashemite centuries. He cited as illustrative of 19th century travel books an 1874 London-published book referencing "Southern Palestine, or Judea." He cited 18th century travel maps and the 14th century "Travels of Sir John Mandeville" stating that "Jerusalem is in the land of Judea," and the 4th century works of Church Father Eusebius. Co-author Verlin's book *Israel 3000 Years* cites an historian quoting Saewulf, an Anglo-Saxon pilgrim to the Holy Land, in 1102: "On this side of the Jordan is **the region called Judea**, as far the sea.."

Philologos concluded:

> Judea and Samaria, although they derive from the Hebrew biblical terms Yehuda and Shomron, have been part of the geographical vocabulary of Christian Europe since the time of Jesus. "The West Bank" has not been. To refuse to refer to the [so-called] West Bank as Judea and Samaria is, whether deliberately or not, **to declare that Jews and Christians have no historical connection to these areas**. To malign others for calling them that is even worse.

One might wonder what the U.N. General Assembly's Resolution 181 in 1947 called these areas. It referred to "the hill country of Samaria and Judea" (Part II, Sec. A, par. 3), not to "the West Bank." Judea and Samaria were these areas actual historical names, not just "biblical names," wrote Israeli Amb. (ret.) Yoram Ettinger, "Second Thought," in Israel Hayom Newsletter, December 16, 2011. He added

> In April 1950, the Jordanian occupation renamed Judea/Samaria as "the West Bank" to assert Jordanian rule and to expunge Jewish connection to the cradle of Jewish history. *Until 1950*, all official Ottoman, British and prior records referred to "Judea and Samaria" and not to the "West Bank."

# X
## "Xenophobic" – Israel With Arab Citizens or a Judenrein Arab State?

"Xenophobia" – "fear or hatred of strangers or foreigners," Webster.

The M.S.M. has had a hand in spreading the misperception that Israel, a country in which its Muslim Arab citizens live in far more freedom and equality than Jewish and Christian "dhimmis" have lived in many Muslim lands, is "xenophobic." [See Section 2, III, IX, XI, XII]

One illustration of the M.S.M. misportraying Israel as xenophobic has been its ridicule of Israeli Yisrael Beitenu party leader Avigdor Lieberman. An October 29, 2006, *Inquirer* staff-writer article called Lieberman the "polarizing" leader of "a far right-wing party" who "bluntly believes that Arabs and Jews can't live together." An *Inquirer* in-house columnist article (Trudy Rubin, 3/15/09) branded him as "notorious for calling on Israel to rid itself of most of its Arab citizens and relocate them to a future Palestinian entity." (For a more accurate view of Lieberman's proposal, *see* "Land Swaps" above.)

Ironically, an article (*A.P.*, 10/31/06) blasting Lieberman's very cabinet appointment as having "effectively ruled out any serious moves to revive Middle East peace negotiations," appended at its tail-end that Hamas, which "won Palestinian parliamentary elections in January," calls "for Israel's destruction," but *that* didn't raise any M.S.M. hackles about ruling out peace talks.

◄ *A.P.* (1/19/07, *Inq.*): "...Hamas, which rejects the existence of a Jewish state in an Islamic Middle East."

◄ And again (*A.P.*, 2/3/09, *Inq.*, A5): "Hamas does not accept a place for a Jewish state in an Islamic Middle East."

*That's* xenophobic.

◄ "Moderate" Abbas' Fatah's constitution includes "...the Zionist occupation in Palestine"; "...uprooting the Zionist existence," "...this struggle will not cease unless the Zionist state is demolished and Palestine completely liberated"; "the Israeli existence in Palestine is a Zionist invasion with a colonial expansive base"; "the Zionist Movement is racial, colonial and aggressive... "; "...our just struggle in order to resist together Zionism and imperialism"; "...the world-wide struggle against Zionism, colonialism and imperialism." *[See* Section 2, I]

◄ *Jerusalem Post* columnist Caroline Glick reported (8/13/09) that Fatah reiterated this xenophobia at its August 2009 General Assembly in Bethlehem by demanding "that **all Jews be expelled** from Judea, Samaria and Jerusalem ahead of the establishment of a Jew-free Palestinian state."

◄ The *A.P.* reported (4/29/09, *Inq.*, A4), that "a Palestinian military court convicted a man of treason and sentenced him to death for selling West Bank land to an Israeli company."

Xenophobia is not an ailment of Jewish Israelis. Xenophobia is a disease of the Middle East's Muslim Arabs, who "reject the existence of a Jewish state in an Islamic Middle East." But there is more than Arab xenophobia here.

There is denial of facts. Israelis are not "strangers and foreigners." As shown in the next section, The Yishuv Has Been There All Along.

And Christians, and other minorities, have suffered from Muslim xenophobia. [*See* Section 2, XIX]

# Y

## The Yishuv Has Been There All Along

An opinion column by house columnist Stu Bykofsky in the *Philadelphia Daily News* (4/5/10) commented upon a statement made by Palestinian Arab activist Hanan Ashwari on her visit to Philadelphia a few days before:

> To me, the most painful thing she said, about Jewish claims on the land, was this: "How can you tell us someone who came from Poland yesterday has more rights than I do?" This is the current, insidious Arab claim that Jews are interlopers and latecomers to the land they have lived on for some 3,500 years. Jews are a **majority** [emphasis original] in Jerusalem since at least the 1860's.

The misperception inherent in referring to today's Palestinian Arabs as "*the* Palestinians*" is that it conveys an image of them as the aboriginal inhabitants of the land called Palestine. As recently as December 2011, Palestinian Arabs have made the claim of their descent from the Jebusites of the Second Millennium B.C.E. [*See* Section 2, IV] Defining "Palestinian" as meaning exclusively Palestinian Arabs is a fairly new usage of the term "Palestinian," begun in earnest in the 1960s. (*See* the section on "Palestinians" above.)

There is a second misperception about a people's presence in Palestine, that people being the Jews. Although many people believe that Jewish presence in the land of Israel came to an end with the Romans' final destruction of the Jewish kingdom Judaea in the year 135, and that the Jews were exiled by Rome (*see, e.g.*, Jimmy Carter, *Palestine: Peace Not Apartheid*, p. 2), and that the Jews did not begin to return in meaningful numbers until the Zionist movement in the late 19th century, that is not the historical fact. The historical fact is that the Jews never left.

The M.S.M.'s insistent mischaracterization of Palestine's attempted 1948 partition between its two populations as the "creation" and "founding" of Israel (see "Creation of Israel" and "Founding of Israel" above) purveys images of newness and artificiality to modern Jewish presence in Palestine. The M.S.M.'s coupling of this with attendant displacement of "Palestinians" heightens these images. But even the A.P., in a December 11, 2011 (*Inq.*, A4) news article stated that during the Mandate "Muslims, Christians, and Jews living there were **ALL** referred to as **Palestinians.**" In reality, the term "Palestinian" was mostly used by Palestine's Jews. [*See* "_P_alestinians" and Section 2, IV]

The fundamental fact which the media obscures through insistently using the terms "Israel's 1948 creation" and "founding," and displacement of "Palestinians," is that all through the long-dark foreign rule centuries following Rome's destruction of ancient Judaea, Jews – not as stray individuals, but as the organized, openly-Jewish, homeland-claiming Yishuv – remained in the land.

The Jews' continuous homeland presence all through those long, dark Hadrian-to-Herzl foreign-rule centuries, largely unknown to Christians and even to Jews in the West, is recounted in Section 2, III. Here we address, not the historical fact of that continuous Jewish presence, but the consequence to Western public perceptions of Arab and Jewish Palestine equities of that presence not being known in the West. As with the M.S.M.'s voicing, through quotation of Israel's adversaries, of canards like "Israel is a colonial Zionist entity" and "Israel was created because of the Holocaust," this canard that the Jews were absent for most of the past two millennia – "How can you tell us someone who came from Poland yesterday has more rights than I do?"– has to be countered through M.S.M. inclusion in news articles of the actual historical facts, either by the M.S.M. stating them on its own account or quoting Israeli or Diaspora Jews.

Many people regard the term "Yishuv" as referring to homeland Jewish communities during just the past few centuries, but the scholars who authored *The Jews In Their Land*, a detailed study conceived and edited by David Ben-Gurion (p. 108), define "Yishuv" as referring to "the Jewish population of the Land" as far back as the biblical kingdoms in the first half of the first millennium B.C.E.

That the Yishuv never left is attested to by writers including historians and Israeli prime ministers.

Eminent mid-20th century British historian James Parkes expressed it this way:

> It was, perhaps, inevitable that Zionists should look back to the heroic period of the Maccabees and Bar Cochba, but their real title deeds were written by the less dramatic but equally heroic endurance of those who had maintained a Jewish presence in The Land all through the centuries, and in spite of every discouragement. (*"Whose Land? A History of the Peoples of Palestine,"* p. 266)

Samuel Katz, in his introduction to *"Battleground: Fact & Fantasy in Palestine"* (pp. xv-xvi) wrote that "the gap between what is generally known and the facts of the continuity of Jewish life in Palestine since the destruction of the Second Temple" is an "astonishing area of Jewish neglect." Then P.M. Begin, in his Foreword to *Battleground's* second edition in 1977, wrote: "The most moving chapter in the book is that on the continuous Jewish presence in Palestine. I was glad to learn that this particular chapter has been disseminated in special editions in several languages."

Israeli Premier Ariel Sharon to the Foreign Press Corps in Israel, 1/11/04:

> The Jewish people was born as a people 4,000 years ago, and as a matter of fact, never left. There were Jews that never left this country. And that one must understand....For years we talked mostly about security. I think that this approach was a mistake....I think that Israel made a mistake and I include my-self in one of those not to speak about the Jewish rights over this country. It's painful....We speak about the history of the Jewish people. And the Jewish people as Jews have existed for 4,000 years and never left this country.

Israeli P.M. Netanyahu (12/1/10):

> A few days ago I heard that the Palestinian Information Min-istry was publishing a study that claims that the Jewish people has no connection to the Western Wall....It is not only a reli-gious bond, it is a religious and national bond, a historic link of the highest level that has been going on for thousands of years, and that too is not trivial because there is a test point here.
>
> I say to Abu Mazen [Mahmoud Abbas] to condemn this, de-nounce the study; turn to your people and tell them: "There is a Jewish people here, it has been here for close to 4,000 years, we recognize this people, we recognize their historic bond with this land and this city." (Israel Prime Minister's Office, "PM Netanyahu's Speech at the 40 Signatures Knesset Discussion," 12/1/10)

Joan Peters, *"From Time Immemorial: The Origins of the Arab-Jewish Conflict Over Palestine,"* p. 83:

> The Jewish presence in "The Holy Land" – at times tenuous – persisted through its bloody history....Buried beneath the propaganda – which has it that Jews "returned" to the Holy Land after two thousand years of separation, where they found crowds of "indigenous Palestinian Arabs" – is the bald fact that the Jews are indigenous people on that land who never left, but who have continuously stayed on their "Holy Land." Not only were there the little-known Oriental Jewish commu-

nities in adjacent Arab lands, but there had been an unceasing strain of "Oriental" or "Palestinian" Jews for millennia [citing "Palestine Royal Commission Report (London 1937), pp. 2-5, 7, 9, particularly p.11, par. 23"]."

It is the absence of an appreciation that the Yishuv has been present in the land all through the centuries that leads to the media lacing its Arab-Israeli conflict reporting with the slew of Jewish presence-delegitimizing pejoratives that it uses: **"West Bank"** for what was known as Judea and Samaria until Jordan's seizure of them from 1948 to 1967; **"East" Jerusalem**, for the part of the never-previously-divided city Jordan had seized and held for those 19 years; Arabs as **"residents"** of **"neighborhoods," "towns"** and **"villages"** throughout the land, but Jews as **"Jewish settlers"** living in **"settlements"** in that "West Bank" and "East" Jerusalem.

# Z

## "Zionist Entity" – Why Calling Israel "Israel" Matters So Deeply

The false image which Israel's enemies purvey by calling Israel "the Zionist entity" is the same as that purveyed when they call Israel "created because of the Holocaust," to portray Jews as "Western colonialists" alien to the Mideast.

For example, a 2/2/06 *Inquirer* staff writer article (*Inq.*, A1, 8) quoted Hamas leader Mashaal: "We shall never recognize the legitimacy of a **Zionist** state created on *our* soil."

An article (*A.P.*, 11/27/07, *Inq.*) quoted Iranian leaders that Israel is "a fake and forged state, called the **Zionist** regime," and an article (*A.P.*, *Inq.*, A3) quoted "a Hamas spiritual leader" referring to "the **Zionist colonizers**."

In a piece titled "Is Fatah Moderate" on its website, the media watchdog CAMERA quotes an English version of Fatah's constitution describing "the Zionist entity" as "racial, colonial and aggressive" (Article 7). Other articles speak of "demolishing the Zionist occupation in Palestine" (Article 22), "complete liberation of Palestine" and "eradication" of "Zionist economic, political, military and cultural existence" (Article 12), and "uprooting the Zionist existence" (Article 19).

[For a similar translation, see www.acpr.org.il/resources/fatehconstitution.]

Is this propaganda, which is spread in part by using the M.S.M. as a megaphone, working? An August 2008 History News Network article by Boston University Professor Richard L. Cravatts, "How to Get the World to Hate Israel," showed that it is. Citing a 2006 survey ranking Israel *last* among nations in public popularity, Dr. Cravatts wrote that to get the world to hate Israel, these are some of the things that you do:

> Even after 60 years of its existence, you question the funda-
> mental right of Israel to even exist and  regularly, though
> falsely, condemn it for being created "illegally"—through the
> "theft" of Palestinian lands and property—and thus decide,
> because of its original sin, it has no "right to exist." You accuse
> the government  of a "brutal," illegal "occupation" of Pales-
> tinian lands, especially Gaza and the West Bank (but for many,
> all of Israel), of being a "colonial settler state," a Zionist
> "regime" or "project," a land-hungry nation, a usurper of prop-
> erty that was lived on and owned by a Palestinian "people"
> "from time immemorial."

A shocking instance of M.S.M. elevation of the "colonial Zionist entity" canard
to the status of legitimate claim occurred in the *N.Y Times'* and *International
Herald Tribune's* August 5, 2005, news article reporting archeologist Eilat
Mazar's unearthing in the City of David part of Jerusalem what may well be
King David's palace:

*N.Y. Times*:

> The find will also be used in the broad political battle over
> Jerusalem – whether the Jews have their origins here and thus
> have some special hold on the place, or whether, as many
> Palestinians have said, including the late Yasser Arafat, the
> idea of a Jewish origin in Jerusalem is **a myth used to justify
> conquest and occupation.**"

*International Herald Tribune*:

> Her discovery is also bound to be used in the other major battle
> over Jerusalem – whether the Jews have their deepest origins
> there and thus have some special hold on the place, or whether,
> as many Palestinians believe – including the late Yasser Arafat
> – that the notion of a Jewish origin in Jerusalem is **a religious
> myth used to justify occupation and colonialism.**

And an article (*A.P.*, 2/3/09, *Inq.*, A5) begged a rather fundamental question:

> Hamas does not accept a place for a Jewish state in an Islamic
> Middle East."

As with Holocaust and ancient Jewish history denial, the M.S.M. allows its
powerful voice to be used for Israel's enemies' dissemination of the "colonial
Zionist entity" canard.  Countering anti-Israel M.S.M. bias in this context be-
gins with demanding that, when a news article quotes a leader or spokesperson
calling Israel "the Zionist colonizers," etc., it state the Jewish people's contin-

uous homeland connection and presence for three millennia, quoting an Israeli or Jewish leader if necessary.

Here's one such Jewish response, in an August 2008 article by Nathan Jeffay, "The Other Middle-East Refugees," in the *Jerusalem Report*. After quoting a spokesman for Israel's Foreign Ministry that "Jewish refugees from Arab countries will be an important factor in peace negotiations," the article continues, quoting spokesmen for the Jewish refugees, that the existence of the Middle Eastern lands' Jewish refugees

> ...cuts to a deeper issue, the nature of the Jewish state. Israel's detractors – including Jewish ones – claim it "is a white European state plunked right in the center of the Middle East, where it has no place"....But confronted with the issue of Jewish refugees, these critics are forced to ask where these Jews came from....They had been in many of the countries of the Middle East for 2,600 years, which is 1,000 years before the advent of Islam....The fact that many of these Middle Eastern Jews now live in Israel shows that it is not, as critics claim, a colonial state displacing a native population, but a country heavily populated by people indigenous to the region, cruelly displaced from nearby countries, This underscores the legitimacy of Israel as a Jewish state...."

The Jewish people has been physically present in the land of Israel itself continuously during the past three millennia. That presence has not been as stray individuals but, throughout, as that of an organized, openly Jewish, homeland-claiming people, "in spite of every discouragement." (*See*, e.g., Verlin, *Israel 3000 Years: The Jewish People's 3000 Year Presence in Palestine*.)

# Summary of Section One

In the concluding chapter of her important book, *The Other War: Israelis, Palestinians and the Struggle for Media Supremacy* (p. 267), journalist Stephanie Gutmann observes "Israel doesn't have the resources to counter" every imbalanced news article in the Western media. True, but a more fundamental motivation for Western Jews to respond to anti-Israel bias by the M.S.M – particularly its delegitimizing of the Jewish people's homeland connection to Israel – is recognizing that this is the Jewish people's struggle, not just Israel's, a struggle in which Israel and its Jewish and Christian supporters are faring poorly indeed.

What we have tried to show through this section's "A-to-Z" treatment is that mainstream Western media anti-Israel imbalance is *not* a random collection of spontaneously occurring *sui generis* inaccuracies. Such could be effectively countered by letters "to the editor" seeing them as stand-alone incidents. Anti-Israel media bias is a set of consensus (we did not say "conspiracy") imbalanced M.S.M. terms and viewpoints that have to be challenged as such – by pro-active steps along with post-occurrence damage control.

And even this is not an end in itself, but a means of securing accurate Western public perception of Arab-Israeli conflict right-and-wrong. The world will have an important say in framing the settlement of the Arab-Israeli [not "Israeli-Palestinian"] Palestine conflict, whenever it comes, and much will ride on Western publics' perceptions of Arab and Jewish Palestine equities. The contenders for that perception are not competing "narratives" of Arabs and Jews, but the narrative of "Palestinians' displacement by Israel's 1948 founding" versus the historical truth.

Israel's Jewish and Christian supporters in the West must undertake two conscious steps. First, we must sharpen our terms and frames-of-reference, purging those that delegitimize the Jewish people's homeland connection to Israel, and then demand that the M.S.M. do the same. Consider the following disastrously delegitimizing M.S.M. terms and frames of reference that, alas, even Israelis and pro-Israel Westerners often use.

**"1967 Borders"** – They aren't. They were subsequent war-vitiated 1949-67 Israel-Jordan ceasefire lines.

**"1948 Creation of Israel," "1948 Founding of Israel"** – No. Israel's attainment of independence wasn't artificial and out-of-the-blue.

**"The War that Followed Israel's Creation"** – No, it wasn't. The 1948 war was a partition-rejecting multi-nation Arab invasion for Israel's destruction.

**"Palestinian Refugees From the War that Followed Israel's Creation"** – No, they weren't. There were multiple reasons why Arabs (not yet called

"Palestinians") left Israel, mainly encouragement by the invading Arab states. And more Jewish refugees, mostly Israel-absorbed, fled vast Muslim lands where Jews had lived for millennia than Arabs left tiny Israel.

**"East Jerusalem"** – No, it's not. Except for Jordan's 1948-1967 seizure, the Old City, City of David, and "eastern" residential areas have been part of just "Jerusalem," which has again had a Jewish majority since 19th century times.

**"East Jerusalem Jewish Settlers"** – No, they're not. Jews have lived in Jerusalem since ancient times, inexorably returning whenever foreign conquerors kicked them out. During the three millennia preceding 1967, nobody called Jews in Jerusalem alien "settlers."

**"Hamas is 'Considered' a Terrorist Group"** – No, it's not. It *is* a terrorist group.

**"Israel was Created Because of the Holocaust"** – No, it wasn't. Israel's independence is the natural culmination of the Jewish people's continuous organized, openly-Jewish, homeland-claiming presence, recognized in the 20th century by pre-Holocaust international forums and documents.

**"Palestinian Refugee Issue"** – No, it's not. In the 1948-49 Arab-Israeli war and its aftermath, a greater number of Middle Eastern Jews fled vast Muslim lands than Arabs fled tiny Israel. Israel's absorption of the Jewish refugees while "host" countries, including today Palestinian Arab-controlled areas of Palestine, continue to confine the Arabs to "refugee camps" does not remove the Jewish refugees (who've had descendants too) from the Arab-Israeli conflict's refugee issue.

**"'Jewish State' Recognition Demand is a New Stumbling Block"** – No, it's not. The land of Israel as the Jewish people's homeland has been central to Jewish peoplehood since Moses' time.

**"Palestinian Militants"** – No, they're not. Mass murderers who prey on civilians using rockets, mortars and bombs are terrorists, period.

**"Suicide Bombers"** – No, they're not. They're mass murderers of civilian men, women and kids.

**"Millions of Palestinian Refugees and Their Descendants"** – No, there weren't. Palestine's 1947 entire population, at least a third of it Jews, was less than two million. Not all the Arabs lived in the part that became Israel, and not all of them left. Some half-million Arabs left tiny Israel. A greater number of Jews, most of whom fled to Israel, fled vast Muslim lands.

**"Moderate Abbas and Fatah"** – No, they're not. They demand Israel's retreat to the 1949 ceasefire lines, removal of Jews from Judea, Samaria and all of Jerusalem, while demanding a "right of return" for millions of Arabs into shrunken Israel. They reject "two states for two peoples." They demand impossible peace-talk pre-conditions.

**"Hard-Line Netanyahu"** – No, he's not. He accepts the "two-state solution" with a Muslim Arab state alongside Jewish Israel. He instituted a 10-month Judea-Samaria building ban. He calls continuously for resumption of direct talks without pre-conditions.

**"Nakba"** – No, it wasn't, unless it's your view that the homeland Jewish army having thrown back a multi-nation Arab invasion for its destruction and annihilation of its people was a "catastrophe." The Palestinian Arabs' real Nakba was their turning down their own state because there would also have been a Palestinian state of the Jews.

**"Occupied Territories," "Palestinian Territories"** – No, they're not. The League of Nations Palestine Mandate recognized the Jewish people's right to reconstitute its Jewish National Home in Palestine (including Judea and Samaria, and originally including what became Transjordan), and called for close settlement of the Jews on this land, where Jews had lived, claiming it as their homeland, for three thousand years. They're disputed, not "occupied" or "Palestinian" territories.

**"Israeli Offensives in Gaza"** – No, they're not. Israel eventually responding to near-daily rocketing of its civilians by going after the rocket-launching terrorists in their lairs is a defensive response to that rocketing, not an aggressive "Israeli offensive."

**"The Palestinians"** – No, they're not. Palestine is a place, not a people. Palestine's Arabs are Palestinian Arabs, just as Israeli Jews are Palestinian Jews. The media acknowledges that during the Mandate Christians, Muslims and Jews in the land were all called Palestinians. In fact, until the 1960's "Palestinian" was used mainly in reference to Palestine's Jews.

**"Retaliation"** – No, it's not. To "retaliate" is to return injury-for-injury, like-for-like. Labeling Israel's response against terrorists who rocket and bomb Israeli civilians "Israeli retaliation" drags Israel's obligatory, justified protection of its citizens down to the moral mud of intentionally targeting civilians. .

**"Road Map Requires Palestinian Authority To Rein In Militants"** – No, it doesn't. It requires the Palestinian Authority to confront all those engaged in terror and to dismantle terrorist capabilities and infrastructure.

**"Rockets Fired At Israel, Into Israel"** – No, they're not. They're fired at civilians in towns and cities in Israel, using target shifting and volleying to try to evade Israel's new Iron Dome interception.

**"Israeli Said 'Militants'"** – He almost certainly didn't. If he did, print the direct quote of him saying so.

**"Seized By Israel in June 1967"** – Don't say that to Jews who remember the anguish Israeli and Diaspora Jews went through in May 1967.

**"'Jewish Settlements' Versus 'Palestinian' Neighborhoods ... Towns ...**

**Villages"** – No, they're not. Wherever the eventual political border will run, Jews are not outsiders, but actually have far longer connection to the land of Israel, including Judea, Samaria and "East" Jerusalem, than Arabs. Most place names are of Hebrew, Greek or other non-Arab origin.

**"Suspected Militants"** – Don't use that expression for those who blow themselves up seeking martyrdom.

**"P.A. Is For and Israel Against the 'Two-State Solution'"** – Wrong on both counts. Israel agrees with the U.S. on "two states for two peoples, Jewish and Arab." Abbas and other P.A. leaders have said over and over "We shall never recognize a Jewish state."

**"Israel's Deadly Raid On an Aid Flotilla Bound for Gaza"** – No, it wasn't. It was Israeli enforcement of a legal blockade against seaborne armaments for the terrorist Gaza regime of Hamas, which "claims responsibility" for relentlessly rocketing civilians in Israel, and a long line of "suicide" bombers.

**"The Cave of the Patriarchs is a 'West Bank Shrine,' and Rachel's Tomb is 'a Mosque' "** – No, they're not. They're Jewish, and they long antedate Islam.

**"The West Bank"** – No, it's not. "Judea and Samaria" are not just "biblical names," but the names the Israeli hill country of Israel was known by from ancient times, including in the U.N.'s 1947 partition resolution, until after Transjordan invaded in 1948 (and was ousted by Israel in 1967).

**"'Whistle-Blower' Vanunu"** – No, he's not. He betrayed and endangered his countrymen, surrounded as they are by enemies sworn to their destruction, by revealing his country's military secrets.

**"Israel is Xenophobic"** – No, it's not. Israeli Arabs are full Israeli citizens. The xenophobes are the Palestinian Arabs, who would expel every last Jew from Judea, Samaria and Jerusalem.

**"Israel Is a European Colonial Zionist Entity With No Place In The Islamic Middle East"** – No, it's not. The Jewish people, as such, has lived in the land of Israel without interruption for longer than 3,000 years. The Zionist movement is a modern expression of a diaspora connection to the land, including through aliyah, that never ceased. Much of Israel's population today is descended from Jews expelled in the mid-20th century from Middle East lands in which they had unbroken family roots going back hundreds and even thousands of years.

The Jewish state of Israel is none of the dark, depraved things its enemies and the M.S.M. paint it. It is a miraculous revival of sovereign dignity of a people which never relinquished its ancient homeland connection to its land. Surrounded by foes dedicated to its annihilation, it has accomplished much that is good for itself and the world. See Section 2, X, "The Untold Story of Israel's Accomplishments and Humanitarianism."

## Books Referenced in Section 1

Bar-Illan, David, *Eye On The Media* (Jerusalem, Jerusalem Post, 1993)

Bell, J. Boyer, *Terror Out of Zion: The Violent and Deadly Shock Troops of Israel's Independence, 1929-1949* (New York, St. Martin's Press, 1977)

Ben-Arieh, Yehoshua, *Jerusalem in the 19th Century: The Old City* (New York, St. Martin's Press, 1984)

Ben-Gurion, David (ed.), *The Jews In Their Land* (Garden City, Doubleday & Co., 1966)

Bright, John, *A History of Israel* (Louisville, Westminster John Knox Press, 2000)

Carter, Jimmy, *Palestine: Peace Not Apartheid* (New York, Simon & Schuster, 2006)

Gilbert, Martin, *Jerusalem: Rebirth of a City* (New York, Viking 1985)

Gutmann, Stephanie, *The Other War: Israelis, Palestinians and the Struggle for Media Supremacy* (San Francisco, Encounter Books, 2005)

Katz, Samuel, *Battleground: Fact & Fantasy in Palestine* (New York, Steimatsky-Shapolsky, 1985)

Karsh, Ephraim, *Palestine Betrayed* (New Haven, Yale University Press, 2010)

Morris, Benny, *A History of the First Arab-Israeli War* (New Haven, Yale University Press, 2008)

Myre, Greg and Griffin, Jennifer, *This Burning Land: Lessons from the Front Lines of the Transformed Israeli-Palestinian Conflict* (Hoboken, John Wiley & Sons, Inc., 2010)

Parkes, James, *Whose Land? A History of the Peoples of Palestine* (New York, Taplinger Publishing Co., 1971)

Peters, Joan, *From Time Immemorial: The Origins of the Arab-Jewish Conflict Over Palestine* (New York, Harper & Row, 1984)

Tal, Eliyahu, *Israel in Medialand* (Jerusalem, Jerusalem Post, 1988)

Verlin, Jerome, *Israel 3,000 Years: The Jewish People's 3,000 Year Presence in Palestine* (Philadelphia, Pavilion Press, Inc., 2010)

# Section 2
## Background for Understanding Misreporting of News

## I. Documents:  Muslim, Arab, Israeli and International
### The Qur'an

When the core of your enemy's doctrine and religion considers you an "unbeliever"– to be, at best, subjugated to *dhimmi* (second class) status, never to be befriended or trusted – it is required that they engage in warfare against you and excuse your annihilation as part of a religious duty, *jihad*; under such circumstances, achieving co-equal co-existence becomes impossible. "Islam" is a religion that celebrates the "peace" that will come only when everyone is Muslim or, at least, agrees to become "submissive" to the hegemon126y of the Islamic state. This is the insurmountable problem that has bedeviled all so-called "peace process" efforts to-date with democratic-state, western-oriented State of Israel.

Islam means to "submit." The Qur'an teaches Muslims that *they* are superior, while non-Muslims – known as infidels – are inherently inferior and must be dominated. The Torah's promise that the Jews will return to the Land and make it thrive – including the recent success of tiny Israel, the state of the Jews – defies what Allah has told Muslims what will happen, and is perceived as an affront and delegitimizing to their religion and their honor, particularly because they have not been able to defeat Israel militarily.

The root of the problem may be in the Qur'an itself.  Here are some notable excerpts of Quaranic doctrine regarding "infidels," Jews and Christians, and peacemaking:

> The only true faith in God's sight is Islam. Qur'an 3:19

> Believers, take neither the Jews nor the Christians for your friends. They are friends with one another. Whoever of you seeks their friendship shall become one of their number. God does not guide the wrong-doers. Qur'an 5:51

> The unbelievers among the People of the Book [Bible] and the pagans shall burn forever in the fire of Hell. They are the vilest of all creatures. Qur'an 98:6

> He that chooses a religion over Islam, it will not be accepted from him and in the world to come he will be one of the lost. Qur'an 3:85

This Book is not to be doubted.... As for the unbelievers, it is the same whether or not you forewarn them; they will not have faith. God has set a seal upon their hearts and ears; their sight is dimmed and grievous punishment awaits them. Qur'an 2:1/2:6-2:10

You are the noblest community ever raised up for mankind. You enjoin justice and forbid evil. You believe in God. Had the People of the Book [Jews and Christians] accepted the Faith, it would surely have been better for them. Some are true believers, but most are evil-doers. Qur'an 3:110-111

Let not believers make friends with infidels in preference to the faithful since he who does this cuts himself from God unless it be to protect yourself against them in this way . Qur'an 3:28

God's curse be upon the infidels! Evil is that for which they have bartered away their souls. To deny God's own revelation, grudging that He should reveal His bounty to whom He chooses from among His servants! They have incurred God's most inexorable wrath. An ignominious punishment awaits the unbelievers. Qur'an 2:89-2:90

Lord...Give us victory over the unbelievers. Qur'an 2:286; 3:148

I shall cast terror into the hearts of the infidels. Strike off their heads, strike off the very tips of their fingers. Qur'an 8:12

When the sacred months are over slay the idolaters wherever you find them. Arrest them, besiege them, and lie in ambush everywhere for them. Qur'an 9:5

Prophet, make war on the unbelievers and the hypocrites and deal rigorously with them. Hell shall be their home: an evil fate. Qur'an 9:73

Believers, make war on the infidels who dwell around you. Deal firmly with them. Know that God is with the righteous. Qur'an 9:123

Muhammad is God's apostle. Those who follow him are ruthless to the unbelievers but merciful to one another. Qur'an 48:29

> Those that make war against God and His apostle and spread disorder in the land shall be slain and crucified or have their hands and feet cut off on alternate sides, or be banished from the land. Qur'an 5:33

> When you meet the unbelievers in the battlefield strike off their heads and, when you have laid them low, bind your captives firmly. Qur'an 47:4

> Let not the unbelievers think that they will ever get away. They have not the power to do so. Muster against them all the men and cavalry at your command, so that you may strike terror into the enemy of God and your enemy... Qur'an 8:59-60

*Sharia:* Muslim or Islamic law, both civil and criminal justice as well as regulating individual conduct both personal and moral. The custom-based body of law based on the Qur'an and the religion of Islam. Because, by definition, Muslim states are theocracies, religious texts are law, the latter distinguished by Islam and Muslims in their application, as *sharia* or *sharia* law.

*Wala' wa Bara':* "loyalty and enmity." This doctrine requires Muslims to maintain absolute loyalty to Islam and to one another, while disavowing (even hating) all things un-Islamic, including persons (*i.e.*, infidels); it portrays non-believers as enemies to be shunned and subjugated (*see* Qur'an 4:89, 4:144, 5:51, 5:54, 60:4, 6:40, 9:23, and 58:22). For instance, Qur'an 3:28 commands "believers not to take infidels for friends and allies instead of believers...unless you but guard yourselves against them, taking precautions." According to mainstream exegete Tabari, a prominent Muslim scholar, "taking precautions" means:

> If you [Muslims] are under their [non-Muslims'] authority, fearing for yourselves, behave loyally to them with your tongue while harboring inner animosity for them...[but know that] God has forbidden believers from being friendly or on intimate terms with the infidels rather than other believers— except when infidels are above them (in authority). Should that be the case, let them *act friendly* towards them while preserving their religion.

After interpreting Qur'an 3:28 as meaning that Muslims may "protect" themselves "through outward show" when under non-Muslim authority, Ibn Kathir, perhaps Islam's most celebrated exegete, quotes a close companion of Muhammad saying "Let us smile to the faces of some people while our hearts curse them."

*Taqiyya*: This doctrine revolves around deceiving the infidels; it is pivotal to upholding loyalty and enmity whenever Muslim minorities live among non-Muslim majorities: "Only when you are in their [non-Muslims'] power, fearing for yourselves, are you to demonstrate friendship for them with your tongues, while harboring hostility toward them. But do not join them in the particulars of their infidelities, and do not aid them through any action against a Muslim."

Muslims are "obligated to befriend a believer, even if he is oppressive and violent towards you; Muslims must be hostile to the infidel, even if he is liberal and kind to you" (Sheikh al-Islam, Ibn Taymiyya: 1263-1328)

*Hudna*: (also known as a *hudibiyya* or *khudaibiya*) is a tactical cease-fire that permits Arabs to rebuild; this allows them to be more effective when they decide to resume the war, affording them what they would anticipate to be an advantage. Hamas and Hizbollah considered the ending of the wars in Lebanon and Gaza to be merely *hudnas*.

*Jihad*: literally "struggle," revolves around fighting and killing the infidel enemy, "holy war"; if it costs the Muslim fighter his life, he will gain martyrdom. Violent *jihad* warfare against unbelievers is a constant element of mainstream Islamic theology. According to Daniel Pipes, an authority on Islam, *jihad* is "holy war" or more precisely "It means the legal, compulsory, communal effort to expand the territories ruled by Muslims at the expense of territories ruled by non-Muslims."

*Dar Al Islam v. Dar Al Harb*: Islamic law divides the world into these two abodes. *In Dar al-Islam*, the citizenry abide by the ordinances, rules, edicts, and assembly of Islam. The Muslim state guarantees the safety of life, property, and religious status (only if the religion is not idolatrous) of minorities (*ahl al-dhimma*), provided there has been submission to Muslim control. In contrast, *Dar al-Harb* (the abode of war) denotes territory that is not governed by the assembly of Islam, the territory Muslims strive to conquer. *Jihad* can be invoked for the sole purpose of turning *Dar al-Harb* into *Dar al-Islam*. The conflict only is destined to end with the hegemony of Islam, so that the religion reigns supreme. That is the ultimate goal of Islam, to establish worldwide *Sharia* law; non-believers (infidels) are treated as *dhimmi* (second-class citizens under rule of Muslims, with limited rights). Thus, mainstream Islam (as per teachings of Muhammad) mandates that non-Muslims have three choices: conversion, subjugation or death.

Palestinian-Arabs groups have expanded on these Qur'anic concepts. Note below that the PLO, Fatah and Hamas emblems all omit any reference to Israel in their maps of "Palestine" claiming all of Palestine for themselves.

## Palestine Liberation Organization (PLO) Charter (ratified 1964 and 1968)

The PLO is one of the best-known terrorist organizations in the world. It was formed in 1964—three years before Israel gained control of Judea/Samaria and Gaza in a defensive war in 1967—by the Arab League, with the stated-goal of "liberation of Palestine" through armed struggle." If its goal was a Palestinian Arab state on these territories, Jordan and Egypt could have ceded it authority to establish a state. But the goal of the PLO was to destroy Israel. The largest faction of the PLO is the Fatah party. The largest component of the Palestinian Authority is the PLO. The PLO Charter states the following:

> Article 2: Palestine, with the boundaries it had during the British Mandate, is an indivisible territorial unit.

> Article 9: Armed struggle is the only way to liberate Palestine. This is the overall strategy, not merely a tactical phase. The Palestinian Arab people assert their absolute determination and firm resolution to continue their armed struggle and to work for an armed popular revolution for the liberation of their country and their return to it.

> Article 15: The liberation of Palestine, from an Arab viewpoint, is a national (*qawmi*) duty and it attempts to repel the Zionist and imperialist aggression against the Arab homeland, and aims at the elimination of Zionism in Palestine. Absolute responsibility for this falls upon the Arab nation—peoples and governments—with the Arab people of Palestine in the vanguard. Accordingly, the Arab nation must mobilize all its military, human, moral, and spiritual capabilities to participate actively with the Palestinian people in the liberation of Palestine. It must, particularly in the phase of the armed Palestinian revolution, offer and furnish the Palestinian people with all possible help, and material and human support, and make available to them the means and opportunities that will enable them to continue to carry out their leading role in the armed revolution, until they liberate their homeland.

Article 19:  The partition of Palestine in 1947 and the establishment of the state of Israel are entirely illegal, regardless of the passage of time, because they were contrary to the will of the Palestinian people and to their natural right in their homeland, and inconsistent with the principles embodied in the Charter of the United Nations, particularly the right to self-determination.

Article 20:  The Balfour Declaration, the Mandate for Palestine, and everything that has been based upon them, are deemed null and void. Claims of historical or religious ties of Jews with Palestine are incompatible with the facts of history and the true conception of what constitutes statehood. Judaism, being a religion, is not an independent nationality. Nor do Jews constitute a single nation with an identity of its own; they are citizens of the states to which they belong.

Article 21:  The Arab Palestinian people, expressing themselves by the armed Palestinian revolution, reject all solutions which are substitutes for the total liberation of Palestine and reject all proposals aiming at the liquidation of the Palestinian problem, or its internationalization.

Article 22:  Zionism is a political movement organically associated with international imperialism and antagonistic to all action for liberation and to progressive movements in the world. It is racist and fanatic in its nature, aggressive, expansionist, and colonial in its aims, and fascist in its methods. Israel is the instrument of the Zionist movement, and geographical base for world imperialism placed strategically in the midst of the Arab homeland to combat the hopes of the Arab nation for liberation, unity, and progress. Israel is a constant source of threat vis-à-vis peace in the Middle East and the whole world. Since the liberation of Palestine will destroy the Zionist and imperialist presence and will contribute to the establishment of peace in the Middle East, the Palestinian people look for the support of all the progressive and peaceful forces and urge them all, irrespective of their affiliations and beliefs, to offer the Palestinian people all aid and support in their just struggle for the liberation of their homeland.

## Fatah

Fateh, or *Fatah* (which means "victory" or "conquest") is the largest faction within the Palestinian "resistance." It was formed in 1958; Yasser Arafat was one of its founders and its chairman from 1969 until his death in 2004. It is a nationalistic organization, not religiously based like Hamas. The Fatah constitution was written in 1964 and reaffirmed at its August 2009 convention. It states, *inter alia*:

> Article 4: The Palestinian struggle is part and parcel of the world-wide struggle against Zionism, colonialism and international imperialism.
>
> Article 7: The Zionist Movement is racial, colonial and aggressive in ideology, goals, organization and method.
>
> Article 17: Armed public revolution is the inevitable method to liberating Palestine....
>
> Article (19): Armed struggle is a strategy and not a tactic, and the Palestinian Arab People's armed revolution is a decisive factor in the liberation fight and in uprooting the Zionist existence, and this struggle will not cease unless the Zionist state is demolished and Palestine is completely liberated.

## The Khartoum Resolution of 1967

Heads-of-state from eight Arab countries met for a summit in Khartoum, Sudan shortly after the 1967 Six-Day War. The resulting formulation became known as the "Three No's" and has continued to form the basis of the policies of most Arab states toward Israel: "NO peace with Israel; NO recognition of Israel; NO negotiations with Israel."

Since then, only two Arab states have signed peace treaties with Israel: Egypt in 1979 and Jordan in 1994.

## The Hamas (Islamic Resistance Movement) Covenant (1988)

Hamas is an acronym meaning "Islamic Resistance Movement." It was founded in 1987 by Sheikh Ahmed Yassin as the Muslim Brotherhood's local political arm. Hamas is unabashedly and stridently anti-Israel and anti-Semitic. Its covenant contains the following statements:

> Introduction: Israel will exist and will continue to exist until Islam will obliterate it, just as it obliterated others before it.... Our struggle against the Jews is very great and very serious. It needs all sincere efforts. It is a step that inevitably should be followed by other steps. The Movement is but one squadron that should be supported by more and more squadrons from this vast Arab and Islamic world, until the enemy is vanquished and Allah's victory is realized.

> Article 7: The Prophet, Allah's prayer and peace be upon him, says: 'The hour of judgment shall not come until the Muslims fight the Jews and kill them, so that the Jews hide behind trees and stones, and each tree and stone will say: "Oh Muslim, oh servant of Allah, there is a Jew behind me, come and kill him"

> Article 8: Allah is its target, the Prophet is its model, the Koran its constitution: Jihad is its path and death for the sake of Allah is the loftiest of its wishes.

> Article 11: The Islamic Resistance Movement believes that the land of Palestine is an Islamic *Waqf* trust consecrated for future Muslim generations until Judgment Day. It, or any part of it, should not be squandered: it, or any part of it, should not be given up....This is the law governing the land of Palestine in the Islamic *Sharia* (law) and the same goes for any land the Muslims have conquered by force, because during the times

of [Islamic] conquests, the Muslims consecrated these lands to Muslim generations till the Day of Judgment.

Article 13: Initiatives, and so-called peaceful solutions and international conferences, are in contradiction to the principles of the Islamic Resistance Movement... There is no solution for the Palestinian question except through Jihad. Initiatives, proposals and international conferences are all a waste of time and vain endeavors.

Article 15: "...It is necessary to instill the spirit of Jihad in the heart of the nation so that they would confront the enemies and join the ranks of the fighters. It is necessary that scientists, educators and teachers, information and media people, as well as the educated masses, especially the youth and sheikhs of the Islamic movements, should take part in the operation of awakening [the masses]. It is necessary to instill in the minds of the Muslim generations that the Palestinian problem is a religious problem, and should be dealt with on this basis.

Article 31: Under the wing of Islam, it is possible for the followers of the three religions—Islam, Christianity and Judaism—to coexist in peace and quiet with each other. Peace and quiet would not be possible except under the wing of Islam. Past/present history is the best witness to that.

## Palestinian Basic Law (ratified 2002)

The Palestinian Basic Law was promulgated to function as a temporary constitution for the Palestinian Authority until such time as the establishment of an independent state.

Article 4: 1. Islam is the official religion in Palestine. Respect and sanctity of all other heavenly religions shall be maintained. 2. The principles of Islamic Shari'a shall be the main source of legislation. 3. Arabic shall be the official language.

This language is the foundation for Palestinian rejectionism and explains why they: incite hatred and violence against Jews and Israelis in their schools, mosques, and media; shun peace talks and direct negotiations; violate their international obligations under agreements such as the Oslo Accords; engage in deliberate terrorism against Israeli civilians; and call for boycotts, divestment, sanctions, and "lawfare" against Israelis in foreign courts. This Basic Law is essentially a theocracy, and provides the basis for treating Jews as *dhimmis*; necessarily, it denies the recognition of their state.

## Basic Israeli Documents Bearing on the Making of Peace

Israel was founded on guiding principles contained in the Bible, Jewish law, values and traditional sources.

In the Torah (The Five Books of Moses, the first five books of the Bible), the first mention of God's explicitly assigning the Land Of Israel to Abraham and his descendants comes in Genesis 12:7. When Abraham was looking for a burial cave for Sarah, he finds the cave called "*Machpelah*", which is owned by Efron the Hittite. Gen. 23. God reaffirms to Jacob the land of Israel that he assigned to Abraham and Isaac is assigned to him and his descendants. When God speaks to Moses first, the encounter takes place at the burning bush. There (Exodus 3:16-17) the God of Abraham, Isaac and Jacob speaks to Moses and says (17): "...I will take you out of the misery of Egypt to the land of the Canaanites (who were the dominant tribe), the Hittites (from whom Abraham bought the cave), the Amorites, the Perizzites, the Hittites and the Jebusites (who inhabited the Jebusite city where later, under David, the city of Jerusalem would be built), to a land flowing with milk and honey." When Moses finally leads the People out of Egypt, he does so on God's instruction to lead them to the Promised Land. This is reinforced repeatedly to the People, *e.g.,* Ex. 13:5 and 11. When Joshua takes over for Moses, Deut. 34:9, he assumes all of the responsibilities which God had given to Moses. Joshua led the children of Israel into the Promised Land, the date of which is precisely recorded in scripture using their calendar at that time: the 10th day of the first month (later called *Nisan*), forty years after the Exodus from Egypt (Joshua 4:19; 5:6). This has been calculated to be the year 1422 B.C.E.

Leviticus 19:34 instructs: "The stranger who resides with you shall be to you as one of your citizens; you shall love him as yourself, for you were strangers in the land of Egypt; I the Lord am your God." The Passover Haggadah instructs that, because the Jewish People "were strangers in the land of Egypt," Jews are not to oppress others in their midst (*i.e.*, not to treat others the way they were treated).

In stark contrast to the various Arab, Palestinian and Muslim documents above, the State of Israel has offered its outstretched hand to its neighbors in cooperation and friendship from the ***outset:***

## Declaration of the Establishment of the State of Israel (May 14, 1948)

The Land of Israel was the birthplace of the Jewish people. Here their spiritual, religious and political identity was shaped. Here they first attained to statehood, created cultural values of national and universal significance and gave to the world the eternal Book of Books.

After being forcibly exiled from their land, the people kept faith with it throughout their Dispersion and never ceased to pray and hope for their return to it and for the restoration in it of their political freedom.

Impelled by this historic and traditional attachment, Jews strove in every successive generation to re-establish themselves in their ancient homeland. In recent decades they returned in their masses. Pioneers, *ma'pilim* [Hebrew: immigrants coming to Eretz-Israel in defiance of restrictive legislation] and defenders, they made deserts bloom, revived the Hebrew language, built villages and towns, and created a thriving community controlling its own economy and culture, loving peace but knowing how to defend itself, bringing the blessings of progress to all the country's inhabitants, and aspiring towards independent nationhood.

In the year 5657 [1897], at the summons of the spiritual father of the Jewish State, Theodore Herzl, the First Zionist Congress convened and proclaimed the right of the Jewish people to national rebirth in its own country.

This right was recognized in the Balfour Declaration of the 2nd November, 1917, and re-affirmed in the Mandate of the League of Nations which, in particular, gave international sanction to the historic connection between the Jewish people and Eretz-Israel and to the right of the Jewish people to rebuild its National Home.

The catastrophe which recently befell the Jewish people—the massacre of millions of Jews in Europe—was another clear demonstration of the urgency of solving the problem of its homelessness by re-establishing in Eretz-Israel the Jewish State, which would open the gates of the homeland wide to every Jew and confer upon the Jewish people the status of a fully privileged member of the comity of nations.

Survivors of the Nazi holocaust in Europe, as well as Jews from other parts of the world, continued to migrate to Eretz-Israel, undaunted by difficulties, restrictions and dangers, and never ceased to assert their right to a life of dignity, freedom and honest toil in their national homeland.

In the Second World War, the Jewish community of this country contributed its full share to the struggle of the freedom- and peace-loving nations against the forces of Nazi wickedness and, by the blood of its soldiers and its war effort, gained the right to be reckoned among the peoples who founded the United Nations.

On the 29th November, 1947, the United Nations General Assembly passed a resolution calling for the establishment of a Jewish State in Eretz-Israel; the General Assembly required the inhabitants of Eretz-Israel to take such steps as were necessary on their part for the implementation of that resolution. This recognition by the United Nations of the right of the Jewish people to establish their State is irrevocable.

This right is the natural right of the Jewish people to be masters of their own fate, like all other nations, in their own sovereign State.

ACCORDINGLY WE, MEMBERS OF THE PEOPLE'S COUNCIL, REPRESENTATIVES OF THE JEWISH COMMUNITY OF ERETZ-ISRAEL AND OF THE ZIONIST MOVEMENT, ARE HERE ASSEMBLED ON THE DAY OF THE TERMINATION OF THE BRITISH MANDATE OVER ERETZ-ISRAEL AND, BY VIRTUE OF OUR NATURAL AND HISTORIC RIGHT AND ON THE STRENGTH OF THE RESOLUTION OF THE UNITED NATIONS GENERAL ASSEMBLY, HEREBY DECLARE THE ESTABLISHMENT OF A JEWISH STATE IN ERETZ-ISRAEL, TO BE KNOWN AS THE STATE OF ISRAEL.

WE DECLARE that, with effect from the moment of the termination of the Mandate being tonight, the eve of Sabbath, the 6th Iyar, 5708 [15th May, 1948], until the establishment of the elected, regular authorities of the State in accordance with the Constitution which shall be adopted by the Elected Constituent Assembly not later than the 1st October 1948, the People's Council shall act as a Provisional Council of State, and its executive organ, the People's Administration, shall be the Provisional Government of the Jewish State, to be called "Israel".

THE STATE OF ISRAEL will be open for Jewish immigration and for the Ingathering of the Exiles; it will foster the development of the country for the benefit of **all** its inhabitants; it will be based on freedom, justice and peace as envisaged by the prophets of Israel; **it will ensure complete equality of social and political rights to all its inhabitants irrespective of religion, race or sex; it will guarantee freedom of religion, conscience, language, education and culture; it will safeguard the Holy Places of all religions**; and it will be faithful to the principles of the Charter of the United Nations. (emphasis added)

THE STATE OF ISRAEL is prepared to cooperate with the agencies and representatives of the United Nations in implementing the resolution of the General Assembly of the 29th November, 1947, and will take steps to bring about the economic union of the whole of Eretz-Israel.

WE APPEAL to the United Nations to assist the Jewish people in the building-up of its State and to receive the State of Israel into the comity of nations.

WE APPEAL - in the very midst of the onslaught launched against us now for months - to the Arab inhabitants of the State of Israel to preserve peace and participate in the upbuilding of the State on the basis **of full and equal citizenship and due representation** in all its provisional and permanent institutions. (*emphasis added*)

**WE EXTEND our hand to all neighbouring states and their peoples in an offer of peace and good neighbourliness, and appeal to them to establish bonds of cooperation and mutual help with the sovereign Jewish people settled in its own land. The State of Israel is prepared to do its share in a common effort for the advancement of the entire Middle East.** *(emphasis added)*

WE APPEAL to the Jewish people throughout the Diaspora to rally round the Jews of Eretz-Israel in the tasks of immigration and upbuilding and to stand by them in the great struggle for the realization of the age-old dream - the redemption of Israel.

PLACING OUR TRUST IN THE "ROCK OF ISRAEL", WE AFFIX OUR SIGNATURES TO THIS PROCLAMATION AT THIS SESSION OF THE PROVISIONAL COUNCIL OF STATE, ON THE SOIL OF THE HOMELAND, IN THE

CITY OF TEL-AVIV, ON THIS SABBATH EVE, THE 5TH
DAY OF IYAR, 5708 (14TH MAY,1948)

## International Documents Regarding the Making of Peace

During World War I, British policy became gradually committed to the concept of establishing a Jewish home in Palestine (*Eretz Yisrael*). After discussions in the British Cabinet and consultations with Zionist leaders, the decision was publicized in the form of a letter from Arthur James Lord Balfour to Lord Rothschild, dated November 2, 1917. This letter represented the first political recognition of Zionist aspirations by a Great World Power. The Balfour Declaration states: "His Majesty's Government view with favour the establishment in Palestine of a national home for the Jewish people, and will use their best endeavours to facilitate the achievement of this object, it being clearly understood that nothing shall be done which may prejudice the civil and religious rights of existing non-Jewish communities in Palestine or the rights and political status enjoyed by Jews in any other country."

The defeat of the Ottoman Empire in 1918 led to dissolution of its vast lands in the Middle East. At the initial Paris Peace Conference in 1919, the victorious Allies began adjusting their differences and territorial appetites. At a meeting of the Allies in London in February 1920, it was decided to put Palestine under British Mandatory rule. At the San Remo Conference, held in San Remo, Italy in April 1920, the Allies agreed to divide the former Arab provinces of the Ottoman Empire along the lines of the Sykes-Picot Agreement: France received the mandates for Syria and Lebanon, and Britain obtained mandates for Iraq, Transjordan (which it created in 1920 from the Mandate for Palestine) and Palestine. Most significantly, the Conference confirmed the pledge contained in the Balfour Declaration regarding the establishment of a Jewish national home in Palestine. The Zionists (including attendees Chaim Weizmann, Nahum Sokolow and Herbert Samuel) argued convincingly to Britain to incorporate the Balfour Declaration into the preamble of the Palestine Mandate.

In July 1922, the League of Nations entrusted Britain with the Mandate for Palestine. Recognizing the historical connection of the Jewish people with Palestine, Britain was called upon to facilitate the establishment of a Jewish national home in Palestine-*Eretz Yisrael*. In September 1922, the Council of the League of Nations and Britain decided that the provisions for setting up a Jewish national home would not apply east of the Jordan River, which constituted **three-fourths of the Mandate territory**, eventually becoming the Hashemite Kingdom of Jordan. Thus, the Mandate for Palestine, a historical League of Nations document, formulated the Jewish legal right to settle anywhere in western Palestine, between the Jordan River and Mediterranean Sea, an entitlement unaltered in international law. The entire League of Nations, 51 members, unanimously declared on July 24, 1922: "Whereas recognition has been given to the historical connection of the Jewish people with Palestine and to the grounds for reconstituting their national home in that country."

There was no focus or anything heard about a distinct Palestinian Arab people...because it did not exist. The international decision to create Palestine "as a national home for the Jewish people" was made in recognition of the Jewish people's aboriginal title and continuing links to the land. The Allies strongly believed they had also done justice to the claims of the Arab people via the creation or recognition of several new Arab states, including that of Jordan which was formed from 75% of the Palestine Mandate, and even today consists of 70% Palestinian Arabs.

## U.N. Partition Resolution

In 1947, the U.N. General Assembly adopted Resolution 181, which sought to divide the remaining Palestine Mandate into "Jewish" and "Arab"(not "Palestinian") states. The Jews accepted but Arabs rejected this Resolution, and when Israel declared its independence at the Mandate's expiration, invaded with the intent to destroy it.

## U.N. Resolution 242

On Nov 22, 1967, the U.N. Security Council unanimously adopted Resolution 242, establishing the principles that have been the framework for negotiation of an Arab-Israeli peace settlement following the June 1967 Six Day War.

A much-quoted, yet often misinterpreted clause is the call for the "Withdrawal of Israeli armed forces from territories occupied in the recent conflict." This clause is linked to a calling for "termination of all claims or states of belligerency" and the recognition that "every State in the area" has the "right to live in peace within secure and recognized boundaries free from threats or acts of force." The resolution does **not** make Israeli withdrawal a prerequisite for Arab action.

The "withdrawal" clause does **not** specify how much territory Israel is required to relinquish. The Security Council very deliberately did **not** say Israel must withdraw from "**all the**" territories captured after the Six-Day War. The Arab states pushed for the word "all" to be included, but this was specifically rejected; nevertheless, they said they would interpret the resolution as if it had included the word "all."

Lord Caradon, the British Ambassador who drafted the approved resolution, declared after the vote: "It is only the resolution that will bind us, and we regard its wording as clear." On October 29, 1969, the British Foreign Secretary told the House of Commons that the withdrawal envisaged by the resolution would not be from "all the territories." He later stated: "It would have been wrong to demand that Israel return to its positions of June 4, 1967, because those positions were undesirable and artificial."

U.S. Ambassador Arthur Goldberg, another of the drafters, explained: "The notable omissions–which were not accidental–in regard to withdrawal are the words 'the' or 'all' and 'the June 5, 1967 lines' ... the resolution speaks of withdrawal from occupied territories without defining the extent of withdrawal."

The Arab states also objected to the call for "secure and recognized boundaries" because they feared this implied negotiations with Israel, which they had ruled-out at the Khartoum Arab League conference in August 1967 with their three "No's." Ambassador Goldberg explained that the "secure and recognized boundaries" phrase was specifically included because the parties were expected to make "territorial adjustments in their peace settlement encompassing less than a complete withdrawal of Israeli forces from occupied territories, inasmuch as Israel's prior frontiers had proved to be notably insecure."

In sum, the Resolution clearly calls on the Arab states to make peace with Israel. The principal condition is that Israel withdraw from "territories," intentionally omitting "the"and "all," " occupied" in the 1967 war. Since Israel withdrew from approximately 94% of these "territories" when it gave back the Sinai to Egypt (1982), the Gaza Strip (2005) and portions of Judea/Samaria (2005), it has already substantially, if not wholly, fulfilled its obligation under U.N.S.C.R. 242.

## Oslo Accords

On September 13, 1993 representatives of the State of Israel and the PLO signed the "Declaration of Principles On Interim Self-Government Arrangements", a document also known as the "Oslo Accords". They were signed at a Washington ceremony hosted by U.S. President Bill Clinton on September 13, 1993, during which Palestinian leader Yasser Arafat and Israeli Prime Minister Yitzhak Rabin ended decades as sworn enemies with an uneasy handshake. This agreement was the fruit of secret negotiations between Israel and the Palestinians, represented by the PLO, following the Madrid Conference in 1991.

The Oslo Accords contain a set of mutually agreed-upon general principles regarding a five year interim period of Palestinian self-rule. So-called "permanent status issues" are deferred to later negotiations, to begin no later than the third year of the interim period. The permanent status negotiations were intended to lead to an agreement that would be implemented to take effect at the end of the interim period.

The main points of the Oslo Accords (or Declaration of Principles = DOP):

Transfer of Powers to the Palestinian Arabs:

The DOP features an agreement in principle regarding a transfer of power and responsibilities to the Palestinians in Judea/Samaria and Gaza, so they may have control over their own affairs.

The DOP does not prejudge the Permanent Status:

The DOP specifically states that permanent status issues, such as Jerusalem, refugees, settlements, security arrangements and borders are to be excluded from the interim arrangements and that the outcome of the permanent status talks should not be prejudged or preempted by the interim arrangements. During this period, the Israeli government retains sole responsibility for foreign affairs, defense and borders. Israel's position on Jerusalem remains unchanged. When the DOP was signed, Prime Minister Rabin stated that "Jerusalem is the ancient and eternal capital of the Jewish people." An undivided Jerusalem under Israeli sovereignty, with religious freedom for all, is and remains a fundamental Israeli position.

Security remains an Israeli responsibility:

In the DOP, Israel and the PLO agree that during the interim period, Israel will remain responsible for security along the international borders and the crossing points to Egypt and Jordan. Israel will also retain responsibility for and the overall security of Israelis in Judea/Samaria and Gaza, the Israeli settlements in those areas, and freedom of movement on roads.

Implementation of the DOP was specified to involve the following phases:

Gaza-Jericho: Self-rule in the Gaza Strip and the Jericho area, including a withdrawal of Israeli forces from those areas (the "first redeployment"), is to serve as a first step in the implementation of the DOP. The details of the Gaza-Jericho aspect of the DOP were negotiated and concluded in an agreement signed in Cairo between Israel and the PLO on May 4, 1994.

Preparatory Transfer of Powers and Responsibilities: In the rest of Judea/Samaria, five specific spheres—education and culture, health, social welfare, direct taxation and tourism—are to be transferred to Palestinian representatives through early empowerment. Additional spheres may be transferred as agreed by the sides. The DOP proposed that this transfer of powers take place immediately following the implementation of the Gaza-Jericho agreement.

The Interim Agreement and Elections: A modalities agreement regarding the election of a Palestinian Council and a comprehensive Interim Agreement specifying the structure and powers of the Council will be negotiated. The Interim Agreement will detail the self-government arrangements in Judea/Samaria and Gaza. Concurrent with the elections, Israeli forces are to be redeployed outside populated areas to specified locations. The Palestinian Council will have a strong police force in order to guarantee public order and internal security. Central to the DOP are two economic annexes which outline economic cooperation between Israel and the Palestinians, both bilaterally and in the multilateral context.

The Permanent Status: Negotiations between Israel and the Palestinians on the permanent status will commence as soon as possible but not later than the beginning of the third year of the interim period (May 1996). These talks will determine the nature of the final settlement between the two sides. It is understood that these negotiations will cover remaining issues including Jerusalem, refugees, settlements, security arrangements, borders, relations and cooperation with other neighbors, and other issues of common interest. Under the DOP, the permanent status will take effect 5 years after the implementation of the Gaza-Jericho agreement, namely May 1999.

A letter on key issues, addressed to Prime Minister Yitzhak Rabin, was signed by Yasser Arafat on September 9, 1993. The letter says specifically that:

(1) The PLO recognizes the right of the State of Israel to exist in peace.

(2) The PLO accepts U.N. Security Council Resolutions 242 and 338

(3) The PLO commits itself to the Middle East peace process...all outstanding issues...will be resolved through negotiations

(4) ...the PLO renounces the use of terrorism and other acts of violence and will assume responsibility over all PLO elements and personnel in order to assure their compliance, prevent violations and discipline violators.

(5) ...those articles of the Palestinian Covenant which deny Israel's right to exist, and the provisions of the Covenant which are inconsistent with the commitments of this letter are now inoperative and no longer valid.*

(6) ...the PLO undertakes to submit to the Palestinian National Council for formal approval the necessary changes in regard to the Palestinian Covenant.

Rabin gave a letter in exchange to Arafat, also dated September 9, saying:

...Israel has decided to recognize the PLO as the representative of the Palestinian people and commence negotiations with the PLO within the Middle

East peace process.

The Israelis kept their commitments, including teaching their children a curriculum of peace and turning over to the Palestinian Arabs civil administration of areas in the territories. Not only did the Palestinian Arabs not abide by their obligations, they vastly **increased** their levels of incitement and terrorist attacks, culminating in the devastating and bloody Second Intifada. The PLO never revoked the pertinent articles in its Covenant. Hamas unequivocally refuses to recognize the Oslo Agreements. The media consistently failed to point out, excused and at best whitewashed, the repeated and violent Palestinian transgressions.

### "The Road Map To a Two-State Solution"

The "Roadmap For Peace" or "Road Map" (formally "A Performance-Based Roadmap to a Permanent Solution to the Israeli-Palestinian Conflict") was a plan formulated in 2003 by a "quartet" of international entities: the United States, the European Union, Russia, and the United Nations, to resolve the Israeli-Palestinian conflict after it became clear that the Oslo Accords had failed. It was first outlined in a speech by President George W. Bush on June 24, 2002, in which he stated: "The Road Map represents a starting point toward achieving the vision of two states, a secure State of Israel and a viable, peaceful, democratic Palestine. It is the framework for progress towards lasting peace and security in the Middle East...."

Media references to the Road Map frequently cite only Israeli obligations, and when Palestinian obligations are cited they are often couched as "**to rein in militants**." However, while forms of the word "**terror**" appear ten times in the road map, forms of the word "**militants**" never appear even once.

The Road Map has three "phases."

The P.A.'s Phase I obligations in the Road Map include:

> Palestinian leadership issues unequivocal statement reiterating Israel's right to exist in peace and security and calling for an immediate and unconditional ceasefire to end armed activity and all acts of violence against Israelis anywhere. All official Palestinian institutions end incitement against Israel.

> Palestinians declare an unequivocal end to violence and terrorism and undertake visible efforts on the ground to arrest, disrupt, and restrain individuals and groups conducting and planning violent attacks on Israelis anywhere.

> Rebuilt and refocused Palestinian Authority security apparatus begins sustained, targeted, and effective operations aimed at confronting all those engaged in terror and disman-

tlement of terrorist capabilities and belowstructure. This includes commencing confiscation of illegal weapons and consolidation of security authority, free of association with terror and corruption.

Arab states cut off public and private funding and all other forms of support for groups supporting and engaging in violence and terror.

## Arab Rejection of Peace Proposals With Israel

As Israeli P.M. Benjamin Netanyahu observed in his speech before the U.S. Congress in May 2011, the conflict has never been about the establishment of a Palestinian State (Jordan, which was formed from 75% of the land from the Palestine Mandate, has a population which is 70% "Palestinian" Arab), but rather the existence of the tiny Jewish state of Israel (5.5 million Jews) surrounded by 22 Arab-Muslim nations (population 350 million). Netanyahu went on to describe the incessant incitement against Israel and Jews perpetrated in Judea/Samaria and Gaza by the P.A. and Hamas, and their fanciful requirement that the descendants of Palestinian refugees from the 1948 war they initiated be allowed to "return" to their "homes" inside Israel proper: " My friends, this must come to an end. President Abbas must do what I have done. I stood before my people—I told you it wasn't easy for me—I said 'I will accept a Palestinian state.' It is time for President Abbas to stand before his people and say 'I will accept a Jewish state.' Those six words will change history."

However, several days after Netanyahu's speech, Abbas made the following comments: "With regard to Palestinian recognition of a Jewish state, or whatever, this has never been an issue. Throughout the negotiations between Israelis and us, from 1993 until a year ago, we never heard the words 'Jewish state.' Now they have begun to talk about it, and our response 'Go to the U.N. and call yourselves what you want. We are not the party to address. Not only that— we refuse to recognize a Jewish state. Try to wrest it out of the U.N. or anyone else. Why does Israel insist on demanding from us and us alone? It did not demand this from the Arabs, from Egypt, from Jordan, or from any Arab country with which it negotiated? Only from us. We know the reason, and we say: 'No, we refuse.' " Abbas reiterated this sentiment on August 28, 2011, on the eve of the September U.N. statehood bid, as he criticized demands made by the International Quartet and urged them to back-off: "Don't order us to recognize a Jewish state. We won't accept it."

The Arab nations have repeatedly and persistently rejected peace with Israel and a western "Palestine" Arab state of their own: (a) when it was proposed in 1937 by the Peel Commission; (b) when it was offered by the U.N. in 1947 (the Jews accepted the 1947 partition plan, but the Arabs rejected it and instead launched a war against the fledgling Jewish state by five invading Arab armies); and (c) when it was offered to P.A. President Yasser Arafat by President Clinton and Israeli Prime Minister Ehud Barak at the Camp David Conference in 2000. Arafat's response was a non-response, he walked away; soon thereafter, he initiated the deadly "Second Intifada." Palestinian P.M. Abbas similarly rejected Israeli Prime Minister Ehud Olmert's offers for a state on all of Gaza and 93% of Judea/Samaria with some land swaps in 2008. Again, the M.S.M. fails to report this history.

The M.S.M. also fails to note that, during the Israel War for Independence in 1948-49, Arab armies illegally annexed the areas which became known as "the West Bank" (Jordan) and the Gaza Strip (Egypt), which the U.N. had designated as a state for the Arabs. No new, separate, "Palestinian" state was ever demanded for or on those territories, despite their being in Arab hands. In fact, when the Palestine Liberation Organization was formed in 1964 at the Arab League Summit in Cairo, its covenant made no mention of "liberating" these lands from Egypt or Jordan. Instead, the PLO leadership stated unequivocally that its goal was to "push the Jews into the sea." That still remains the goal of the P.A. and Hamas, the elected government of Gaza. It is a myth that the Arabs will make peace with Israel in exchange for territory. There is but one Jewish state on the planet. Israel comprises just 0.1% of the land mass of the Middle East, yet it is the one expected by the rest of the world to cede territory.

When P.A. officials address Arab audiences, they openly state that their goal is the destruction of Israel, not simply the conquest of the 1967 territories (*i.e.*, "West Bank" and Gaza) and that they advocate the "Strategy of Phases"; this envisions gaining some of the territories, and then using them as a forward operating base or launching pad to invade and annihilate the rest of Israel. The M.S.M. rarely, if ever, reports what Arab/Palestinian officials say to their audiences in Arabic about their goals to destroy the Jewish state.

And Hamas's leaders–like their counterparts in the Muslim Brotherhood– make no bones about their incessant intention to destroy Israel. In December 2011 at a speech in Gaza, Hamas leader Ismail Haniyeh proclaimed, "We say today explicitly so it cannot be explained otherwise, that the armed resistance and the armed struggle are the path and the strategic choice for liberating the Palestinian land, from the (Mediterranean) sea to the (Jordan) river, and for the expulsion of the invaders and usurpers (Israel)....We won't relinquish one inch of the land of Palestine."

P.A. maps and emblems in official publications and schoolbooks define all of Israel as "Occupied Palestine," omitting "Israel," depicting a single entity, "Palestine." Songs taught to children in P.A. schools and summer camps refer to "returning" to cities in pre-1967 Israel. Both P.A.- and Hamas media, mosques and schools consistently espouse hatred of Jews and denial of their bond with the Holy Land. How often does the M.S.M. cover this?

Thus, in essence, the Palestinian Arabs expect Israel to recognize their rights to a state, but deny that same right to Israel as the nation-state of the Jewish people. They do not merely desire a Palestinian Arab state in Judea/Samaria and Gaza, which they could have had over 60 years ago. Their unambiguous goal is the total eradication of Israel. This is an existential battle between one side's rigid, deeply-engrained, life-controlling religious-based teachings which forbid a non-Muslim state in their midst to be tolerated...especially a Jewish one, run by people whom Allah tells the Muslims in the Qur'an are to be hated, despised, and at best permitted to live as *dhimmis* (second class citizens) under their hegemony, and whose continued existence is a constant repudiation of what Allah forecasts. They are now intensely envious of the success and prowess of the tiny state. Moreover, under Islamic law, any land that was once Muslim (that they conquered from other peoples) must always belong to Muslims; thus, "Palestine" is Muslim land. Muslims have proven that they are willing to fight to the death for these ideas to achieve the goal of destroying Israel and the West. Israel's goal, on the other hand, is simply to live in peace and security with her Muslim neighbors. Unfortunately, the cold reality is that the hardened Arab and Muslim mind-set prevents any other scenario, no matter how much we in the tolerant Judeo-Christian western/democratic liberal tradition wish it were different.

### Israel's Peace Process Position

In an address to the Knesset in May 2011, Israeli Prime Minister Netanyahu laid out six key points that could pave the way to resolving the conflict—points, he said, all Israelis could agree on:

> (1) The Palestinians recognize the State of Israel as the national homeland of the Jewish people.
>
> (2) The agreement between Israel and the Palestinians must end the conflict and all demands on the State of Israel.
>
> (3) The problem of the Palestinian refugees will be resolved outside of Israel and not within its borders.
>
> (4) A Palestinian state must be demilitarized, with practical security arrangements, including long-term presence along the Jordan River.
>
> (5) Israel will retain the settlement blocs.
>
> (6) Jerusalem will remain the united and sovereign capital of the State of Israel.

Not surprisingly, the P.A. immediately rejected them.

Sources:
PA Charter
Hamas Charter
Jewishvirtuallibrary.org
YNetnews.com
Peel Commission Report
"What is Jihad?" (by Daniel Pipes in *NY Post* 12-31-02)
Israel Ministry of Foreign Affairs
*The Al Qaeda Reader*
*The Politically Incorrect Guide to Islam (And The Crusades)* by Robert Spencer (2005)
*Myths and Facts: A Guide to the Arab-Israel Conflict* by Mitchell C. Bard *(2006)*
Yale University Law School*: The Avalon Project*
Palestinianbasiclaw.org

# II. **Documents: Resources for Countering Anti-Israel-Media Bias**

◄ David Bar-Illan, late editor of *The Jerusalem Post,* compiled his ground-breaking "Eye On The Media" columns into a book with that title (Jerusalem, Jerusalem Post, 1993); copies are still available on Amazon. "Top 50 Reviewer" Shalom Freedman called it "A courageous pioneering work of truthtelling." Freedman's (11/4/04) review:

> The late David Bar-Ilan for a number of years wrote a weekly column in the *Jerusalem Post* exposing distorted media coverage against Israel. Among the culprits were the *Guardian*, *Reuters* and *A.P.*, the *L.A. Times* the *N.Y. Times*, and most of the major newspapers and media services. Bar-Ilan detected that a major anti-Israel bias had developed since the Six-Day War. He wrote fairly, always got his facts right, and time and again pointed out errors. At the time each of these struggles seemed a "life and death" one and Bar-Ilan's writings were a source of comfort and strength to a large number of supporters of Israel. This work is excellent not only for those interested in the Middle East conflict but for anyone who wants to see how the media may distort the news, and rewrite it in accord with its own bias and agenda.

◄ *Israel in Medialand*, compiled and edited by Eliyahu Tal (Jerusalem,

Jerusalem Post, rev. ed. 1989), both focuses on M.S.M. coverage of the "intifada" that broke out in late-1987, and probes fundamental news reporting issues; it is also available on Amazon.

◄  Anti-Israel media bias has been documented in journalist Stephanie Gutmann's *The Other War: Israelis, Palestinians and the Struggle for Media Supremacy* (San Francisco, Encounter Books, 2005). She analyzed coverage of big news stories like those on the claimed Jenin massacre and Mohammed al-Dura shooting; talks to "those in the trenches" like the Jerusalem Post's Khaled Abu Toameh and Israeli press official Danny Seaman; and assesses how well Israel and Jews in the West are fighting back in that other war.

◄  CAMERA (www.camera.org) and HonestReporting (www.honestreporting.com) are the major watchdogs contesting international M.S.M. anti-Israel bias.

◄  News source-specific bias trackers monitor the *L.A. Times* (David Frankenthal's jtbla.com), the *Washington Post* (EyeOnThePost.com) and the *Inquirer* ("Brith Sholom Media Watch," a focus on Israel coverage e-mailed weekly by one of this book's co-authors since 2001; jverlin1234@comcast.net).

◄  Husband-wife journalists Greg Myre and Jennifer Griffin lived for eight years, including during the second "intifada," in a Jewish Jerusalem neighborhood, reporting for *A.P.* and Fox News, respectively. Their 2011 book *This Burning Land: Lessons from the Front Lines of the Transformed Israeli-Palestinian Conflict,* includes discussion of Mideast reporting word-choices confronting reporters, and provides a view of Israeli and Palestinian Arab claims as seen through the sharp eyes of this pair of journalists.

# III.  History:  The Jewish People's Continuous Presence in Palestine

"'Jewishness'is more than just a religion. It is an intertwined and intricate mixture of ancestry, religion, history, culture, country, tradition, attitude, ethnicity, peoplehood and nationhood."

The Holocaust is not the only era of Jewish history which the Jewish people's enemies target as historically conjured. To counter seemingly-endless propaganda denying the Jewish people's historical connection to its homeland, Jews must forcefully make these three historical points:

(1)  ancient Jewish homeland history happened;

(2)  the Romans, after finally defeating ancient Judaea, did not "exile" the Jews from the land; and

(3)  Jews have continuously resided in Palestine, from Israelite origins through

the long dark foreign-rule centuries to the modern era.

The following condensed summary is extracted from Verlin, *Israel 3000 Years: The Jewish People's 3000 Year Presence in Palestine*, Philadelphia, Pavilion Press, Inc., 2011 (www.pavilionpress.com), and the authorities quoted and cited therein.

## Ancient Homeland Jewish History Happened

We are not solely dependent on the Hebrew Bible as evidence that the ancient Israelite kingdoms existed. Archeological evidence – including of the Israelites' enemies – abounds and continues to be unearthed.

Archeologists are divided whether the Israelites arrived in Canaan by conquest or arose from within the Canaanite population, but agree that Israelite presence in the land can be traced back as far as the late second millennium B.C.E. A population surge occurred in the Judean and Samarian hill country c. 1200 B.C.E. that continued to exist there without interruption into the era of the Israelite Biblical kingdoms. The first reference to "Israel" is in Egyptian Pharaoh Merneptah's 1210 B.C.E. stele, seemingly referring to it as an ethnic group on the far borders of Canaan.

Repeated archeological searches through the 20th century failed to find remains of 10th century B.C.E. Jerusalem, the time and place of King David. "Minimalists" began to quip that King David "was as real as King Arthur." Then, in an electrifying finding in 1993 at Tel Dan in northern Israel, archeologists unearthed a stone inscribed by a 9th century B.C.E. Israelite enemy king, Hazael of Aram-Damascus, boasting of his victories over the northern kingdom of Israel and "the House of David." This "House of David" inscription, referencing the southern kingdom of Judah by its founder's name just a century after his lifetime, shifted debate from whether King David was a real historical figure to whether he had merely been a tribal chieftain of a dusty hill village. Then, in 2005, Israeli archeologist Eilat Mazar unearthed in the oldest City of David section of Jerusalem an enormous 10th century B.C.E. public building that may have been King David's fabled Biblical palace.

This discovery was supplemented by 10th century B.C.E. findings, including a Hebrew alphabet, also that year at Tel Zayit on what had been the Philistine border. "A border town of such size and culture," the American archeologist, Prof. Ron E. Tappy, stated, "suggested a centralized bureaucracy, political leadership and literacy levels that seemed to support the Biblical image of the united kingdom of David and Solomon in the 10th century B.C.E." And this was supplemented by explosive findings in 2008 at Elah Fortress-Khirbet Qeiyafa, also on the Philistine border, of an almost certainly Israelite late 11th/early 10th century B.C.E. fortress with "the most massive gate ever found in any Biblical city to date," and a pottery shard containing the earliest Hebrew writing ever discovered. Hebrew University's Prof. Garfinkel, excavator of Elah Fortress:

> The Biblical text, the single-phase city at Khirbet Qeiyafah, and the radiometric dates each stands alone as significant evidence clearly indicating that the Biblical tradition does bear authentic geographical memories from the 10th century B.C.E. Elah Valley. There is no ground for the assumption that these traditions were fabricated in the late 7th century or in the Hellenistic period.

Massive remains of the northern kingdom of Israel have been unearthed at its capital, Samaria, and elsewhere. A stone erected by a 9th century B.C.E. Moabite king, boasting of victories over Israel's Omride dynasty, shows that "the kingdom of Israel reached far east and south of its earlier heartland in the central hill country." And then there is a dark stone monument, "the Monolith inscription" erected by Assyrian king Shalmaneser III, 858-824 B.C.E., recording the forces of an alliance arrayed against him, including, as apparently the largest component, "2,000 chariots, 10,000 foot soldiers of Ahab, the Israelite."

The smaller Jerusalem-based southern kingdom of Judah grew substantially following the northern kingdom's destruction by Assyria in 722 B.C.E. Hezekiah's famous water tunnel, with its still extant inscription marking the spot where the diggers from both ends finally met, was part of his preparation for Judah's 701 B.C.E. war with Assyria, which ended in bitter defeat. An enormous mural found in the 1840's at Sennacherib's palace in Nineveh depicts in photographic detail Assyrian sacking of the Israelite city Lachish. The final blow was delivered by Assyria's successor, Babylonia, which destroyed Jerusalem and the Temple in 586 B.C.E. A pottery shard with a message from a Judahite outpost officer to his commander in Lachish is among the last glimpses available of the Biblical kingdom, as its towns and cities were snuffed-out one by one. "And may my Lord know," the outpost officer wrote, "that we are watching for the signals of Lachish according to all the signs that my Lord gave, for we do not see Azekah."

Not all the people were exiled to Babylon. A majority remained on the land. Babylonia, like Assyria, did not long survive its destruction of a Biblical kingdom. Within half-a-century, exiles began to return under Babylonia-conquering Cyrus of Persia, whose policy it was to restore captive peoples to their homelands and grant them autonomy. And so what had been the Biblical kingdom of Judah soon became the Jewish Persian province Yehud. There, the Temple, which had stood for four hundred years, was soon rebuilt as the Second Temple, which stood for six hundred. Following its conquest by Alexander, Yehud became Judaea and fell first under control of Alexander's Egyptian-based Ptolemid successors and, in 200 B.C.E., his Seleucid successors. It was against them that the Maccabees led a two-decade revolt, commemorated by Hanukkah, culminating in 142 B.C.E. in the independence of the Jewish Hasmonean kingdom Judaea.

It was this people, the Israelites of Judah and Israel, who became the Jews of Yehud and Judaea, who during that time and in that homeland place distilled their deepest beliefs into the Hebrew Bible that has so influenced the world from ancient times to our own.

During subsequent decades, Hasmonean Judaea expanded, restoring most of the land of Israel and adding adjacent areas to Jewish control. But in 63 B.C.E., the Romans arrived, and through a bloody three-month siege of Jerusalem, . – Pompey brought Judaea under Rome's thumb. In the Roman-Parthian War following Caesar's assassination in 44 B.C.E., the Judaeans revolted but, after a 5-month bloody Jerusalem siege in 37 B.C.E., Rome restored its control and placed Herod "the Great" on Judaea's throne. Among his many building activities, Herod rebuilt the Temple. Its western retaining wall, the Western Wall, survives to this day. As Roman rule became increasingly oppressive and corrupt, the Jews were stirred to rebel. The "Great Revolt" broke out in 66 C.E. and culminated in Jerusalem and the Temple's destruction in 70 C.E. Massada fell in 73 C.E. Echoes of this revolt survive in the world today in "Judaea Capta" coins and the still-standing Arch of Titus in Rome. It was in this Roman-ruled Judaea, while the Temple still stood, that Jesus lived and left his mark on the world.

Incredibly, in 132 C.E., Judaea's Jews revolted again, led by Bar-Kochba, backed by the sages led by Akiba. So ferocious was this Bar-Kochba Revolt that Rome brought back its ablest general, Severus, from Britain, where he was governor, to suppress it. It took him four years. Roman historian Dio Cassius described the carnage wrought on both sides: "The whole of Judaea became desert....Many also of the Romans were slain in the war. Wherefore Hadrian, writing to the Senate, would not use the Emperor's wonted opening form of words, 'I and the army are well.' "

### The Romans Did Not "Exile" the Jews; They Remained Through the Centuries

Jimmy Carter stated a widely-held perception when he wrote ("Historical Chronology," beginning on page 1 of *Palestine: Peace Not Apartheid*) for the year 135 C.E.: "Romans suppress a Jewish revolt, killing or forcing almost all Jews of Judaea into exile." Even the Zionists, to the exasperation of empathetic mid-20th century British historian James Parkes, emphasized "exile and return," rather than making the case, as Parkes put it, that the "heroic endurance of those who had maintained a Jewish presence in The Land all through the centuries, and in spite of every discouragement," wrote the Zionists' "real title deeds."

Upon defeating Bar-Kochba, the Romans did not exile Judaea's surviving Jews; they remained in the land, initially still as its majority people. The Romans and their Byzantine heirs ruled what they renamed as "Palestine"[in memory of the long-gone Philistines, not today's Palestinian Arabs] until the Arab conquest in 638. Archeologists are continually unearthing remains of Roman-Byzantine era synagogues throughout the land. Historian Michael Avi-Yonah:

> ...the Jews were able to maintain their status in the country, and shared in the material prosperity of the Byzantine period. The numerous synagogues of the 4th to 7th centuries attest to this.

It was during this era that Jewish scholars in Yavne, Tiberias and Galilee compiled the great religious works, the Mishnah and then Palestinian Talmud. The Romans recognized the patriarch as head of the homeland Jewish community, the Yishuv, until his dismissal in the 5th century, apparently for having violated a "no new synagogues" ban. The Sanhedrin, which continued in existence, exercised authority over Western diaspora Jewish communities. Even the Babylonian scholars yielded to those in the homeland on setting the calendar. Self-mustered battalions of 20,000 or more homeland Jews fought alongside the invading Persians of 614 against the Byzantine Empire.

The Yishuv aided the Arab invaders of 638 and received rewards, including being appointed guardians of the Temple Mount and restoring of their synagogue in Hebron at the entrance to the gate of the Cave of the Patriarchs. Three foreign Muslim dynasties, initially Arab but progressively controlled by Turks, ruled until the First Crusade. We know today of a hundred 9th century Jewish communities spread all over the land. The Crusaders of 1099 acknowledged that "Jew, Turk and Arab" confronted them in Jerusalem, of whom "the Jew is the last to fall," and that Haifa's Jews fighting alone "with great courage" held them off for a month. Return of Diaspora Jews, spurred by Yehuda Halevi, Maimonides and others, continued during Crusader rule. Benjamin of Tudula recorded surviving Crusader-decimated Jewish communities. Christian pilgrims recounted the land's indelible Jewish connections, including the continued name of "the region called Judea" between the Jordan and Sea.

Saladin-led Turks defeated the Crusaders at the Horns of Hattin battle of 1187. Following waves of Asian and Mongol invaders in the Crusaders' wake, non-Arab Mamluks gained control of large areas including Judea by 1260; they ruled, first from Turkey and then from Egypt, until the Ottoman Turkish conquest in 1517. Records of the Mamluk-era Yishuv in Jerusalem reveal that a 1491 Christian pilgrim recorded "not many Christians, but many Jews" who claim the Holy Land and "refuse to leave." The four Jewish holy cities – Jerusalem, Safad, Tiberias and Hebron – were established, Acre and other towns had Jewish communities, and agricultural villages in the Galilee flourished..

During the 400-year corrupt and oppressive rule of the Ottoman Turks, the fortunes of Jews and others in the land waxed and waned, but by the mid-19th century, the land's population had dropped to less than one-quarter million, its smallest in all of recorded times.

But then the Yishuv began to revive. By the mid-1800's, still during Ottoman rule, Jews again became Jerusalem's largest population segment; before the end of the 19th century, Jews became Jerusalem's majority over Muslims and Christians combined (a dominance that has subsequently increased). New Jewish communities led the breakout from the Old City's walls. Near Jaffa, the Yishuv founded Mikveh Israel, the land's first modern agricultural school, in 1870 and Petah Tikva, the land's first modern agricultural settlement, in 1878. WhenTheodor Herzl convened the First Zionist Congress in Switzerland in 1897, there were already Jewish pioneers at work, rclaiming The Land by reclaiming he land. It was to an already reviving Yishuv that Zionists came.

# IV.  History:  "Palestine" is the Name of a Place, Not of a People

"Palestinian" *used to denote* primarily Palestine's Jews; "Palestine"is a place, not a people.

In 135 C.E., the Roman Empire finally ended the Jerusalem and Second Temple-centered Jewish kingdom Judaea in its fourth of four wars. To disassociate the capital and land of Judaea from Jews, Roman Emperor Hadrian renamed Jerusalem as "Aelia Capitolina" ("Aelia" was part of Hadrian's name and "Capitolina" referenced the Roman god Jupiter) and Judaea as "Palestina" (derived from the Greek name "Paleshet" denoting "the land of the Philistines"). The Philistines had been an Aegean "Sea People" who had conquered the southeastern Mediterranean coast in the late 2nd millennium B.C.E., shortly after the Israelite conquest of the interior hill country, and fought the Israelites in Biblical battles. Half a millennium before Hadrian renamed Judaea in their memory, the Philistines had been destroyed by the same Babylonian Empire that had destroyed the Biblical kingdom of Judah. The Romans weren't referring to Arabs.

*From the 2nd into the 20th century*, Palestine was never a native-ruled place, but only an undifferentiated part of the empire of foreign conqueror. The post-World War I international conferences that carved up the Ottoman Empire into European-controlled mandates included a Mandate for Palestine, which the League of Nations entrusted to Britain. That Mandate expressly recognized the Jewish people's historical connection with Palestine and its right to reconstitute there its Jewish National Home. It called for "close settlement" of Jews on the land. During this post-Turkish empire Mandate, it was Palestine's Jews who used the term "Palestinian" when referring, e.g., to the *Palestine Post* (today's *Jerusalem Post*), the Palestine Symphony, and United Palestine Appeal. The U.N.'s 1947 Resolution 181 sought "partition" into "the *Jewish* state" and "the Arab state"; it did not reference "Jewish" and "Palestinian" states.

In 1947, British Foreign Secretary Ernest Bevin recognized "the creation of a sovereign Jewish state" was "the essential point of principle" for the Jews:

> There are in Palestine about 1,200,000 Arabs and 600,000 Jews. **For the Jews, the essential point of principle is the creation of a sovereign Jewish state.** For the Arabs the essential point of principle is to resist to the last the establishment of Jewish sovereignty in any part of Palestine." (Great Britain, Parliamentary Debates, Commons, vol. 433, col. 988, quoted in Bell, *Terror Out of Zion*, New York, St. Martin's Press, 1977, p. 188)

Following failure of the 2000 Camp David negotiations, then-Israeli P.M. Ehud Barak postulated why Arafat had rejected what he considered to be an "extremely generous" peace offer: "At the deepest level, Arafat does not accept the...right of the State of Israel to exist as a Jewish state" (Myre & Griffin, *This Burning Land,* p. 20). And U.S. Special Envoy George Mitchell repeatedly stated thereafter that the Road Map's "Two-State Solution" calls for "two states for two peoples," one of them the *Jewish* state of Israel.

Amb. (ret.) Yoram Ettinger has defined "Who Are the Palestinians?" ("Second Thought," from 12/14/11 "Israel Hayom," http://bit.ly/up8bJm):

> Contrary to political correctness, Palestinian Arabs have not been in the area west of the Jordan River from time immemorial....
>
> Most Palestinian Arabs are descendants of the 1845-1947 Muslim migrants from the Sudan, Egypt, Lebanon, Syria, as well as from Iraq, Saudi Arabia, Bahrain, Yemen, Libya, Morocco, Bosnia, the Caucasus, Turkmenistan, Kurdistan, India, Afghanistan and Balochistan.

In 1695, Hadriani Relandi, a Dutch scholar, geographer, cartographer and philologist, extensively surveyed Palestine. His book, published in Latin as *Palestina, ex monumentis veteribus illustrata,* drew strong conclusions, summarized in a Think-Israel article, http://www.think-israel.org/goldreich.palestina.html. Ettinger wrote these included:

> Not one settlement in the Land of Israel has a name that is of Arabic origin. Most of the settlement names originate in the Hebrew, Greek, Latin or Roman languages. In fact, till

today, except for Ramlah, not one Arabic settlement has an original Arabic name. Till today, most of the settlement names are of Hebrew or Greek origin, the names distorted to senseless Arabic names. There is no meaning in Arabic to names such as Acco (Acre), Haifa, Jaffa, Nablus, Gaza, or Jenin and towns named Ramallah, El Halil and El-Kuds (Jerusalem) lack historical roots or Arabic philology. In 1696, the year Relandi toured the land, Ramallah, for instance, was called Bet'allah (from the Hebrew name Beit El) and Hebron was Hebron (Hevron) and the Arabs called Mearat HaMach

Most of the land was empty, desolate, and the inhabitants few in number…. Most of the inhabitants were Jews and the rest Christians. There were few Muslims, mostly Nomad Bedouins….

The interesting part was that Relandi mentioned the Muslims as nomad Bedouins who arrived in the area as construction and agricultural labor reinforcement, seasonal workers…
.

The book totally contradicts any post-modern theory claiming "Palestinian heritage," or Palestie nian nation. The book strengthens the connection, relevance, pertinence, kinship of the Land of Israel to the Jews and the absolute lack of belonging to the Arabs, who robbed the Latin name Palestina and took it as their own."

The *Jerusalem Post's* David Bar-Illan noted why, during much of the 20th century, the term "Palestinian" was most commonly used in reference to Palestine's Jews; he also depicted why, in the 1960's, a total change in meaning altered "Palestinian" to mean Palestine's Arabs, henceforth "the Palestinians":

The Arab residents of this country during the British Mandate resented the appellation Palestinian. They called themselves Arab, and named all their institutions – from the Arab Higher Committee on down" – Arab," not Palestinian. Only the Jews, when referring to themselves and their institutions in English, used the name Palestinian: The Palestine Post (still the incorporated name of this newspaper), the Palestine Symphony, the United Palestine Appeal are typical examples….Applying the term Palestinian to Arabs of Palestine probably began in the 1960's, but neither Security Council resolution 242 of 1967 nor 338 of 1973 mentions Palestinians at all. It was only in the mid-1970's that the term became popular [p. 166-67 of Eye On The Media compilation].

...there is a distinct public-relations disadvantage in being a part of the Arab nation: it is difficult to elicit sympathy for people who belong to a nation of 200 million people which possesses land almost twice the size of the US. Nor is it easy to portray them as an underdog against four million Israelis occupying a tiny two-by-four country.

Distinct Palestinian nationalism was born, then, to separate the Arabs of Palestine from other Arabs. The Arab-Israeli conflict thus became the struggle of the "Palestinian nation" against the Israeli occupiers. [Eye On the Media compilation, p. 370]

# V.  History:  Jerusalem, A Jewish City

During the past 3000 years, Jerusalem has been the capital city of three sovereign nations – Judah, Judaea and Israel – all of them Jewish. Between Judaea's final fall in 135 and modern Israel's independence in 1948, a succession of foreign empires *seriatim* ruled Jerusalem; although they persecuted and at times tried to banish its Jews, Jews relentlessly returned, again becoming the city's majority population group during 19th century Ottoman Turkish rule; the Jews tenaciously maintained their physical presence in Jerusalem from ancient times through the long post-Biblical foreign-rule centuries. The land's *next* native state after 135 C.E. was modern Israel in 1948.

In contrast, Palestinian Arabs have never ruled Jerusalem. Foreign Arabs ruled the city for part of the time between their 638 defeat of European Byzantines and Muslims' 1099 defeat by European Crusaders, and part of the city between Jordan's 1948 invasion and its ouster by Israel in 1967. Thus, there is no historical or demographic basis to justify viewing Jews as Jerusalem "settlers." The history of the Jews in Jerusalem is part of that of the Jews in their land, summarized in Section 2, IV.

## Chronology

Around 1000 B.C.E., the Israelites under King David conquered Jerusalem (then comprising today's City of David) from the Canaanites, making it the capital of the Israelite kingdom. After the death of David's son Solomon, who had built the Temple just to the north of the original city, the Israelite kingdom split into the Biblical kingdoms of Israel and Judah; Jerusalem remained the capital of Judah, the seat of the kings of the House of David for more than 400 years. A half-century after Babylonia's destruction of Jerusalem and the Temple, Persians under Cyrus defeated Babylonia and allowed captive peoples to return to their lands. Jews, under leaders including Ezra and Nehemiah, rebuilt the Jerusalem Temple in what became the Jewish Persian province Yehud. Following Alexander's death soon after he defeated the Persians, Yehud (which became known as Judea) fell first under the Ptolemies and then the Seleucids. In the mid-second century B.C.E., Maccabee-led Jews regained independence from the Judaism-suppressing Seleucids, rededicating the Temple in a commemoration observed to this day as Hanukkah. The Second Temple stood for six centuries. It was destroyed by Rome at the end of the Great Revolt in 70 C.E. Ancient Jewish sovereignty flickered again in the ferocious Bar Kochba Revolt of 132-135.

Contrary to quite widespread belief (even among Jews), the Romans did not "exile" the Jews from Judaea after finally extinguishing ancient Jewish sovereignty in 135. Though Jews were banned from Jerusalem for part of the remaining Roman-Byzantine rule, they remained in the land, initially still as its majority people. One Roman emperor even began preparations to rebuild the Temple. In 614, self-mustered battalions comprised of 20,000 or more homeland Jews fought alongside autonomy-promising Persian invaders. The Yishuv soon thereafter aided Muslim conquerors, and received rewards in Hebron and Jerusalem. The population remained mostly Christian, Samaritan and Jewish well into the Muslim dynasty era.

In 1099, invading Christian Crusaders acknowledged that Turks, Arabs and Jews confronted them at Jerusalem, of whom "the Jew is the last to fall." Jewish immigration continued during Crusader times. Benjamin of Tudula and other travelers mentioned Jews residing in Jerusalem and elsewhere in the land.

Following Mongol invasions in the Crusaders' wake, Turk-Circassian Mamluks gained control in the mid-1200's and ruled the Near East first from Turkey and then from Egypt until defeated by Ottoman Turks in 1517. During these centuries, the presence of Jews in Jerusalem was organized and open..

In 1335, a Verona monk visiting Palestine was quoted by a rcheologist Dan Bahat as having noted that "there was a long-established Jewish community at the foot of Mount Zion in the area known as the Jewish Quarter," and that

> A pilgrim who wished to visit ancient forts and towns in the Holy Land would have been unable to locate these without a good guide who knew the Land well or without one of the Jews who lived there. The Jews were able to recount the history of these places, since this knowledge had been handed down from their forefathers and wise men. So when I journeyed overseas I often requested and managed to obtain an excellent guide among the Jews who lived there.

"The Jews who lived there" were uniquely "able to recount the history of these places since this knowledge had been handed down from their forefathers and wise men." And here are further 14th and 15th century references to Jews as Jerusalem homelanders:

**1338:** Visitor Isaac Ibn Chelo noted "students of medicine, astronomy and mathematics" and "excellent Jewish calligraphers in the city," talents evidencing that secular as well as religious scholarship existed in Jerusalem, even in medieval times.

**1384-1395:** Christian travelers noted that Jerusalem's Jews had their communal residential areas.

**1428:** Pope blocked the Yishuv attempt to buy Mt. Zion buildings.

**1438:** Italian rabbi settled in Jerusalem, becoming spiritual leader.

**1440:** Mamluks imposed tax on Jerusalem's Jews, and many left.

**1470:** 150 Jewish families in Jerusalem.

**1474:** Muslims destroyed an old synagogue, and demanded bribes for a new "Street of the Jews" and "Gate of the Jewish Quarter."

**1480:** Monk writes of Jews in Jerusalem and Gaza (again in 1484).

**1481:** Jewish visitor cites Jews in Gaza, Hebron, Jerusalem.

**1483:** Travelers reported Jews living in Jerusalem and Hebron.

**1488:** Rabbi Ovadiah arrives, finds 70 families, many widows.

**1491:** Christian pilgrim: in Jerusalem "not many Christians, but many Jews," who claim the Holy Land, and "refuse to leave." Author Joan Peters quoted him as stating that there were more Jews than Christians in Jerusalem, and that they consider the country their land.

**1495:** 200 families, following lifting of Italian ship ban.

**1496:** Destruction and rebuilding of Rambam synagogue.

**1497:** Christian traveler: "In Jerusalem dwell many Jews."

**1499:** Christian traveler: "...very many Jews in Jerusalem." Author Samuel Katz quoted this pilgrim that the Jews there spoke Hebrew, and another "that they hoped soon to resettle the Holy Land." This occurred despite a ban on new synagogue construction; no Jew could erect or repair a house without a special permit (*i.e.*, bribe).

### Surviving as a Jewish *Dhimmi* Residing in Jerusalem

During these centuries, life of Jews under Ottoman occupation was not un-fettered; documents tell of extortion and trade restrictions, such as Jewish mer-chants being subjected to extortion and forbidden to sell in the square. Indeed:

> Time and again Jews were charged with offenses against the Muslim faith and had to buy their way out of trouble. Consequently they were always deep in debt; and if anyone fell behind in his payments, his belongings were often auc-tioned off, even sacred articles and ancient scrolls of the Law. These were usually bought by Christian dealers who sold them in Europe.

Life in Jerusalem improved under Sulieman (1520-1566). Between 1536 and 1542, he built the walls and pools of Solomon, repaired sewers and cis-terns. Jews lived in quarters coterminous with the Jewish Quarter of our time. Ulrich Prefat of Slovenia's chronicled (1546-47): "Many Jews dwell in Jerusalem and there is a special street of the Jews."

Bahat, showing synagogue photographs, described a religious-site link be-tween Jerusalem's 16th century Jews and today's:

> When the Jews were expelled from Spain in 1492 many found their way to the Turkish Empire, where they succeeded in at-taining high positions. Their influence helped many Spanish Jews to settle in Jerusalem after 1516. The newcomers built a new synagogue, named Eliyahu Hanavi, and soon after-wards three more synagogues were built. This group of four synagogues still exists (though used as a garbage dump during the Jordanian occupation of 1948-67), and is once again re-stored.

These Sephardim were only one of Jerusalem's Jewish groups.

> [T]here were four congregations: Sephardi, Ashkenazi, Mo-roccan (North African), and Musta'arabim. The largest was the Sephardi, with its exiles from Spain and Portugal. Next came the Ashkenazi, comprised of 15 very old families (de-scendants of Jews who had come in the days of Maimonides) as well as more recent arrivals from Europe, including immi-grants from Italy. The Musta'arabim...were descendants of the Land's early inhabitants.

Jerusalem's was a vibrant Jewish community. "In 1587 a rabbi wrote: 'The Land is steeped in learning as it never was in ancient days. There is a religious school (Talmud Torah) with more than a hundred youngsters...also a college'."

Life worsened towards the end of the 16th century, when Abu Sufain became governor of Jerusalem. In 1586, the three-century-old Nachmanides synagogue was seized and converted into an Arab warehouse; oppression and onerous taxation worsened. "There was a typical incident in 1643: the governor inflicted a burdensome tax on the community, and since the community was quite incapable of paying it, he jailed all its notables....This happened again and again during the period, forcing the Jews to leave the city. By 1663, most of them had gone to Ramleh, abandoning their property in Jerusalem." The oppression wasn't even all rational. In 1637, Muslims threatened to kill Jerusalem's Jews unless it started raining within three days. (It did.)

In 1674, Jesuit Father Michael Naud wrote that "Jews of Jerusalem" were

> ...paying heavily to the Turk for their right to stay here....They prefer being prisoners in Jerusalem to enjoying the freedom they could acquire elsewhere....The love of the Jews for the Holy Land, which they lost through their betrayal (of Christ), is unbelievable. Many of them come from Europe to find a little comfort, though the yoke is heavy.

> The custom of extorting money from pilgrims remained unchanged for centuries, as told in 1751 by a Swedish traveler, Frederick Hasselquist: "As 4,000 persons (Christians) besides as many Jews come from all quarters of the world, this sum (a total of 25 piasters for each pilgrim) may be a considerable revenue for the Turks; and indeed they receive no other from this uncultivated and almost uninhabited country."

Tal quoted Francois Rene de Chateaubriand in *Journal of Jerusalem* (1811): "Christians and Jews alike lived in great poverty and in conditions of great deprivation. There are not many Christians but there are many Jews and these the Muslims persecute in many ways." Peters quoted an 1834 letter that a 40,000 strong Muslim mob "rushed on Jerusalem....The mob entered, and looted the city for five or six days. The Jews were the worst sufferers, their homes were sacked and their women violated." Peters' chapter *"Dhimmi* in the Holy Land" provides a litany of like-persecutions of Jews and Christians during the Ottoman era. At one point, after detailing numerous brutal incidents:

> In the following few decades (1848-1878) scores of incidents involving anti-Jewish violence, persecution and extortions filled page after page of documented reports from the British Consulate in Jerusalem. A chronology would be overwhelming, but perhaps a few extracts [*see* Peters, p. 191 ff] from those complaints will show the pattern of terror that continued right into the period of the major Jewish immigration

beginning about 1878.

Tal quoted an 1843 traveler: "In Jerusalem, [the Jew's] case is a very hard one. He is oppressed and robbed by the Turks in a most unmerciful manner; in short, for him there is neither law nor justice." And Karl Marx in 1854: "Nothing equals the misery and suffering of the Jews who are the constant object of Muslim oppression and intolerance."

A restraining factor in Muslim-on-*Dhimmi* Jerusalem violence was this, quoted by Peters from an 1859 British consulate document:

> The Mohammedans of Jerusalem are less fanatical than in many other places, owing to the circumstances of their numbers scarcely exceeding *one quarter* of the whole population, and of their being surpassed in wealth (except among the Effendi class) in trade and manufactures by both Jews and Christians.

Jewish determination not to be driven from Jerusalem prevailed. Bahat quoted a 1656 monk: "In Jerusalem there also live many Jews who came from all over the world." Ben Zvi referred to the anonymous author of a famous letter, "Hurvot Yerushalayim" ("The Ruins of Jerusalem"): "More of our people now inhabit the city of our Lord than have done so since Israel was exiled from its Land. Daily many Jews come to settle there, in addition to the pilgrims who come to pray to Him who stands beyond our Wall...." In 1700, Rabbi Judah the Pious led 1,000 Jews from Poland who settled in Jerusalem and began building the Hurva synagogue. In 1751, the Kabbalist Shalom Sharabi came from Yemen. "In 1777, Rabbi Isaiah Bardaki arrived from Poland to become leader of the Jewish community and Austrian vice-consul."

Mark Twain, *The Innocents Abroad* (1869), caught the intensity of the Jews' attachment to Jerusalem: "Everywhere precious remains of Solomon's Temple. That portion of the ancient wall ...which is called the Jews' Place of Wailing, where the Hebrews assemble every Friday to kiss the venerated stones and weep over the fallen greatness of Zion."

## Population Statistics

Karl Marx discussed Jerusalem in an article published in the New York Daily Tribune on April 15, 1854, noting that the city's "sedentary population numbers about 15,500 souls, of whom 4,000 are Mussulmans [Muslims] and 8,000 Jews," thereby confirming that there has been a Jewish majority in Jerusalem since the 1850s. (Jewish Review of Books)

The low population of this most famous of cities, through 19th century times, may appear surprising. Its significance was noted by Dr. Ben-Arieh, focusing upon the time-period (1800-1870) in which the entire population dwelt in the

Old City (*Jerusalem in the Nineteenth Century: The Old City*, p. 279):

Taken in their entirety, the demographic statistics we have dealt with (1800-1870) at such length may seem fairly insignificant. But, as with many important towns in past ages, the character of Jerusalem was determined by a relatively small population. The period we have been reviewing (1800 – 1870) marked the rise of the Jewish element in the city to the point where Jews came to outnumber all other Jerusalemites, as they have continued to do ever since.

## Jerusalem's Population

| Year | Jews | Muslims | Christians | Total | Source |
|------|------|---------|------------|-------|--------|
| 1800 | 2,250 | 4,000 | 2,750 | 9,000 | Ben-Arieh p. 279 |
| 1830 | 3,000 | | | 11,000 | Verlin p. 134 citing Parkes |
| 1836 | 3,250 | 4,500 | 3,250 | 11,000 | Ben-Arieh p. 279 |
| 1838 | 6,000 | 5,000 | 3,000 | 14,000 | Verlin p. 134 citing Gilbert, Tal |
| 1839 | 5,500 | | | | Verlin p. 134 citing British Consul |
| 1839 | 6,500 | | | | Verlin p. 134 citing Scot Clergyman |
| 1840 | 5,000 | 4,650 | 3,350 | 13,000 | Ben-Arieh p. 279 |
| 1840 | 5,000 | 6,000 | 4,000 | 15,000 | Verlin p. 134 citing Parkes |
| 1844 | 7,120 | 5,760 | 3,390 | 16,270 | Verlin p. 134 citing Tal |
| 1844 | 7,120 | 5,000 | 3,390 | 15,510 | Jewish Virtual Library |
| 1850 | 6,000 | 5,400 | 3,600 | 15,000 | Ben-Arieh p. 279 |
| 1854 | 8,000 | 4,000 | 3,000 | 15,000 | Verlin p. 134 citing Tal |
| 1860 | 8,000 | 6,000 | 4,000 | 18,000 | Ben-Arieh p. 279 |
| 1864 | 8,500 | 5,000 | 4,500 | 18,000 | Verlin p. 134 citing Peters |
| 1870 | 11,000 | 6,500 | 4,500 | 22,000 | Ben-Arieh p. 279,358 |
| 1872 | 10,600 | 5,000 | 5,300 | 20,900 | Verlin p. 134 citing Parkes |
| 1876 | 12,000 | 7,560 | 5,470 | 25,030 | Jewish Virtual Library |
| 1876 | 12,000 | 7,560 | 5,470 | 25,030 | Verlin p. 134 citing Tal |
| 1878 | 11,000 | | | | Verlin p. 134 citing Bahat |
| 1880 | 17,000 | 8,000 | 6,000 | 31,000 | Ben-Arieh p. 358 |
| 1890 | 25,000 | 9,000 | 8,000 | 42,000 | Ben-Arieh p. 358 |
| 1896 | 28,112 | 8,560 | 8,748 | 45,420 | Jewish Virtual Library |
| 1896 | 28,000 | 8,600 | 8,700 | 45,300 | Verlin p. 134 citing Gilbert |
| 1899 | 30,000 | 7,700 | 10,900 | 48,600 | Verlin p. 134 citing Parkes |
| 1900 | 35,000 | 10,000 | 10,000 | 55,000 | Ben-Arieh p. 358 |
| 1910 | 45,000 | 12,000 | 13,000 | 70,000 | Ben-Arieh p. 358 |
| 1911 | 30,800 | 10,000 | 15,000 | 55,800 | Verlin p. 134 citing Tal |
| 1916 | 26,571 | | | | Ben-Arieh p. 358 |
| 1 917 | 31,147 | | | | Ben-Arieh p. 358 |

## Jerusalem's Population (cont'd)

| Year | Jews | Muslims | Christians | Total | Source |
|------|------|---------|------------|-------|--------|
| 1922 | 34,300 | 13,500 | 14,700 | 62,500 | Ben-Arieh p. 358 |
| 1922 | 33,971 | 13,411 | 4,699 | 52,081 | Jewish Virtual Library |
| 1931 | 51,222 | 19,894 | 19,335 | 90,451 | Jewish Virtual Library |
| 1947 | 99,320 | 36,850 | 31,300 | 167,300 | Verlin p. 134 citing Tal |
| 1948 | 100,000 | 40,000 | 25,000 | 165,000 | Jewish Virtual Library |
| 1967 | 195,700 | 54,963 | 12,646 | 263,309 | Jewish Virtual Library |
| 1987 | 340,000 | 121,000 | 14,000 | 475,000 | Jewish Virtual Library |
| 1990 | 378,200 | 131,800 | 14,400 | 524,400 | Jewish Virtual Library |
| 1990 | 353,200 | 124,200 | 14,000 | 491,500 | Verlin p. 134 citing Tal |
| 2000 | 530,400 | 204,100 | 14,700 | 758,300 | Jewish Virtual Library |
| 2009 | 479,756 | 278,568 | 15,476 | 773,800 | Jewish Virtual Library |

Sources: Yehoshua Ben-Arieh, *Jerusalem in the Nineteenth Century: The Old City,* St. Martin's Press, New York, 1984

Jewish Virtual Library, www..jewishvirtuallibrary.org/jsource/History/jerupop.html

Jerome R. Verlin, *Israel 3000 Years: The Jewish People's 3000 Year Presence in Palestine,* Pavilion Press, Inc., Philadelphia, 2011

## Scriptural References

Muslims believe Jerusalem is mentioned in the Qur'an (if not by name) and the Hadith (explicitly). Its holiness has both historical origins (promoted by al-Fadhail, focused on the history of cities) and political import (promoted by the Umayyad dynasty, embellishing its sanctity). The al-Aqsa Mosque has been classified as the third holiest site in Islam by medieval scripts and in modern-day political tracts. For example, Sahih Bukhari (one of the six canonical hadith collections of Sunni Islam) quoted Abu al-Dardaa (one of Muhammad's traveling companions) as having ranked the potency of prayer by its venue: "The Prophet of Allah Muhammad said a prayer in the Sacred Mosque [in Mecca] is worth 100,000 prayers; a prayer in my mosque [in Medina] is worth 10,000 prayers; and a prayer in al-Masjid al-Aqsa is worth 1,000 prayers." Although Mohammed never set foot in the city, Muslims believe – during the Night Journey – Muhammad was transported to al-Aqsa from the Sacred Mosque (the Ka'aba) in Mecca. Muhammad led prayers towards this site until the seventeenth month after the emigration to Medina in 622, when God directed him to turn towards Mecca.

In contrast, Jerusalem is unambiguously mentioned more than 600 times in the Hebrew Bible. Jews pray facing Jerusalem and, while in Jerusalem, pray facing the Temple Mount; Muslims pray facing Mecca and, if in Jerusalem, pray with their backs toward the city and its famous mosques.

## Modern Era

In a chapter entitled "Defending Israel's Legal Rights to Jerusalem" in a volume, *Israel's Rights as a Nation-State in International Diplomacy* (published jointly by the Jerusalem Center for Public Affairs and the World Jewish Congress), Amb. Dore Gold wrote of

> ...the simple truth that the Jewish people actually restored their clear-cut majority in Jerusalem not in 1948 or in 1967 but in 1863, according to British consular records. Prussia's consulate was reporting a Jewish plurality already in 1845, when the Jews constituted the largest religious group in Jerusalem. This transformation in Jerusalem occurred well before the arrival of the British Empire in the First World War and the issuing of the Balfour Declaration. It even preceded the actions of Theodor Herzl and the First Zionist Congress. Indeed, in 1914 on the eve of the First World War there were 45,000 Jews in Jerusalem out of a total population of 65,000. The Jewish majority in Jerusalem reflected the simple fact that the Jewish people had been streaming back to their ancient capital for centuries, despite the dangers to their physical well-being that this entailed and the discriminatory taxes imposed by the Ottoman Empire on its non-Muslim subjects. In the mid-nineteenth century, Baghdad and Damascus were Arab cities, but Jerusalem was already a Jewish city.

In a 1924 pamphlet, "A Brief Guide to Al-Haram Al-Sharif Jerusalem" published by the Supreme Muslim Council, the two principal edifices are described as the Dome of the Rock and the mosque against the south wall. The guide states:

> The site is one of the oldest in the world. Its sanctity dates from the earliest (perhaps from pre-historic) times. Its identity with the site of Solomon's Temple is beyond dispute. This, too, is the spot, according to the universal belief, on which "David built there an altar unto the Lord, and offered burnt offerings and peace offerings." (2 Samuel XXIV, 25)

Jerusalem has never been the capital of any Arab entity, and it was a backwater throughout most of Arab history. Moreover, it never served as a provincial capital – despite 1300 years of Muslim Arab rule – nor was it ever either a Muslim cultural center or considered an ancestral home of Muslims. When Jordan illegally controlled eastern Jerusalem (including the Old City and Temple

Mount) from 1948 until the Six-Day War in 1967, it was not designated a capital of any Arab entity. Indeed, during the city's 1948-1967 divided rule (the first in its longer than 3000-year history), the Jordanian-controlled section became an underdeveloped provincial and isolated town. The PLO's National Covenant, as written in 1964, never mentioned Jerusalem; only after Israel regained control of the entire city did the PLO "update" its Covenant to include Jerusalem ("One Nation's Capital Throughout History," Myths & Facts, Inc. & Eli E. Hertz, 2011, p. 9).

Under the 1949 armistice agreement with Israel, Jordan pledged to allow free-access to all holy places, but failed to honor that commitment. For 19 years, Jews and Christians residing in Israel were barred from their holy places; Christian Arabs living in Israel were denied access to churches and other religious sites in the Old City and nearby Bethlehem, while Jews were prevented from praying at the Western Wall. The Old City was rendered devoid of Jews, including the historic Jewish Quarter where Jewish families had lived for generations, and Jordan destroyed more than 50 synagogues. Jewish sites, such as the ancient Jewish Mount of Olives cemetery, were desecrated.

During Jordan's reign, there was a precipitous decline in the holy city's Christian population – from 25,000 to 11,000 – a pattern that was consistent with what transpired in other Arab countries, where there is no religious freedom. It was only after the Six-Day War that the Jewish Quarter was liberated and rebuilt, and free access to holy places was reestablished. This is why Israel is refuses to relinquish control of its historic religious and political capital – over the millennia – to any external governing body.

## VI. **History: The Arab Myth of "Temple Denial"**

For Jews, the Temple Mount, or *Kotel*, (site of Solomon's Temple, Second Temple and Western Wall) is the holiest place on earth. Temple Denial is the assertion, serving to delegitimize Israel and the Jewish people, that no Jewish Temple ever existed in Jerusalem. This pernicious lie is pivotal to efforts to steal the history and identity of the Jewish people to justify eradicating Jews from the Middle East.

Many Palestinian, Arab and Muslim leaders have consistently and provocatively denied Jewish history, religion and custom, both in ancient Judea/Israel and particularly in Jerusalem. This campaign intensified after Israel gained control over the Temple Mount in 1967. P.A. religious and political leaders, officials and academics refer to the Temple as the "alleged Temple." The major political impact of this posturing is that countries refuse to recognize Jerusalem's centrality to Judaism and as Israel's declared capital by failing to locate their embassies there.

This Big Lie – that the Temple never existed and the Jews have no history in the Land of Israel – contradicts Jewish sources (Bible, Talmud, Psalms, prayers), Christian sources (which in essence would constitute denial of Jesus's existence), early chroniclers (such as Josephus and the archeological record), and even the Qur'an itself. In Sura 17:2-7, the Qur'an mentions the "Children of Israel's" two periods of independence in the land and the destruction of both the First and Second Temple: "...to enter the Temple even as they entered it for the first time, and to lay waste...." Many prominent classical Islamic theological texts refer to the Jewish connection to the Temple. [*See* also Sura 17:1, the "Farthest Mosque" which refers to the al-Aqsa Mosque on the Temple Mount.]

Notably, the Supreme Muslim Council, led by the virulently anti-Semitic Grand Mufti of Jerusalem Haj Amin al-Husayni, which controlled the Temple Mount in the Palestine Mandate period, published yearly guide books to the al-Haram al-Sharif (Arabic for Temple Mount), in 1924, 1925, 1929, 1935 and 1950, all stating that its "identity with the site of Solomon's Temple is beyond dispute. This, too, is the spot, according to the universal belief, on which David built there an altar unto the Lord and offered burnt offerings and peace offerings." However, by 1954, the Muslim *waqf*, the religious authority that ruled the Dome of the Rock and al-Aqsa Mosque, abruptly removed these references.

In 1930, the League of Nations issued its, "Report of the Commission Appointed by His Majesty's Government in the United Kingdom of Great Britain and Northern Ireland, with the Approval of the Council of the League of Nations, to Determine the Rights and Claims of Moslems and Jews in Connection with the Western or Wailing Wall at Jerusalem" (Dec. 1930). The report found: "It was Solomon who built the first Temple of Jerusalem, the grandeur and beauty of which have become widely renowned, thanks to the holy books and the historians. The Temple was situated on Mount Moriah on the platform, now known as the Harem-esh-Sherif area."

Since the 2000 Camp David Summit, when P.A. President Yasser Arafat told President Bill Clinton that "Solomon's Temple was not in Jerusalem, but Nablus," this outrageous historical revisionism has become part of the Arab/Muslim bitter delegitimization campaign. Palpable is their intent to deny the Jewish people its human rights, its civil rights, its history, its access and authority over its holiest sites, and even its State of Israel. Among the false claims of the Palestinian Arabs and Muslims is that the remains of the Second Temple – the Western Wall – are in fact remnants of the al-Aqsa Mosque. Customary after Muslim conquest of "infidels" was deliberate humiliation of the vanquished; this phenomenon has served as the basis for the mosque-controversy at the 9-11 site in New York City. Thus, the al-Asqa Mosque was deliberately built atop the Temple after the Muslim conquest of Jerusalem. Yet, the M.S.M. rarely comments on these myths perpetrated by Arab/Muslims regarding the holiest site in Judaism, the sacred cradle of the Judeo-Christian tradition.

Sources:

"The PA Denies Jewish History in Jerusalem: The Jewish Temple is "The Alleged Temple" (Itamar Marcus and Nan Jacques Zilberdik, *Palestinian Media Watch*, Aug. 2011)

"The Mounting Problem of Temple Denial" (David Barnett, in *Middle East Review of International Affairs/MERIA* Aug. 2011)

"A Brief Guide to Al-Haram Al-Sharif Jerusalem," published by the Supreme Muslim Council (1924)

"Report of the Commission Appointed by His Majesty's Government in the United Kingdom of Great Britain and Northern Ireland, with the Approval of the Council of the League of Nations , to Determine the Rights and Claims of Moslems and Jews in Connection with the Western or Wailing Wall at Jerusalem," (Dec. 1930)

"From Jerusalem to Mecca and Back: The Islamic Consolidation of Jerusalem (Dr. Yitzhak Reiter, 2005)

Israeli Foreign Minister Shlomo Ben-Ami's Interview with Ari Shavit, *Haaretz,* Nov. 25, 2001

# VII. Israel: International Recognition of the Jewish National Home Prior to the Establishment of the State of Israel

World War I pitted Britain and its allies against Germans and the Ottoman Empire. In 1917, when the U.S. entered the war on the side of the British, President Woodrow Wilson declared that self-determination should guide any post-war reorganization of territories formerly controlled by Ottomans.

British policy became gradually committed to establishing a Jewish home in Palestine (*Eretz Yisrael*). Following discussions in the British Cabinet and consultations with Zionist leaders, a formal decision was issued on November 2, 1917, in the form of a letter from British Foreign Minister Lord Arthur Balfour to Lord Rothschild; it represented the first political recognition of Zionist aspirations by a great world power. The Balfour Declaration states: "His Majesty's Government views with favour the establishment in Palestine of a national home for the Jewish people, and will use their best endeavours to facilitate the achievement of this object, it being clearly understood that nothing shall be done which may prejudice the civil and religious rights of existing non-Jewish communities in Palestine or the rights and political status enjoyed by Jews in any other country."

Defeat of the Ottoman Empire in 1918 led to dissolution of its vast lands in the Middle East. At the initial Paris Peac e Conference in 1919, the victorious Allies began adjusting their differences and territorial appetites. At a meeting of the Allies in London in February 1920, Palestine was placed under British Mandatory rule. At the San Remo (Italy) Conference in April 1920, the former Arab provinces of the Ottoman Empire were divided along the lines of the Sykes-Picot Agreement: France received the mandates for Syria and Lebanon, and Britain obtained mandates for Iraq, Transjordan (which it created in 1920 from the Mandate for Palestine) and Palestine. Most significantly, the conference confirmed the pledge contained in the Balfour Declaration regarding a Jewish national home in Palestine and incorporated it into the preamble of the conference's policy document. The Zionists (including attendees Chaim Weizmann, Nahum Sokolow and Herbert Samuel) emerged victorious.

In July 1922, the League of Nations formally entrusted Britain with the Mandate for Palestine. Recognizing the historical connection of the Jewish people with Palestine, Britain was called upon to facilitate the establishment of a Jewish national home in Palestine-*Eretz Yisrael*. In September 1922, the Council of the League of Nations and Britain decided that the provisions for setting up a Jewish national home would not apply to the area east of the Jordan River, constituting three-fourths of the territory in the Mandate (initially called Transjordan and eventually becoming the Hashemite Kingdom of Jordan). Thus, the Mandate for Palestine, a legal League of Nations document, formalized the Jewish legal right to settle anywhere in western Palestine, between the Jordan River and the Mediterranean Sea. The entire League of Nations—51 members—unanimously declared on July 24, 1922: "…[R]ecognition has been given to the historical connection of the Jewish people with Palestine and to the grounds for reconstituting their national home in that country."

Concomitantly, however, there was no focus upon or anything heard about a distinct Palestinian Arab people—because they did not exist. In fact, Arab leaders rejected the notion of a unique "Palestinian Arab" identity, insisting that "Palestine" was merely a part of "Greater Syria." Moreover, for generations, when one was called a "Palestinian," reference was made to the region's Jewish residents. [*See* Section 2-IV.] The international decision to create in Palestine "a national home for the Jewish people" was made in recognition of the Jewish people's rightful title—noting ownership of the most legitimate "birth certificate" (the Bible) of any nation in the world – and continuous links to the land. The Allies strongly believed at the time that they had also done justice to the claims of the Arab people via the creation or recognition of several new Arab states, including that of Jordan, which was formed from 75% of the Palestine

Mandate and 70% of which now consists of Palestinian Arabs. The M.S.M.'s coverage largely fails to acknowledge (let alone appreciate the import of) this irrefutable historical background. [*See* " 'The Palestinians' – Really, the Jews."]

Sources:
*Jewish Virtual Library*
L. Stein, *The Balfour Declaration* (1961)
C. Weizmann, *Trial and Error* (1949)
D. Lloyd George, *The Truth About the Peace Conference*, (1938)
J. Nevakivi, *Britain, France and the Arab Middle East* (1969)
H. Sachar, *The Emergence of the Middle East, 1914-1924* (1969)

# VIII. Israel: America's Stalwart and Reliable Ally

Considering the upheaval in the Middle East – unstable governments, autocratic, theocratic, undemocratic dictatorships, an uncertain seasonal-shift following the "Arab Spring" – Israel is an oasis of liberty and stands out as a beacon of Western democratic values, and a reliable ally of the United States.

## The Alternatives

Compare:

Egypt:  The beneficiary of billions of dollars of American aid, with its dictator, President Hosni Mubarak overthrown, may be next ruled by the Muslim Brotherhood or other Muslim extremists, who are fanatical radicals, antagonistic to the West, will not vote with the U.S. at U.N., are obsessed anti-Semites, and sworn enemies of Israel. Per a Zogby International poll in July 2011, only 5% of Egyptians have favorable views of the U.S.

Saudi Arabia:  Tyrannical kingdom, hostile to values of U.S., funds Wahhabi radicals to engage in terrorism and to undermine U.S. interests at the U.N, OPEC, and infiltrating U.S. universities.  Per July 2011, Zogby poll, 30% of Saudis have favorable views of the U.S.

Iran:  A most hostile autocractic theocracy with ayatollahs/mullahs, ardent enemies of the West and western values, serial violator of human rights, major sponsor of terrorism through its proxies Hamas and Hizbullah, killing Americans (the "Great Satan") in Iraq and Afghanistan, and threatening to wipe Israel (the "Little Satan") off the map.  Iran is pursuing nuclear weapons in violation of the U.N. and international law.

Jordan:  Weak minority-ruled monarchy, unstable, aligned with Saddam Hussein in first Gulf War; Palestinian Arabs constitute 70% of its population.

Syria:  Repressive police state of Bashar al-Assad since 2000, previously of his father (Hafez al-Assad for 29 years) of the minority Alawite sect; since 2011 civil uprising, the regime has engaged in a bloody crackdown on dissent, killing and torturing thousands, defying Arab League and international law.

Lebanon: Unstable government structure with power divided among Christians, Muslim and Druse; weak military unable to control its borders; Hizbullah terrorist enclave in south amassing thousands of missiles and weapons in defiance of U.N. after 2006 conflict with Israel; under sway of Syria.

## Israel's Shared Values with the U.S.

In stark contrast, Israel is a peaceful, reliable democracy based on shared values, and is a true friend of the U.S., voting with the U.S. at the U.N. more often than any other nation. According to General John Keegan, former chief of U.S. Air Force Intelligence, Israel's contribution to U.S. intelligence was "equal to five CIA's." According to Senator Daniel Inouye (D-HI), former Chairman of Senate Appropriations Committee: "The intelligence received from Israel exceeds the intelligence received from all NATO countries combined. The Soviet military hardware that was transferred by Israel to the U.S. tilted the global balance of power in favor of our country."

Israel's bombing of the Iraqi nuclear reactor in 1981 ultimately saved the U.S. from a nuclear confrontation with Iraq. In addition, U.S. soldiers in Iraq and Afghanistan have benefited from Israel's experience in combating terrorism, improvised explosive devices (IED's), car bombs, and suicide bombers. Israel has developed and contributed in the development of security/armored protection for American tanks and military transports. Moreover, Israel has battle-tested U.S. military systems in real time: F-16 jet fighters include more than 600 Israeli-designed modifications, saving billions of dollars in research and development.

Israel is a leading designer of unmanned aerial vehicles (UAV's), the "Iron Dome" and other "star wars" types of missile defense systems, satellite and communications technology, and telecommunications, all of which benefit U.S. security. Though not a NATO member, Israel secures NATO's southeastern flank, has hospitable harbors, outstanding military installations, air- and sealift capabilities, and personnel trained to maintain sophisticated equipment.

The $3 billion Israel receives per year from the U.S. is exclusively designated for military assistance and, by law, 70% must be spent in the U.S., generating thousands of jobs. Finally, due to Israel's ability to be America's "unsinkable aircraft carrier," thousands of U.S. troops need not be stationed in the Middle East to protect U.S. interests.

Andrew J. Shapiro, Assistant Secretary of State for Political-Military Affairs, told the Washington Institute for Near East Policy, in November 2011, that the U.S. supports Israel's qualitative military edge:

> Israel [is] a country with security challenges that few countries in the world can contemplate....As Israel looks to the future, it should know that America will be there by its side.

> The cornerstone of America's security commitment to Israel has been an assurance that the United States would help Israel uphold its qualitative military edge. This is Israel's ability to counter and defeat credible military threats from any individual state, coalition of states, or non-state actor, while sustaining minimal damages or casualties.

> Today, in these budget-constrained times, some are now asking the question why should we keep providing aid to Israel?...We support Israel because it is in our national interests to do so....If Israel were weaker, its enemies would be bolder. This would make broader conflict more likely, which would be catastrophic to American interests in the region. It is the very strength of Israel's military which deters potential aggressors and helps foster peace and stability.

> The United States also experiences a number of tangible benefits from our close partnership with Israel. For instance, joint exercises allow us to learn from Israel's experience in urban warfare and counterterrorism. Israeli technology is proving critical to improving our homeland security and protecting our troops. One only has to look at Afghanistan and Iraq, where Israeli armor plating technology is being used on U.S. military vehicles and innovative equipment, such as the specially designed "Israeli bandage," is being used to treat our troops.

> The links between our two governments and U.S. and Israeli defense companies have yielded important, groundbreaking innovations that ultimately make us all safer. This involves sensors, unmanned aerial vehicle technology, surveillance equipment, and detection devices to seek out IED's that support our forces. Additionally...our security assistance to Israel also helps support American jobs, since the vast majority of security assistance to Israel is spent on American-made goods and services."

Robert D. Blackwell and Walter B. Slocombe, who served under Democratic and Republican administrations in diplomatic, defense and national security positions, presented the Washington Institute for Near East Policy with a thesis asserting that U.S. aid to Israel is not merely a gesture between allied nations, but an act that serves definitive U.S. national interests worldwide and does not take a toll on its relations with its Arab allies. Their report (October 2011), "Israel: A true ally in the Middle East," states that Israeli underappreciated contributions to U.S. national interests include enhanced counter-terrorism, intelligence, missile defense, advanced radar systems, unmanned aerial systems, armored vehicle protection, defense against short-range rockets, robotics, advice and expertise on behavioral screening techniques for airport security, and technology "to solve some of the most vexing technical and strategic problems" useful in urban warfare. According to the authors:

> Israeli-developed defense equipment, some of which benefited from generous U.S. aid, now used by the U.S. military include short-range unmanned aircraft systems that have seen service in Iraq and Afghanistan; targeting pods on hundreds of Air Force, Navy and Marine strike aircraft; a revolutionary helmet-mounted sight that is standard in nearly all frontline Air Force and Navy fighter aircraft; lifesaving armor installed in thousands of mine-resisted ambush protected (MRAP) armored vehicles used in Iraq and Afghanistan; and a gun system for close-in defense of naval vessels against terrorist dinghies and small-boat swarms. Moreover, U.S. and Israeli companies are working together to produce Israel's Iron Dome, the world's first combat-proven counter-rocket system. Counter-terrorism and intelligence cooperation is deep and extensive, with the United States and Israel working to advance their common interest in defeating the terrorism of Hamas, Hezbollah and Al Qaeda and its affiliate groups, and preventing nuclear proliferation in the region. There are joint Special Forces training and exercises and collaboration on shared targets. This intimate relationship reinforces overall U.S. intelligence efforts by providing Washington with access to Israel's unique set of capabilities for information collection and assessments on key countries and issues in the region. Such was the case, for example, when Israel passed to the United States conclusive photographic evidence in 2007 that Syria, with North Korean assistance, had made enormous strides toward "going hot" with a plutonium-producing reactor.

The authors recognize important differences have arisen over the decades—with periodic policy flare-ups—on topics ranging from Israel's preventive action against Iraq's nuclear reactor to Israeli sales of weaponry and military technology to China; some of the most contentious disputes have been over actions affecting the Middle East "peace process." Far more often, however, the U.S. and Israel have collaborated on the most salient "anchors of American national interests in the Middle East": the Arab-Israel peace treaties. They determined the cost-benefit calculus yields the conclusion that "costs" to the U.S. in the Arab world for its support of Israel are not much different than the "costs" to U.S. for support of other beleaguered (and sometime imperfect) friends, including West Berlin in the Cold War, Kuwait in 1990-91 and Taiwan today. The authors concluded:

> But the long-standing U.S. commitment to Israel has not prevented development of close ties with Arab nations, which understand—however much they disagree with U.S. support for Israel—that they benefit from a good relationship with the United States on other issues. Nor has it made the Arab oil-exporting states any less conscious of their own economic and strategic interest in a reasonably stable flow of oil to world markets, or their eagerness to buy first-class military equipment from the United States or to enjoy the benefits of U.S. protection against Iranian or other aggression. Would Saudi Arabia's policies toward the United States, for example, be markedly different if Washington entered into a sustained crisis with Israel over the Palestine issue? Would Riyadh lower the price of oil? Would it stop hedging its regional bets concerning U.S. attempts to coerce Iran into freezing its nuclear weapons programs? Would it regard current U.S. policy toward Afghanistan more positively? Would it view American democracy promotion in the Middle East more favorably? Would it be more inclined to reform its internal governmental processes to be more in line with U.S. preferences? No. In sum, we believe that Israel's substantial contributions to U.S. interests are an underappreciated aspect of this relationship and deserve equal billing to shared values and historical responsibility as rationales for American support of Israel.

In short, Israel is an asset of the U.S., sharing technology and developing life-saving, high-tech ideas, products, and industries. In contrast, the Arab-Muslim world subverts U.S. national interests, contributing terrorism and global jihad, and using oil as a threat.

## Borders – Suddenly, a Point-of-Contention

In a June 19, 2011, op-ed, carried, *inter alia*, by the *Inquirer*, former U.S. Permanent Representative to the U.N. John Bolton, echoing Goldberg's and Caradon's statements, counseled that this U.S. position should remain unchanged:

> These "land for peace" resolutions (242 and 338) make no mention of "the 1967 borders" or any other specific line, and for very compelling reasons. Those who drafted these texts understood that the '67 [*i.e.*, '49] lines could never meet Israel's legitimate quest, in 242's words, "to live in peace within secure and recognized boundaries free from threats or acts of force." It has been America's policy to support those Israeli aspirations, and should remain so today.

Sources:

"U.S. Support for Israel's Qualitative Military Edge" (Andrew J. Shapiro, *Washington Institute for Near East Policy*)

"Israel: A Strategic Asset for the United States" (Robert D. Blackwill and Walter B. Slocombe, *The Washington Institute for Near East Policy, from LA Times*, October 31, 2011)

# IX. Israel: An Open Democracy that Respects Human Rights

Israel is a pluralistic society: 80% of Israelis are Jews, comprised of Sephardic/native Jews (who have lived there since antiquity) and Jews of different ethnicities and races (who have emigrated from the Middle East, Ethiopia, India, Russia, Europe and the Americas); Jewish refugees from Arab and Muslim countries and their descendants make up over half of the Jewish population. Israel's non-Jewish minorities make up 20% percent of the population. Among these groups are Arab Muslims (one-million strong), Arab Christians, Druze, Baha'i, Bedouins, Asians and Circassians.

The essence of Israel's openness is embodied within the Declaration of the Establishment of the State of Israel (May 14, 1948), which affirms:

> The State of Israel...will foster the development of the country for the benefit of **all** its inhabitants; it will be based on freedom, justice and peace as envisaged by the prophets of Israel; **it will ensure complete equality of social and political rights to all its inhabitants irrespective of religion, race or sex**; it will guarantee freedom of religion, conscience, lan-

guage, education and culture; it will safeguard the Holy Places of all religions; and it will be faithful to the principles of the Charter of the United Nations. ...We appeal—in the very midst of the onslaught launched against us now for months—to the Arab inhabitants of the State of Israel to preserve peace and participate in the upbuilding of the State on the basis of **full and equal citizenship and due representation** in all its provisional and permanent institutions. [emphasis added]

These equality-promising words have been implemented in the political, civil, religious and economic spheres. Israeli Arabs are not excluded or persecuted in the Jewish state; Arabic, like Hebrew, is an official language in Israel. Israeli law expressly forbids discrimination on the basis of race, creed or sex; there is no segregation. Under Israeli law, all (including Arab minorities) are provided full civil rights, citizenship, and the right to vote; indeed, Israel is one of the few places in the Middle East where Arab women may vote. Israel permits freedom of speech, assembly and movement. The Arab citizens of Israel have more rights – and enjoy more freedom, education, access to healthcare, and economic opportunity – than do Arabs of any Arab state.

All can and do serve in all branches of government (holding elected and appointed positions), including the Knesset (parliament), judiciary (including the Supreme Court) and administrative branches (cabinet and diplomatic corps). Indeed, some of the Israeli government's harshest critics are Israeli Arabs who are members of the Knesset. Some have even called for the elimination of Israel and have openly collaborated with avowed enemies of Israel.

The situation in Judea/Samaria differs, however, due to countless acts of Arab terrorism. To make Israel safe for ALL of her citizens, Jews and non-Jews. Israel was compelled to impose such precautions as restricting movement of Arab residents living beyond the "Green Line." The devastation from the wave of violence from the Second Intifada, therefore, prompted creation of check-points, special roadways, and the security fence.

Were Israel to give Palestinian Arabs full citizenship, Judea/Samaria would necessarily be annexed, an action which no Israeli government is yet prepared to take, especially absent a peace treaty or agreement to end the conflict. Israel has given Palestinian Arabs increasing authority over their internal affairs and, indeed, the P.A. maintains civilian control of 95% of Palestinian Arabs in the territories. They are not citizens of Israel, but they have the right to petition Israel's highest courts, and have frequently been successful.

Harvard Law Professor Alan Dershowitz placed the Israeli legal system in perspective in a speech before the American Israel Public Affairs Committee's Annual Meeting (May 23, 1989):

One does not judge a democracy by the way its soldiers immediately react, young men and women under tremendous provocation. One judges a democracy by the way its courts react, in the dispassionate cool of judicial chambers. And the Israeli Supreme Court and other courts have reacted magnificently. For the first time in Mideast history, there is an independent judiciary willing to listen to grievances of Arabs—that judiciary is called the Israeli Supreme Court.

It has been falsely claimed that Israel forbids Israeli Arabs from buying land in Israel. During the early $20^{th}$ century, the Jewish National Fund was established to purchase land in the territory of Palestine for Jewish settlement and land reclamation; these lands and others acquired after Israel's 1948 War of Independence were subsumed by the government. In 2002, the Israeli Supreme Court ruled the state cannot allocate land based on religion or ethnicity, and may not prevent Arab citizens from living wherever they choose. All citizens (regardless of race, religion or sex) can lease government land, which constitutes 92% of Israel's total land mass and is managed by the Land Management Authority; it is not for sale to anyone, Jew or Arab. The remaining 8% of the territory is privately-owned; the *Waqf* (the Muslim charitable endowment), for instance, owns land that is expressly for the use and benefit of Muslim Arabs.

The sole legal distinction between Jewish and Arab citizens of Israel is that the latter are not required to serve in the Israeli army. This is to spare Arab citizens the need to take up arms against their brethren. Nevertheless, Bedouins have served in paratroop units and other Arabs have volunteered for military duty. Compulsory military service is applied to the Druze and Circassian communities at their own request.

Some economic and social gaps between Israeli Jews and Arabs result from the latter not serving in the military; veterans qualify for many benefits not available to non-veterans. Moreover, the army aids in the socialization process. Arabs do have an advantage in obtaining some jobs during the years Israelis are in the military, however, and industries such as construction and trucking have come to be dominated by Israeli Arabs. Israeli law prohibits discrimination in employment; all Israeli workers are eligible to join and establish labor organizations.

Access to Israel's world-class quality healthcare system is equal for Arab and Israeli citizens. Israel also accepts Arabs from Judea, Samaria and Gaza, including terrorists, for medical treatment, often without charge. Hundreds of thousands of Arab children attend Israeli schools; at the time of Israel's independence, there was one Arab high school in the country whereas, today, there are hundreds of Arab schools. Israel is the only place in the Middle East where LGBT Arabs are not discriminated against, or live in fear of their lives.


## Apartheid

Jimmy Carter linked Israel with "apartheid" in titling his 2006 book *Palestine: Peace Not Apartheid,* but he wasn't the first. Tal (*Israel in MediaLand,* 1989) observed:

> [V]arious critics of Israel have sometimes attempted to draw false comparisons between the apartheid regime in South Africa and democratic Israel....A particularly offensive and blatant example occurred in the report by Peter Jennings, the ABC News anchorman (January 19, 1988).

"Apartheid" regime refers to systematic, deliberate segregation of groups on the basis of race or ethnicity and denial of basic civil rights to those groups by those in-power. Such discrimination existed in South Africa, where the white minority ruled over the overwhelmingly black majority. It enshrined racial separation into law, denying blacks the rights of voting and citizenship; dictating where they could work, live and travel; and jailing and killing those who protested these policies.

Judge Richard J. Goldstone, a former justice of the South African Constitutional Court exonerated Israel of the apartheid charge. Goldstone had chaired the U.N.'s "Commission of Inquiry Regarding the Prevention of Public Violence and Intimidation"—also known as the "Goldstone Commission"—which had been highly critical of Israel's conduct during its 2008-2009 "Cast Lead" operation in Gaza in the wake of thousands of rocket and missile attacks from Gaza into Israel following Israel's unilateral evacuation of Gaza in 2005, but which he has largely recanted.

In an October 31, 2011, *N.Y. Times* op-ed entitled, "Israel and the Apartheid Slander," Judge Goldstone stated: "The charge that Israel is an apartheid state is a false and malicious one that precludes, rather than promotes, peace and harmony." Acknowledging the greater "complexity" of Judea/Samaria, he nonetheless concluded that "the reality" is that Israel is "in a state of war with many of its neighbors who refuse to accept its existence"; that "the security barrier was built to stop unrelenting terrorist attacks"; and that "road restrictions get more intrusive after violent attacks and are ameliorated when the threat is reduced." He identified a "critical distinction between an Israel that has "agreed in concept to the existence of a Palestinian state" and whose citizens currently "remain under threat of attacks from the West Bank and Gaza"...

and a South Africa in which "enforced racial separation was intended to permanently benefit the white minority."

Palestinian Arabs generally dispute Israel's right to exist and many actively seek its destruction; in contrast, black South Africans sought to destroy apartheid, not their country. Further illustrating the distance between Israeli society and apartheid, in the late-1980's and early-1990's, Israel rescued more than 20,000 Ethiopians from oppression, absorbing them into Israel and giving them religious freedom.

## The Security Barrier

Israel's security barrier has been an especially attractive target for those who accuse Israel of practicing apartheid. Comparable to other attempts to harm and to delegitimize Israel, criticisms of the barrier are based on fallacies and lies. It was not built to be, nor is it in fact an "apartheid wall." Approximately 97% of the 400-mile barrier built along the edge of Judea/Samaria is a chain-link fence; the remaining 3% (10 miles) is a concrete wall designed to repel sniper fire that was prevalent in particular areas. The fence was built in 2003 in direct response to an intensifying campaign of hundreds of suicide/homicide bombings, terrorist attacks, and rocket attacks on Israeli citizens, tourists—including Americans—perpetrated by Palestinian Arabs, sponsored and armed by the Palestinian Authority, Hamas, and other groups, including Syria and Iran.

Though many have protested the fence and intentionally or ignorantly label it a "wall," it is in fact similar to barriers that dozens of other democracies and other states have built on their borders: U.S. and Mexico, India and Pakistan, Spain and Morocco, North and South Korea, Saudi Arabia and Yemen. Only 5-8% of Judea/Samaria and only three-tenths of 1 percent of Palestinian Arabs are on the "Israeli" side of the fence (many of whom prefer to live in Israel than under the corrupt P.A.). Those harboring grievances about this barrier have petitioned the Israeli Supreme Court, which has ruled in several cases that the fence had to be rerouted. The fence was built to stop terrorists (not Arabs, in general) from penetrating and infiltrating into Israel. In the years since the construction of the fence, terrorist attacks have decreased dramatically (by over 90%). The fence is Israel's legitimate, rightful and sensible defense against an amoral, ruthless and bloodthirsty terrorist aggressor. Terrorism is a deadly obstacle to peace; the fence is an obstacle to terrorism, and has saved—and will continue to save—countless lives on both sides.

## Israel and the P.A. on Jews and Arabs in Each Other's State

Undemocratic, theocratic Arab states discriminate against minorities and non-Muslims; subjugate women (sometimes prohibiting them from driving and entering schools and professions); permit "honor killing" of women; hang homosexuals; execute those who sell land to a Jew; shut-down newspapers; prohibit free speech and assembly; and, lest we forget, force their citizens to be "human shields." The M.S.M. should inform the public of the party that merits condemnation rather than disseminating "apartheid" slurs hurled at Israel by Palestinian Arabs. Instead, the M.S.M. perpetuates rather than combats hypocrisy, dubbing right-wing Israeli politicians as racist, extremist, polarizing, ultra-nationalist, notorious, inflammatory and contentious. (*See* "Land Swaps")

Unless one counts Gaza as such, a Palestinian Arab state west of the Jordan does not yet exist. But pronouncements of Palestinian Arab leaders portend what would be the position of Jews in it. In 2009, P.A. President Mahmoud Abbas' Fatah faction held a General Assembly in Bethlehem, at which Fatah adopted resolutions stating its policies. Commentator Caroline Glick's August 13, 2009, *Jerusalem Post* column, "Fatah's Message," reported that one Fatah resolution "demanded that **all Jews be expelled from Judea, Samaria and Jerusalem** ahead of the establishment of a Jew-free Palestinian state." Regarding Arabs living in Israel, however, Fatah's position is different. Tom-GrossMedia.com reported on August 14, 2009 that "A resolution approved by the assembly stated that Fatah will not give up the armed struggle until all the descendants of those claiming to be of Palestinian Arab origin can live inside Israel."

Israel cannot claim to have solved all her social problems in a mere 63 years of existence, particularly considering the hostile enemies within and surrounding her. To place this into perspective, some suggest that even America, despite having been independent for over 235 years, has yet to integrate (fully and fairly) its diverse communities; more than six decades after civil rights legislation was adopted, discrimination has not been eradicated.

Israel holds civil rights in high regard, including a traditionally dynamic, robust free press similar to America's. Its elected officials are cooperative with the media and reporters are free to go almost anywhere. Consequently, Israel is one of the most open societies in the world, yet, she receives a disproportionate, obsessive and imbalanced level of attention by the M.S.M., especially when compared to the relative silence regarding the closed, government-controlled media in the Arab/Muslim world. Israel should be praised; instead, her foibles are held to an impossible standard.

Sources:

Israel Ministry of Foreign Affairs

Standwithus.com

Jewishvirtuallibrary.com

# X.  Israel:  Untold Story of Accomplishment and Humanitarianism

Contrary to how she is consistently portrayed in the M.S.M., Israel is one of the most amazing, innovative and accomplished countries in the world. Her accomplishments are incredible, despite: (1) being a little more than sixty-years-old; (2) having a population of 7.1 million (less than 1/1000$^{th}$ of the world's total); (3) being one of the smallest countries by land mass; (4) having to be constantly on a war-footing to defend herself from continual attacks from implacable enemies that have sought her destruction for her entire existence; (5) tapping an economy continuously under strain by having to spend more per-capita on her own protection than any other county on Earth; and (6) having absorbed more immigrants relative to her population than any other country. In *Start Up Nation*, authors Dan Senor and Saul Singer address this issue, the "trillion dollar question": How is it that Israel, a country living under these trying circumstances and with few natural resources, can produce more start-up companies than large, peaceful, stable nations like Japan, China, India, South Korea, Canada and the U.K.?

For her size, Israel has contributed disproportionately worldwide to advancements and innovations in: health and wellness, medicine, technology, computing, agriculture, biotechnology, pharmaceuticals, and military (enhancing security and thwarting terrorism)…certainly by a significantly greater magnitude than all her Arab neighbors combined. By contrast, the greatest modern contributions the Arabs have made are: oil (which it serendipitously has in vast reserves under its lands) and terrorism.

## The Key Factors

A "cause and effect" explanation for Israel's successes:

- Israel's $100 billion economy is larger than those of all of its immediate neighbors combined.

- Israel has the highest percentage of home computers per-capita in the world.

- Israel designed the airline industry's most impenetrable flight security (as per industry analysts).

- Israel has the highest ratio of university degrees to the population in the world.

- Israel produces more scientific papers per-capita than any other nation by a large margin (109 per 10,000 people) as well as one of the highest per-capita rates of patents filed.

• Israel has the largest number of startup companies in the world, in proportion to her population; in absolute terms, Israel has the largest number of startup companies than any other country in the world, except the U.S. (3,500 companies, mostly in hi-tech).

• Israel has the largest number of biotech startups on a per-capita basis.

• Israel has the highest concentration of high-tech companies in the world (with more than 3000 high-tech companies and startups), apart from America's Silicon Valley.

• Israel is ranked #2 in the world for venture capital funds (right behind the U.S.).

• Israel has the largest number of NASDAQ listed companies outside the United States and Canada.

• Israel has the highest average living standards in the MidEast.

• Israel's per-capita income in 2010 was over $29,600.00, 28th in the world (per the International Monetary Fund), exceeding that of Italy, New Zealand, Czech Republic and Russia.

• Israel's workforce holding university degrees (24%) ranks third in the industrialized world, after the United States and Holland; 12% hold advanced degrees.

• Israel has the third-highest rate of entrepreneurship—and the highest rate among women and among people over 55–in the world.

• Israel was the first nation in the world to adopt the Kimberly process, an international standard that certifies diamonds as "conflict free."

• Israel has the world's second-highest publication per-capita of new books.

• Israel is the only country in the world that entered the 21st century with a net gain in number of trees, made more remarkable because this was achieved in desert-like environment.

• Israel leads the world in the proportion of scientists and technicians in the workforce (145 per 10,000); this is far greater than that in America (~85), Japan (~70) and Germany (~60). Israel has more than 25% of its workforce employed in technical professions, placing her first in this category as well.

- Israel is the only country to have revived an unspoken language.
- Israeli homes use solar energy for hot water in the highest percentage in the world (93%).
- Israel's scientific institutions are ranked 3rd in the world.
- Israel is ranked 2nd in space sciences.
- Israel's rate of entrepreneurship among women is ranked 3rd highest in the world.
- Israel leads the world for patents in medical equipment.
- Israel has produced 10 Nobel Prize winners: 4 in chemistry, 3 in peace, 2 in economics, 1 in literature, more per-capita than has any other country in the world (more than China, Mexico and Spain combined).
- Israel is the only liberal democracy in the Middle East.
- Israel elected the world's second elected female leader in modern times in 1969, Golda Meir as Prime Minister.
- Israel airlifted a total of 22,000 Ethiopian Jews at risk in Ethiopia, to safety in Israel in 1984 and 1991.
- Israel has more museums per-capita than any other country.

## The Resulting Technological Achievements

This is a sampling of the accomplishments to which Israel and her people can lay claim:

- The cell-'phone was developed in Israel by Israelis working in the Israeli branch of Motorola, which has its largest development center in Israel.
- Most of the Windows NT and XP operating systems were developed by Microsoft-Israel.
- The Pentium-4 microprocessor, Centrino and Atom chip were designed, developed and produced in Israel.
- The Pentium microprocessor was most likely made in Israel.
- Voice-mail technology was developed in Israel.
- Both Microsoft and Cisco built their only R&D facilities outside the US in Israel.
- The technology for the AOL Instant Messenger ICQ was developed in 1996 by four young Israelis.

• In October 2011, Collplant, an Israeli company, announced it is using tobacco (complicit in causing myriad cigarette-related illnesses) to develop and grow human collagen, which is the material generated by the human body to facilitate functions such as wound healing, bone repair, nerve regeneration, and tendon/ligament regrowth. Collplant is currently the only company in the world generating collagen for use in the body from non-animal sources; it is testing whether a drug (Vergenix) hastens healing of chronic diabetic ulcers, a common problem in these patients.

• Israeli scientists developed the first fully-computerized, non-radiation, diagnostic instrumentation for breast cancer.

• Israelis developed a computerized system for ensuring proper administration of medications, thus removing human error from medical treatment. (Treatment mistakes in U. S. hospitals are responsible for 7000 deaths annually.)

• Israel's Given Imaging developed the first ingestible video camera, so small it fits inside a pill; it is used to view the small intestine from the inside, yielding diagnoses of cancer and digestive disorders.

• Israeli researchers developed a device that directly helps the heart pump blood, an innovation carrying potential to save lives in patients with congestive heart failure; it is synchronized with a camera that helps doctors diagnose the heart's mechanical operations through sophisticated sensors.

• Israel developed a new acne treatment, the Clear Light device, which produces a high-intensity, ultraviolet-light-free, narrow-band blue light that causes acne bacteria to self-destruct…all without damaging surrounding skin or tissue.

• Israelis were the first to develop and install a large-scale solar-powered and fully-functional electricity generating plant, in southern California's Mojave desert.

A major Israeli source of pride is the enormous number of inventions and innovations that have taken root on her soil over 63 years, despite challenges of geography, size and diplomacy. In December 2011, the Bloomfield Science Museum in Jerusalem highlighted the top-20 inventions generated by the ever-churning Israeli mind (as reported by the *Jerusalem Post*, 2/27/11):

1. The **Better Place** electric-car network, Israeli **Shai Agassi's** brainchild, is implementing the Israeli pilot that will provide a model for a worldwide electric car grid.

2. **BriefCam** video-synopsis technology lets viewers rapidly review and index original full-length video footage by concurrently showing multiple objects and activities that actually occurred at different times. This technology drastically cuts the time and manpower involved in event-tracking, forensics and evidence-discovery.

3. **Decell Technologies** is a global leader in providing real-time road traffic information based on monitoring the location and movement of phones and GPS devices. Swift-i Traffic, Decell's premium product, is incorporated in leading navigation systems, fleet management services, mapping operations and media channels in several countries.

4. **The EarlySense** continuous monitoring solution allows hospital nurses to watch and record patients' heart rate, respiration and movement remotely through a contact-free sensor under the mattress. The system's builtin tools include a wide range of reports on the status of patients, including alerts for falls and bedsore prevention.

5. **EpiLady**, the first electric hair remover (epilator), secured its leading position in the international beauty care market and, since 1986, has sold almost 30 million units.

6. **Hazera Genetics**, a project of two professors at the Hebrew University Faculty of Agriculture, yielded the cherry tomato. a tasty salad ingredient that ripens slowly and doesn't rot during shipment.

7. **HydroSpin** is developing a unique internal pipe generator that supplies electricity for water monitoring and control systems in remote areas and sites without accessibility to electricity.

8. **Intel Israel** changed the face of the computing world with the 8088 processor (the "brain" of the first PC), MMX and Centrino mobile technology. Israeli engineers at Intel in the 1990s had to convince skeptical bosses to take a chance on MMX technology, an innovation designed to improve computer processing. It's now considered a milestone in the company's history.

9. **Leviathan Energy** innovated the Wind Tulip, a cost-effective, silent, vibration-free wind turbine designed as an aesthetic environmental sculpture, producing clean energy at high-efficiency from any direction.

10.  **MobileEye** combines a tiny digital camera with sophisticated algorithms to help drivers navigate more safely. The steering system-linked device sounds an alert when a driver is about to change lanes inadvertently, warns of an impending forward collision and detects pedestrians. It has contracts with GM, BMW and Volvo, among others.

11.  **Netafim** is a worldwide pioneer in smart-drip and micro-irrigation, starting from the idea of Israeli engineer **Simcha Blass** for releasing water in controlled, slow drops to provide precise crop irrigation. The kibbutz-owned company operates in 112 countries with 13 factories throughout the world.

12.  **Ormat Technologies** designs, develops, builds, owns, manufactures and operates geothermal power plants, supplying clean geothermal power in more than 20 countries.

13.  **Panoramic Power** provides a current monitor solution that enables enterprises and organizations to reduce their operational and energy expenses using a breakthrough power flow visibility platform.

14.  **PrimeSense** revolutionizes interaction with digital devices by allowing them to "see" in three dimensions and transfer control from remote controls and joysticks to hands and body. It is the leading business provider of low-cost, high-performance 3D machine vision technologies for the consumer market.

15.  **Pythagoras Solar** made the world's first solar window, which combines energy efficiency, power generation and transparency. This transparent photovoltaic glass unit can be easily integrated into conventional building design and construction process.

16.  **Solaris Synergy** innovated an environmentally friendly and economically beneficial way to float solar panels on water instead of taking up valuable land, generating energy while protecting and limiting evaporation from reservoir surfaces.

17.  **The Space Imagery Intelligence (IMINT) unit of Elbit Systems** makes a "space camera"—a compact, lightweight electro-optic observation system—for governmental, commercial and scientific applications.

18. **TA Count** real-time microbiology enables the detection and counting of harmful microorganisms in a matter of minutes, rather than the conventional method of cell culture that takes several hours to a few days. The technology applies to the fields of drinking and wastewater, pharmaceuticals and food and beverage production.

19. **Takadu** provides monitoring software to leading water utilities worldwide. The product offers realtime detection and control over network events such as leaks, bursts, zone breaches and inefficiencies.

20. **Turbulence**, the world's first hyper-narrative, interactive movie, is also the name of the company developed by **Prof. Nitzan Ben-Shaul** of Tel Aviv University. The technology allows the viewer to choose the direction of the film's plot by pressing buttons on the PC, Mac or iPad at various moments in the action.

## Gaza Support

Also, greatly underreported by the M.S.M., Israel continues to maintain a humanitarian corridor for the transfer of goods to the Gaza Strip, a hostile entity ruled by Hamas, an organization that has fired at least 10,000 rockets at Israel and has declared its intention to eliminate the Jewish State. (Has any other country in history, faced with such an antagonistic enemy on its doorstep, acted with such selflessness?) Food and supplies are shipped from Israel to Gaza six-days-a-week, channeled through aid organizations or via Gaza's private sector. Among the goods that are regularly delivered to Gaza through Israel are foods (meat, chicken and fish, grains and legumes, fresh vegetables, dairy products, oil, flour, salt and sugar, spices, cakes and candies), toys, cosmetics, animal feed, hygiene products, clothing, school supplies, medicines and medical supplies. Israel coordinated transfer of medical supplies for the disabled (wheelchairs, crutches and first-aid kits).

Other equipment shipped to Gaza include heart-monitors, baby feeding tubes, dental equipment, medical books, ambulance emergency equipment, artificial limbs and infant sleeping bags. In February 2010, Israel facilitated transfer of mammogram equipment for breast cancer diagnosis and the first CT machine in Palestinian Red Crescent Society hospitals in the Gaza Strip. Israel transfers school equipment supplied by UNRWA including notebooks, school bags, writing implements and textbooks, and hundreds of thousands of laptops for Gaza schoolchildren. Israel's conduit is used by internationally recognized organizations including the U.N. and the Red Cross. Israel is not blockading Gaza, which also shares a border with Egypt, despite erroneous and misleading media reports to the contrary.

In 2009, as reported by COGAT (Coordinator of Government Activities in the Territories, Ministry of Defense):

- 738,576 tons (30,576 truckloads) of humanitarian commodities were transferred to Gaza.

- 21,200 international organization staff members entered Gaza.

- 4,883 tons of medical equipment and medicine entered Gaza, in 572 trucks, based on requests made by the P.A. and the international community.

- More than a million tons of humanitarian supplies entered Gaza from Israel (from January 2009 - May 2010), equaling nearly a ton of aid for every man, woman and child in Gaza.

- 22,849 Palestinians exited Gaza, among them 10,544 patients and their companions, for medical treatment in Israel.

- Hundreds of thousands of export items left Gaza, including fruits and flowers.

In June 2010, Israel liberalized the system by which civilian goods (excluding the inflow of weapons and war materiel) enter Gaza and expanded the inflow of materials for civilian projects that are under international supervision. Because of the problematic nature of these dual-use materials, construction materials are currently permitted to be supplied only for P.A.-approved projects that are under the supervision of international bodies.

In September 2011, COGAT reported that:

- 4945 truckloads (136,785 tons) of merchandise were delivered into the Gaza Strip through Kerem Shalom Crossing; this is approximately the same amount as in June, July and August

- 3295 Palestinian individuals exited the Gaza Strip through Erez crossing.

- 66 meetings with private businessmen and other representatives were held.

- 3045 permits were issued to Palestinians for exiting the Gaza Strip; including:

— 1,522 permits for medical treatment (762 patients and 760 for accompanying individuals).

— 57 permits for International Organizations' employees.

— 26 permits for medical conventions.

— 33 permits for attending weddings, funerals and visiting family.

• During September, 1,455 businessmen exited the Gaza Strip.

In December 2011, COGAT reported:

• As of December 1, 2011: the GDP in the Gaza Strip has increased more than 30% compared to 2010, and the unemployment rate is the lowest recorded in the past 10 years.

• Growth reached 31% in the second quarter (the construction industry accounted for the most significant increase in economic growth).

• There is no shortage of commercial goods in the Gaza Strip.

• One hundred exit permits for businesspersons are issued daily, in addition to the passage of Gaza residents for humanitarian reasons and the entry of international organization employees.

• The import of new cars is also permitted, and many luxury cars are imported to Gaza via the Erez crossing.

• 176 projects funded by the international community have been approved for the year; up to the beginning of November, 11,343 truckloads of building materials were delivered to the Gaza Strip for these projects.

• The agricultural export season began on November 21, 2011: exports are expected to be similar to last year (291 truckloads of agricultural produce were exported in 2010).


## Support to Palestinian Arabs

Again, without any significant M.S.M. attention, Israel improved Palestinian Arab quality-of-life in Judea/Samaria, where cities such as Nablus, Ramallah, and Qaliqilya are experiencing growth, stability and security. Culture and leisure activities are increasingly available to these Palestinian Arabs, who enjoy movies, health clubs, malls, restaurants, and music festivals. Access and movement in Judea/Samaria has substantially improved. Many Israeli checkpoints have been reduced, eliminating the restrictions imposed on Palestinian Arabs due to security concerns following terrorist attacks. Remaining checkpoints are now open 24-hours-a-day in most cases. In 2009, Israel issued 54,318 employment permits to Palestinian Arabs for work in Israel; 1,500 high-profile PalestinianArabbusiness-people were given open entry permits to Israel. Israel has also upgraded and improved the capacity of commercial crossings between Israel and Judea/Samaria, and between Israel and Jordan (the Allenby Bridge Terminal). A number of below=structure projects are currently in different stages of implementation in Judea/Samaria. These projects will help improve the standard-of-living for the local population, including among others the upgrading of water, electricity and sanitation below structures.

In September 2011, Israel issued its "Report of the Government of Israel to the Ad-hoc Liason Committee on measures taken by Israel in support of developing the Palestinian economy and socio-economic structure." The report was prepared for a meeting of the Ad Hoc Liaison Committee (AHLC) established in 1996 by the Government of Norway to coordinate international aid for the purpose of building and strengthening the capabilities and institutions of the P.A. The Executive Summary is illustrative and provides as follows:

> The Government of Israel views the bilateral track with the Palestinians as the only way to reach a sustainable solution, based on two states for two peoples. The Government of Israel wishes to maintain the existing legal framework, as long as circumstances allow. After two consecutive years of impressive economic growth in Judea/Samaria, the Palestinian economy now faces a slowdown. According to IMF estimates, in the first half of 2011 real GDP growth amounted to approximately 4% (compared to real GDP for the first half of 2010), a decline from the 8% annual growth rate the previous year. The P.A. now faces a financial crisis. The factors fueling the crisis include: the Palestinian budget's ongoing dependency on foreign aid and the shortfall in aid in 2011; the P.A.'s inability to finance the shortfall through bank loans; the lack of sufficient internal resources to generate income; and a relatively large public sector which consumes a large portion of the budget. The current fiscal situation raises doubts about whether the P.A. will be able to reduce its dependency on foreign aid in the coming years.

> Israel's policy in Judea/Samaria has contributed significantly to growth in the past year. Trade between Israel and the P.A. continuously increased by 7% throughout the first half of 2011, an increase reflected by a 6% increase in tax revenue collection transferred to the PA. A higher volume of commercial goods was shipped from Judea/Samaria via the land crossings to Israel. In the first half of 2011, there was a 31.32% increase in commercial movement of goods via the Allenby Bridge. Palestinian imports (except Israel) amounted to NIS 3,127,395,640, a 17.44% increase compared to the par-

allel period in the previous year. Palestinian exports (except Israel) amounted to USD 45,458,095 in the first half of 2011, a 23% increase compared to the parallel period in the previous year.

## Trade with Muslim World

Trade and commerce have historically been "constants" in the Middle East; if not at war with one's enemies and surrounding tribes, there was always business, markets and the bazaar. The M.S.M. does not report on this facet of daily life. Israeli business quietly thrives in Saudi Arabia and Iraq, and in far-off countries like Indonesia and Malaysia. Company owners on both sides do all they can to avoid harmful publicity. Contacts are made at international conferences overseas, through European and U.S. companies familiar with both sides, and directly over the Internet. Many Israeli companies export products to Saudi Arabia, sometimes accomplished through their U.S.-registered subsidiaries. Israeli companies have also provided equipment such as body armor to U.S. forces stationed in Saudi Arabia. Israel receives raw materials for its plastics industry—polyethylene and polypropylene—from Saudi Arabia and other Gulf countries. Israel's plastics industry, in turn, exports greenhouse sheeting, irrigation drippers, house and garden products, disposable utensils and food packaging to Saudi Arabia. Some of these products are made by Turkish factories established by Israeli companies.

As Dubai was building the Palm Islands—a megalomaniac real estate project delayed by the global economic crisis—Israelis had a hand in providing some of the shingles through an Italian roofing tile company. Companies in the Gulf states rely on sophisticated Israeli technology for security purposes. Israel also exports medical, agricultural and water technologies to the Gulf states.

## Humanitarian Achievements

Israel has a long-standing tradition and heightened sense of humanitarian awareness. This has generated a sense of responsibility for coordinating relief to alleviate disease, hunger, and poverty. Her government and people have offered exemplary levels of aid, both abroad and to her immediate neighbors, through various governmental organizations like Mashav (Israel's Agency for International Development Cooperation) and non-governmental organizations. Israel has provided decades of humanitarian assistance and capacity building in Africa, South America, and its neighboring Arab countries, including Gaza. Starting in the 1950's, Israel adopted an official humanitarian aid agenda, providing vital relief to more than 140 countries; among them are nations that do not maintain diplomatic relations with Israel. Since 1959, Israeli doctors have offered eye camps to treat ocular diseases to people throughout the developing world. In 1970, Israel opened her doors to the world's non-Jewish refugees (saving those in distress and those seeking refuge) from countries including Lebanon, Egypt, Iran, Vietnam, Bosnia, Kosovo, Eritrea and Sudan. Since 1995, Israeli doctors, acting through Save a Child's Heart, have given free life-saving heart operations to kids worldwide, including from the P.A., Iraq, Jordan and other Arab nations. Since the organization first started, 2300 children have been treated. This is virtually ignored by the media.

Unfortunately, due to her own tragic circumstances, Israel has become a world leader in handling mass casualties. No other country can dispatch search-and-rescue teams and field-hospitals as quickly and effectively.

Other recent examples of Israel's frontline actions of extending international aid and training in the wake of natural and man-made disasters and terrorist attacks beyond its borders include:

• 2004: after the tsunami, first-response aid with 60 tons of aid to Indonesia, and 82 tons of relief to Sri Lanka;

• 2005: after the earthquake in Kashmir, the Flying Aid group gave supplies and shelter for thousands of families;

• 2005: after Hurricane Katrina, relief to New Orleans;

• 2009: after a storm in the Philippines, medical teams provided relief;

• January 2010: after the devastating Haiti earthquake, Israel was the first nation on the scene to help to set-up hospitals, rescue people trapped in rubble, and deliver babies; and

• October 2011: after a Turkey earthquake, provided relief despite deteriorated diplomatic relations (after nine Turkish nationals were killed in May 2010 during Israel's interception of a Turkish-flagged "aid flotilla,"– with terrorists on board – attempting to break Israel's lawful naval blockade of Hamas-controlled Gaza).

This assistance to others in need, regardless of their ideology, follows the Jewish injunction of *tikkum olam* – to repair the world – and is all the more remarkable in light of its experiencing unrelenting years of provocation, rocket attacks, bombings and terrorist attacks by enemies committed to its destruction. Israel has generously trained countless trauma surgeons and doctors, police officers, rescue teams and homeland security personnel from around the world.

Sources:

Israel Ministry of Foreign Affairs

COGAT (Coordinator of Government Activities in the Territories, Ministry of Defense)

Facts & Logic About the Middle East (FLAME)

Aish.com

*Start Up Nation*, by Dan Senor and Saul Singer (2009)

"Israel's Top 20 Greatest Inventions of All Time" (*Jerusalem Post*, 12-27-11)

# XI. Opposition: Arab and Muslim Anti-Semitism

The greatest obstacle to peace between Israel and Palestinian Arabs is not the M.S.M.'s obsessive fixation upon Israeli construction in Judea/Samaria and neighborhoods in eastern Jerusalem (which they consider *a priori* part of any future Palestinian state) but, rather, what is rarely mentioned: vituperative, jihadist hatred of Jews. Jihadism in its current incarnation is not exclusively derived from medieval Islamic teachings and sources, but rather is a political amalgam of rank anti-Semitism and Nazi exterminationist aspirations. Islamic hatred motivates actions against Israel, the nation of the Jews. As long as current Islamic teachings prevail (in which Jews are portrayed as "devils" who must be eliminated and Israel is considered an "enemy of God"), any talk about peace between Israel and the Arab-Muslim world in general – and the Palestinian Arabs in particular – is conjectural if not premature or futile. No Israeli concession suffices, including returning land won in defensive wars; the only plausible "final solution" would be national suicide.

### Roots of Islamism

The Qur'an assigns the Land of Israel as a dwelling location for the Jews to which they will be returned as the end of days approaches (Qur'an 17:105), so a faithful Muslim could support the Jewish people's presence in the historic lands of Palestine. But this would contradict the jihadists' schema which, like that of the Nazis, is to erase the source of "evil" that they view as threatening all humanity: Jews and Judaism. Anything outside the Dar al-Islam (the "realm of Islam"), versus its opposite, Dar al-Harb ("house of war") is inherently evil or illegitimate. Thus, for a jihadist to recognize the legitimacy of the Jewish state would be to recognize the existential legitimacy of "evil" itself. An Egyptian cleric, Muhammad Hussein Yaqub, explains this ideology: "If the Jews left Palestine to us, would we start loving them? Of course not....They are enemies not because they occupied Palestine. They would have been enemies even if they did not occupy a thing....Our fighting with the Jews is eternal, and it will end until the final battle...until not a single Jew remains on the face of the earth." ("We will Fight, Defeat and Annihilate Them," al-Rahma TV, January 17, 2009, *MEMRI*).

Hitler's favorite Muslim cleric, the Grand Mufti of Jerusalem, Hajj Amin al-Husseini, was the prototypical modern jihadist. He was the leader of the Arabs in Palestine for twenty years beginning in the 1920's – before the re-establishment of Israel – and was a rabid Jew-hater who brewed a toxic mix of traditional Islamic vilification of Jews with the more modern European forms of Anti-Semitism, as embodied in "The Protocols of the Learned Elders of Zion." His "nephew," the Egyptian-born Yasser Arafat, was trained by the Muslim Brotherhood and took up the jihadist mantle with the founding of Fatah, the Palestine National Liberation Movement, in 1959. Fatah ultimately became the dominant party of the PLO when it was founded in 1964. Fatah means "conquest" and is also the name of the 48th Sura (chapter) of the Qur'an which, according to major Muslim commentators, details the story of the "Treaty of Hudaybiyyah," a "peace" treaty Mohammad concluded with nonbelievers in 628...which he abrogated two years later (when he believed his forces were superior) and proceeded to slaughter the opposing tribe. Adopting this "temporary truce" has become a model and a precedent in Islamic law for all agreements with infidels: never permanent, never lasting more than 10 years. Arafat continually referenced this strategy with regard to his signing of the Oslo Accords. Fatah's definitive objective, as stated in its platform, is "the annihilation of the Zionist entity in all of its economic, political, military and cultural manifestations." Thus, eradication of Israel is not merely political; it is essentially an existential, metaphysical goal against the Jews. Palestine must be *judenrein*.

This is why Arafat's hate-filled rhetoric was directed against Jews, not merely Israelis. In 1992, a year before the Oslo Accords, Arafat stated: "Damn their [the Jews'] fathers. The dogs. Filth and dirt...Treachery flows in their blood, as the Qur'an testifies." One of his Fatah leaders, Sakhr Habash, stated that, once the Palestinian Arabs gained control of Gaza and the West Bank through the Oslo Accords, they would proceed to the "final solution." A mufti Arafat appointed, Ikrima Sabri, preached in October 1994 that Jews were "descendants of pigs and apes" who were involved in a "worldwide Zionist conspiracy," blaming them in Nazi-inspired imagery for all ills of humanity. Another Fatah cleric, Ahmad Abu Halabiya, declared in an October 2000 Friday sermon: "Have no mercy on the Jews, no matter where they are, in any country."

Mustafa Mashhur, leader of the Egyptian Muslim Brotherhood from 1996-2002, wrote the following in a book entitled "Jihad Is The Way" (translated by *PMW*, published in the *Jerusalem Post* in February 2011): "The problems of the Islamic world – such as in Palestine, Afghanistan, Syria, Eritrea or the Phillipines – are not issues of territories and nations, but of faith and religion. They are the problems of Islam and all Muslims, and their resolution cannot be negotiated and bargained by recognizing the enemy's right to the Islamic land he stole, and therefore there is no other option but jihad for Allah, and this is why jihad is the way."

In a video clip from Egypt's Al-Nas TV released on May 7, 2012, radical Muslim preacher Safwat Higazi is seen telling thousands of Muslim Brotherhood supporters at a Cairo soccer stadium: "We can see how the dream of the Islamic caliphate is being realized, God willing, by Dr. Mohamed Mursi" (the movement's presidential candidate), as Mursi and other Brotherhood officials nodded in agreement. "The capital of the caliphate - the capital of the United States of the Arabs - will be Jerusalem," Higazi said, before leading the crowd in chants of "Millions of martyrs march toward Jerusalem."

Mursi responded, "Yes, Jerusalem is our goal. We shall pray in Jerusalem, or die as martyrs on its threshold." This is just further evidence of what the Muslim Brotherhood and its offshoots stand for: the extermination of Israel - and Jews everywhere - as well as the spread and control of radical Islam over the world."

Since the P.A. was established, it has systematically indoctrinated and brainwashed young and old to hate Israelis and Jews. Using media, education, and cultural structures that it controls, the P.A. has actively promoted religious hatred, demonization, conspiracy libels, and the like. The P.A. presents Jews as possessing inherently evil traits. Jews are said to be treacherous, corrupt, deceitful and unfaithful by nature. These Jewish "attributes" are presented as the unchangeable nature of Jews. The P.A. assigns responsibility to the Jews for all the problems in the world: wars, conflicts and civil wars are all said to be triggered by Jews. Indeed, the oppression suffered by Jews throughout history is presented as the legitimate response of nations seeking revenge for the injury caused them by the Jews living among them. The creation of the State of Israel is said to have been a European plot in order to be rid of their Jews and save Europe from the evil of Jewish presence in their countries. Forgeries and fiction masquerading as history are used to document and support the libel that Judaism is essentially racist and evil. Jews are said to be planning and executing heinous crimes, including burning Palestinians in ovens, murder, and using prisoners for Nazi-like experiments. These are packaged to present Israelis and Jews as endangering Palestinians, Arabs, Muslims and all humanity. This ongoing campaign has so successfully instilled hatred that fighting, murder and even suicide-terror against Israelis and Jews are perceived by the majority of Palestinians as "justified self-defense" and as Allah's will.

But perhaps the most implacable of all Arab/Muslim groups embodying jihadist anti-Semitism is Hamas. The organization's 1988 charter is nothing but honest in its aims: to fight, butcher and kill Jews and destroy Israel. Hamas makes no distinction among Jews, Zionists and Israelis; Hamas' war is not merely terminating Jewish "occupation" of perceived Muslim land – including Palestine – but in ridding the planet of Jews altogether. Hamas sees evil rooted not only in Jews, but in Judaism itself; unlike the rest of humanity, the Jews can be neither rehabilitated nor redeemed. Instead, they must be cast into hell and it is Hamas' mission to be the liberator and savior of humanity by doing so. The ultimate, existential fight the Muslims have is with the Jews, who will be defeated, they claim, because Allah has decreed it. Jews are never to be trusted, befriended. The preamble of the Hamas charter quotes the Muslim Brotherhood founder, Hassan al-Banna's declaration that "Israel will exist and will continue to exist until Islam will obliterate it." It is instructive that, when Banna issued this assertion, Israel had not yet been reborn; thus, this is a reference to the Jewish people, not to a political entity. In 2006, Hamas won elections for Palestinian Legislative Council, the legislative body of the P.A., permitted to compete over the strenuous objections of those who knew of this history.

## Manifestations of Islamism

The following two stories illustrate the radical disconnect between Arab/Muslim intolerance and Israeli reverence for humanity, civility and tolerance; they involve Gazans.

The first story is about how Israeli doctors saved a four-month-old Palestinian boy (Mohammed Abu Mustafa) in 2007 who was born without an immune system. Dr. Raz Somech, a pediatric immunology specialist at Tel Hashomer Hospital in Tel Aviv, asked Shlomi Eldar, an Israeli Channel 10 TV correspondent in Gaza, to broadcast a plea to Israelis to help fund a life-saving $55,000 bone marrow transplantation. An anonymous Israeli man whose son, a soldier, had been killed in the line of duty, donated the entire sum, which proved successful. In the 2010 Israeli documentary, "Precious Life," the boy's mother, Raida, revealed in the film that Gazans accused her of collaborating with Israel. During a hospital stay, the mother told Eldar: "For you life is precious, but not for us….After Mohammed gets well, I will certainly want him to be a shahid [martyr]."

The second story concerns a 21-year-old Palestinian woman (Wafa Samir Ibrahim al-Biss), who was detained at a crossing into Israel in June 2005 when something about her gait struck the guards on duty as somewhat amiss. A search revealed that she had been carrying 22 pounds of explosives strapped to her body. She had been attempting to enter Israel to attend a follow-up appointment at the Soroka Medical Center in Beersheva but, upon questioning, she disclosed her intent to detonate the payload at that hospital to kill Israelis. Notably, this would-be suicide/homicide bomber had been treated there five months previously for severe burn injuries received after a gas canister had exploded on a fire while she was cooking at her home. Israel provided her humanitarian medical care otherwise unavailable, of which she readily and ungratefully took advantage.

The Israeli medical system remarkably treats all patients equally (including thousands of Palestinians and Arabs), both terrorist and victim, based on biology not ideology; care is provided while totally aware that some, given the chance, will later try to harm Israelis. Nothing comparable can be envisioned in the Arab-Muslim world, were a Jew in-need.

In sum, failure of the M.S.M. and political leaders to name this evil – as "Islamism" and/or "fascism" – blinds them to the reality that true lasting peace will never be secured in the Middle East. Hamas, Fatah, the PLO, and by extension the P.A., have developed theological and ideological bases that render impossible any negotiation for co-equal peace with a Jewish state. To make peace, for them, would be an act of apostasy or treason. The only type of agreement they can make with the infidel Jews conforms to the PLO's "phased strategy" of destroying Israel in stages. These Islamists cannot and are unwilling to be viable partners in peace with a Jewish state, especially in the Middle East. A thriving Israel on their doorstep, which Allah has deemed inferior, is somehow succeeding despite all their efforts to destroy it and plainly cannot be tolerated; it is a humiliation and embarrassment and deeply challenges their theological tenets.


Unfortunately, to its peril, neither the West nor its liberal-leaning M.S.M. comprehends or will admit to the triumphalist nature of resurgent Islam and its aggressive nature, which calls for jihad and the creation of a universal Islamic State governed by Sharia law. The motivation of Islam is clear, the victory of Islam over all else. Quoting the Qur'an (8:23): "Make war on them ["infidels"] until idolatry shall cease and Allah's religion [Islam] shall reign supreme." Israel is perhaps the first target of Islamist hatred, but it is by no means its last. Appeasement of an Islamist Middle East will not thwart its quest for world dominance. Despite such inattention, the intolerant cannot be tolerated, de-legitimizers cannot be legitimated. Instead, to protect the freedom and liberties Americans cherish in the Judeo-Christian-based democratic tradition, this scourge must be recognized, combated and ultimately defeated...before it consumes Western culture.

Sources:

"How Anti-Semitism Prevents Peace" (David Patterson, Middle East Quarterly, Summer 2011)

Israel Ministry of Foreign Affairs - website

Islamic Hatred Motivates Actions Against Israel (Joseph Puder, The Interfaith Taskforce for America and Israel, Sept. 16, 2011)

Canadian Jewish News (Nov. 4, 2011)

"Palestinian Woman Heading for Treatment at Israeli Hospital Caught Carrying Explosives" (Associated Press, June 20, 2005)

"Palestinian Woman Tries to Blow Herself Up While Going into Israel for Dr. Appeasement" (NBC News, June 22, 2005)

*Palestine Media Watch*

"We will Fight, Defeat and Annihilate Them," al-Rahma TV, January 17, 2009

Hamas Charter (MEMRI (Middle East Media Research Institute)

# XII. Opposition: Arabs Seek Israel's Destruction, Not "Two-State" Peace

The Arab nations consistently and belligerently have rejected peace with Israel *and* an Arab state of their own on Judea/Samaria and Gaza. To appreciate why this has occurred, it is necessary to trace the history of such entreaties during the past century, the degree to which rejectionism has become engrained within the mind of the Palestinian Arab, and the consequences of these findings. Again, these observations that drive day-to-day events are rarely cited within the M.S.M.

### Historical Overview

Creation of a Palestinian State was rejected when it was proposed in 1937 (by the Peel Commission); when it was offered by the U.N. in 1947 (recalling that, while the Jews accepted the "Partition Plan," the Arabs rejected it and instead the armies of five Arab nations launched a war against the fledgling Jewish state); and when it was offered to P.A. President Yasser Arafat by President Clinton and Israeli P.M. Ehud Barak at the Camp David II Conference in 2000. Arafat's response was both a non-response (he walked away without issuing a counter-proposal) and a punctuated-rejection (soon thereafter, he initiated the premeditated bloody Second Intifada). Similarly, in 2008, Israeli P.M. Ehud Olmert offered the P.A. a state, which Abbas also rejected.

In 1949, Judea/Samaria and Gaza, which the U.N. had designated as a state for the Arabs, were annexed (illegally) respectively by Jordan and Egypt. No new, separate, "Palestinian" state was ever created on those territories, despite their being in Arab hands. In fact, when the PLO was formed in 1964 at the Arab League Summit in Cairo, its covenant made no mention of liberating these lands from Egypt or Jordan. The PLO leadership stated unequivocally that its goal was to "push the Jews into the sea." That remains the goal of the P.A. and Hamas, the elected government of Gaza.

There is only one Jewish state on the planet. Israel comprises just 0.1% of the land mass of the Middle East, yet it is the state that is constantly told to and expected to cede territory. When P.A. spokesmen have addressed Arab audiences, they have openly stated that their goal is the destruction of Israel, not simply the reconquest of the 1967 territories (*i.e.*, Judea/Samaria and Gaza); they candidly admit that they advocate the "Strategy of Phases": gain some of the territories, and then use them as a forward operating base to invade and annihilate the rest of Israel. Maps and emblems of the P.A. depict all of Israel as "Palestine," omitting Israel and "green lines." These maps appear in official publications and school textbooks. The songs taught to children in P.A. schools and summer camps refer to "returning" to cities within pre-1967 Israel. Incitement in P.A- and Hamas-run, media, mosques, and schools consistently espouse hatred of Jews and denial of their bond with the Holy Land.

Arafat consistently wore on the sleeve of his uniform a part of the PLO official emblem. That map showed the borders of the intended "State of Palestine" revealing the PLO's intentions to replace the entire State of Israel, including Tel Aviv, Haifa and Jerusalem, and not just the administered areas of Judea, Samaria and Gaza.

The following are quotations from the Arafat-PLO propaganda machine:

> According to the Phased Plan, we will establish a Palestinian state on any part of Palestine that the enemy will retreat from. The Palestinian state will be a stage in our prolonged struggle for the liberation of Palestine on all of its territories. (Abu Iyad, Arafat's second-in-command, 1988)

> After the Palestinian state wins recognition from most of the nations of the world, as expected, the Israeli presence on Palestinian land will be become illegal, and we will fight this with weapons. The battle against the Israeli forces is a right reserved to us. (Farouk Kadoumi, head of PLO's diplomatic desk in, in P.A. newspaper *Al Hayat Al-Jadeeda*, Oct. 15, 1998)

This is Palestine from the (Jordan) river to the Mediterranean Sea, from Rosh Hanikra to Rafah (in Gaza). The gap between Palestinian expectations and the Israeli conspiracy will inevitably lead to a collision. ("Our position" issued by Arafat's Fatah faction of the PLO in *Al Hayat al-Hadeeda*, Dec. 19, 1998)

Both east and west Jerusalem are *waqf*...not only Jerusalem but rather all of Palestine is Islamic *waqf*...from a religious standpoint, it is not accepted that *waqf* be owned by non-Muslims. (Sheik Ekrima Sabri, Arafat's appointed Mufti of Jerusalem, interview by IMRA, June 10, 1998)

The Land of Muslim Palestine is a single unit which cannot be divided. There is no difference between Haifa and Shechem (Nablus), between Lod and Ramallah, and between Jerusalem and Nazareth...the land of Palestine is sacred *waqf* land for the benefit of all Muslims, east and west. No one has the right to divide it or give up any of it. The liberation of Palestine is obligatory for all the Islamic nations and not only for the Palestinian nation. (Prayer sermon broadcast live on P.A. radio, April 30, 1999)

## Intransigence

*Palestine Media Watch* ("*PMW*") is an Israeli research institute studying Palestinian society and its leadership through its Arabic language media; it uniquely illuminates what Palestinian and Arab officials say to their audiences in Arabic. It quoted Adli Sadeq, the P.A. Ambassador to India, as having told the official P.A. daily *Al-Hayat Al-Jadida* on Nov. 26, 2011:

[The Israelis] have a common mistake, or misconception by which they fool themselves, assuming that Fatah accepts them and recognizes the right of their state to exist, and that it is Hamas alone that loathes them and does not recognize the right of this state to exist. They ignore the fact that this state, based on a fabricated [Zionist] enterprise, never had any shred of a right to exist....Hamas, Fatah and the others are not waging war against Israel right now for reasons related to balance of power. There are no two Palestinians who disagree over the fact that Israel exists, and recognition of it is restating the obvious, but recognition of its right to exist is something else, different from recognition of its [physical] existence.

The M.S.M. is generally silent about these real obstacles to the pursuit of peace and/or a viable two-state solution (Arab intolerance and rejectionism) but, in a rare example of reporting on this issue, the *N.Y. Times* published a book review by Isabel Kershner (12/20/2011) entitled, "Finding Fault in the Palestinian Messages That Aren't So Public." The article featured a new book ("Deception: Betraying the Peace Process") by Itamar Marcus and Nan Jacques Zilberdik (the founder and an analyst of *PMW*) which describes the systematic hate-speech used by the P.A., even as they portray themselves—to a gullible, naïve and sometimes unapologetically biased world, and unquestioning and uninquisitive M.S.M.—as pursuing peace. The book exhaustively catalogs the P.A.'s messaging broadcast in Arabic for its domestic audiences (through cultural events, educational media and speeches by political leaders). Hundreds of examples are detailed, glorifying terrorist murders, spreading hate to school-age children, and using libels and lies to demonize Israelis. Included were wild accusations that Israel intentionally spreads AIDS, drug and prostitution among Palestinians, Israel poisoned Arafat, and Israel plans to destroy the al-Aqsa Mosque. At a press conference for the book, the authors and human rights activists warned that the hate speech and incitement against Israel by P.A. leaders is the fundamental impediment to achieving genuine peace.

In December 2011, *MEMRI* (*The Middle East Media Research Institute*), which also monitors and translates Arabic media, reported that a twelfth-grade Saudi textbook titled, "Studies from the Muslim World" includes a chapter (starting on p. 91) on Palestine and the Palestinian cause which deals extensively with the Jews. The chapter presents the conflict over Palestine as a religious—and not political—struggle between the Jews and the Muslims that goes back to the era of the Prophet Muhammad. It states there is no hope of making peace with the Jews because they do not believe in peace, but only strive to spread corruption and instability throughout the world. Jews are portrayed as liars, connivers and cheats by nature, negative traits that are quoted from the Qur'an. Finally, the chapter states that the only way to liberate Palestine from the Jews is through jihad.

Incitement by Palestinian Arab officials is engrained within its culture of death, intolerance, and hatred of Jews and Israelis, throughout schools and mosques, in speeches and in the media. This has included naming of dozens of streets, schools, city squares, youth camps and sports tournaments in honor of killers of Jews. One of the most obscene examples occurred in March 2010, when the P.A. named a square in Al-Bireh, an area near Ramallah, after the female terrorist leader Dalal Mughrabi, who commanded the Fatah terrorists that perpetrated the 1978 coastal road massacre in which 37 Israelis, including a dozen children, were slaughtered. The "dedication" was scheduled for the 32nd anniversary of the event, but it was postponed several days, as a courtesy to

U.S. Vice President Joe Biden who was visiting the region. This occurred only days after the monstrous massacre of five members of a Jewish family, the Fogels, including three young children, as they slept in the home in Itamar by unrepentant Arab terrorists.. To the neutral observer, this demonstrates a sick pride in the murder of Jews and signals a clear rejection of any true desire for peace.

The conflict has never been about a Palestinian State (in fact, Jordan, which was formed from 75% of the land from the Palestine Mandate, has a population which is 70% "Palestinian" Arab) but, rather, the existence of the tiny Jewish state of Israel (5.5 million Jews) surrounded by 22 Arab and/or Muslim nations (population 350 million). In his speech before the U.S. Congress in May 2011, Israeli P.M. Netanyahu observed: "Our conflict has never been about the establishment of a Palestinian state. It has always been about the existence of the Jewish state. That is what the conflict is about....The Palestinians have been unwilling to accept a Palestinian state if it meant accepting a Jewish state alongside it." Netanyahu then proceeded to describe the incessant hateful incitement against Israel and Jews perpetuated in Judea/Samaria and Gaza by Hamas and the P.A., and their fantastical requirement that the descendants of Palestinian refugees from the 1948 war they initiated be allowed to "return" to their "homes" inside Israel proper: "My friends, this must come to an end. President Abbas must do what I have done. I stood before my people—I told you it wasn't easy for me—I said 'I will accept a Palestinian state.' It is time for President Abbas to stand before his people and say 'I will accept a Jewish state.' Those six words will change history."

Several days after Netanyahu's speech, however, Abbas replied: "With regard to Palestinian recognition of a Jewish state, or whatever, this has never been an issue. Throughout the negotiations between Israelis and us, from 1993 until a year ago, we never heard the words 'Jewish state.' Now they have begun to talk about it, and our response 'Go to the U.N. and call yourselves what you want.' We are not the party to address. Not only that—we refuse to recognize a Jewish state. Try to wrest it out of the U.N. or anyone else. Why does Israel insist on demanding from us and us alone? It did not demand this from the Arabs, from Egypt, from Jordan, or from any Arab country with which it negotiated? Only from us. We know the reason, and we say: 'No, we refuse.' " Abbas reiterated this sentiment on August 28, 2011, on the eve of the September U.N. statehood bid, as he criticized demands made by the Quartet and urged them to back-off: "Don't order us to recognize a Jewish state. We won't accept it."

The M.S.M., so-called experts, and governments cannot comprehend that the P.A. refuses to accept whatever compromise may be offered (*e.g.*, concessions, "financial aid, steps toward statehood) because they want "everything" (*i.e.*,all the land for a Palestinian Arab state). Author and commentator Barry

Rubin—Director of the Global Research in International Affairs (GLORIA) Center and editor of the Middle East Review of International Affairs (MERIA) Journal—concluded the P.A. wants

> an independent state on all the West Bank, Gaza Strip and east Jerusalem with no restrictions, no recognition of Israel as a Jewish state, no serious security guarantees, no limits on militarization, no agreement that this means an end to the conflict, no insistence that Palestinian refugees be resettled in the state of Palestine, and nothing to prevent them from pursuing a second stage of wiping Israel off the map entirely.

Per Rubin, various factors have reinforced the Palestinians obstinacy:

> The Palestinians know that the West will always offer more if they are intransigent.

> The more intransigent the Palestinians, the more Israel is blamed.

> Since the P.A. is almost completely supported by foreign aid that is not threatened by its hardline, [economic] pressure does not exist.

> Palestinian public opinion is relatively radicalized and ideological and does not demand a compromise settlement.

> Its rivals 'out-radicalize' and threaten to destroy [them] politically and perhaps even physically if [they] make a deal.

> Due to religious and nationalist ideology, along with misperception of Israel, the P.A. [and even more Hamas] believes that time is on its side, that waiting a couple of generations and many decades doesn't matter.

Thus, Rubin concluded a "perfect" system has been conjured by the world in general (mainly the U.S., Europe, U.N. and Arabic-speaking states and Muslim majority-states):

> The P.A. has no incentive to make peace and will not do so.

> The world insists that 'peace' is an urgent top priority.

> The only variable is Israel, which must be made to give way, but Israel won't do so because of past experience and the fact that the risks are not too high.

## Implications

Such incitement and brainwashing of the Arab Palestinians has poisoned a generation of people to be intolerant, hate Jews, and seek Israel's destruction. This has continued unabated, and is rarely reported by the M.S.M.

The *Jerusalem Post* reported (7/15/11) that "6 in 10 Palestinians Reject 2-State Solution, Survey Finds" (by Gil Hoffman). This poll, conducted by the Palestinian Center for Public Opinion and sponsored by The Israel Project, found (in face-to-face Arabic interviews with Palestinian Arabs in Judea/Samaria and Gaza) that an overwhelming 73% of Palestinian Arabs agree with the *hadith* (Islamic tradition ascribed to Muhammad), quoted by the terrorist group Hamas in its charter about the requirement to conduct a genocide of Jews. The *hadith* states," The Day of Judgment will not come about until Muslims fight the Jews (killing the Jews) when the Jew will hide behind stones and trees. The stones and trees will say 'O Muslims, O Abdulla, there is a Jew behind me, come and kill him."

Other significant findings from the poll were:

80% agree with the statement in the Hamas Charter calling for the creation of Arab and Islamic battalions to fight the Jews, but only 45% said they believed in the charter's statement that the only solution to the Palestinian problem was jihad.

61% reject the idea of a peaceful Palestinian state living alongside Israel as the solution to the Arab/Israeli war, as against 34% who accept it.

66% said that the Palestinians' real goal should be to first set up a Palestinian state alongside Israel and then move towards creating a single Palestinian-controlled state.

72% support denying thousands of years of Jewish history and connection to the land of Israel.

92% insist on Jerusalem being only the Palestinian capital, as against a mere 1% who believe it should be Israel's capital.

3% believe Jerusalem should be the capital of both Israel and a Palestinian state.

4% believe that Jerusalem should be a neutral international city.

62% support a policy of kidnapping Israeli soldiers and holding them hostage.

53% favor teaching songs about hating Jews in Palestinian schools.

64% support seeking a unilateral declaration of Palestinian statehood at the U.N.

Palestinian Arab rejectionism and the utter refusal to recognize Israel as a Jewish state stands at the root of the struggle and behind every so-called core issue, including borders, Jerusalem, settlement building, water rights, and refugees. Genuine reconciliation can only be achieved once the Palestinian Arabs come to terms with the Jewish character of Israel and the fact of Israel's existence as a Jewish state. This will require a paradigm shift which they have never demonstrated the capacity to accept—particularly noting that, as recently as in 2009, Fatah, the supposedly "moderate" party that constitutes the largest faction of the PLO, reaffirmed its official charter which mandates the continuation of the armed struggle until the Palestinian Arabs have achieved the "complete liberation of Palestine, and eradication of Zionist economic, political, military and cultural existence." Palestinian institutions such as the P.A. persistently indoctrinate the Palestinian public (starting with their youngsters) against any type of acceptance of Israel as a Jewish state.

On November 14, 2011, the PLO announced that it will very soon drop the "land swap" formula (now branded as a grave mistake) in any agreement with Israel. Speaking to *Gulf News*, Tayseer Khalid, a member of the PLO Executive Committee, said it was only "mere talk" by Israelis and mediators. "We have never signed an agreement with Israel, which states any shape of land swap formula....Land swap formula is a heresy in the track of negotiations." He also claimed agreements should be reached on core issues (the borders and the withdrawal of Israeli troops) before any land swap formula is addressed, continuing, "It is time for this mistake to get corrected." Khalid also said the PLO believes that the recent setback at the U.N. Security Council (which did not vote to admit "Palestine" as a state) was not the end of the road for the leadership and that other moves are on the PLO agenda: "We will seek a non-member state status for Palestine at the U.N. General Assembly as per the European proposal [Sarkozy Plan]."

Even when Israelis and Palestinian Arabs attempt to meet in eastern Jerusalem, Palestinian political activists belonging to various factions, including Fatah, move to thwart them. In December 2011, such activists twice opposed such meetings under the pretext that they are designed to promote "normalization" between the peoples and threatened to demonstrate in front of the conference hall; the tactic successfully forced the organizers to cancel the meeting.

The thorniest issue is Jerusalem, which is under siege. As former Israeli ambassador, *N.Y Times* bestselling author, and Middle East expert Dore Gold explains in his book, *The Fight for Jerusalem: Radical Islam, The West, And The Future of The Holy City*, the attack on the veracity of its Biblical past by many in the Arab-Muslim worlds, and enabled by the M.S.M., is merely a prelude for compromising its political future: "In Western diplomatic circles it is now being argued that by pushing hard for a Middle East settlement, with the redivision of Jerusalem at its core, the flames of radical Islamic rage will be lowered, stemming the tide of al-Qaeda's ideological spread. Yet the exact opposite is true. In the last decades, radical Islam has been fed by its sense of victory in the face of repeated withdrawals; a redivision of Jerusalem would not only endanger its holy sites, but also unleash new jihadist momentum, on a scale that most political leaders have not begun to consider." Significantly, Gold argues, if Jerusalem is to remain a free city where all faiths can be practiced, it will have to remain under Israeli sovereignty, the only time such freedom has been guaranteed, because the U.N. is weak and untrustworthy and under the thumb of the Muslim states-bloc, and the increasingly extremist Palestinian Muslims are seeking to eliminate all other faiths from Jerusalem – to support their mendacious political narrative—not to tolerate them.

## Prognostication

In three instances (Surahs 2, 5, and 7), the Qur'an tells of Muhammad turning Jews into apes and/or pigs. For instance, Surah 5:60 states, "Those [Jews] who incurred the curse of Allah and his Wrath, and those of whom [some] He transformed into apes and swine." Another section of the Qur'an compares the Jews to donkeys. In a typical Friday prayer and sermon by a Hamas speaker on October 9, 2009 on Al-Aqsa TV:

> Today we look at Al-Aqsa as it sighs beneath the yoke of the Jews, beneath the yoke of the sons of apes and pigs, brothers of apes and pigs. Destroy the Jews and their helpers."
> (*Palestine Media Watch*).

The words of Hezbollah's secretary general, Hasan Nasrallah are telling: "If we searched the entire world for a person more cowardly, despicable, weak or feeble…we would not find anyone like the Jew."

Israel's goal is simply to live in peace and security with her Muslim neighbors. In direct contrast to Israel's "peace curriculum," Palestinian Arabs are not preparing to live civilly with Israel as neighbors; indeed, the opposite is true, and it is insidious. The M.S.M. should not be fooled by the messages the P.A. conveys to the international community through official communication channels in English, while ignoring the very different messages of hate that are routinely directed at the Palestinian people in Arabic.

Yet, Israel is expected to deal with negotiating "partners"who perceive them as sons of apes and pigs. Nevertheless, Israel has tried for more than six decades to come to terms with its Arab-Muslim neighbors under the "land for peace" moniker. Meanwhile, Israel is expected to comply with the chimera of a "peace process," ignoring its consequent existential risk; despite exposure of this myth, Israel is to capitulate to, appease, and excuse the intent and conduct of her enemies, yielding a nirvana of true peace and harmony.

Deceit and duplicity have long concealed the P.A.'s true intentions; speaking the language of "peace" to Western English-speaking audiences belies constant preaching of hate and war to Palestinian Arabs in Arabic. Because *Taqiyya* (deception) is a fundamental concept in Islam, it is quite prevalent in Islamic politics. Consider the P.A.'s official rationalization for refusing to negotiate with Israel, an ongoing claim for more than two years (as of the time of this writing in early 2012). It blames Israeli insistence on building in Judea/Samaria, within areas Israel would retain in any peace agreement. This "deadlock," however, results from a revised policy that the P.A. adopted in 2009 for its 13th Program (as promulgated by its Palestine Strategy Group), titled "intelligent resistance" (*i.e.*, law-fare, boycott campaigns, and propaganda). This is a method by which the P.A. intends to maintain the struggle against Israel without taking terror off the table as the major weapon against Israel. Such political warfare has successfully won-over the international community to the Palestinian cause, which is largely gullible, elitist and politically beholden to the Arab-lobby.

An example of this deception was reported in the summer of 2011 by the organization, Missing Peace, which revealed that the P.A. persistently lies about water issues in order to advance the narrative of Israeli repression and Palestinian victimhood. The P.A. has actually failed to implement approved water projects and ignored undeniable evidence of Palestinian water theft. The M.S.M. generally has ignored this side of the story, failing to dig behind the news.

The December 2011 reconciliation between the P.A. and Hamas, including the announcement that Hamas will join the PLO, is further evidence that P.A. President Abbas was never sincere in pursuing a peace agreement with Israel. In an interview with European reporters about the unity agreement with Hamas, Abbas said: "We set the agreement's pillars and Hamas agreed with us that resistance will be popular and adopt peaceful ways, rather than military resistance." This is pure garbage, belied by this very alliance.

When Hamas celebrated its 24th anniversary in Gaza on December 14, 2011, with a rally attended by 350,000 people, Prime Minister Haniyeh called for continued armed struggle against Israel and for the Muslim Brotherhood to start a war to liberate Jerusalem: "We affirm that armed resistance is our strategic option and the only way to liberate our land, from the sea to the river… .God willing, Hamas will lead the people...to the uprising until we liberate Palestine, all of Palestine." On January 8, 2012, Haniyeh spoke to a cheering crowd of 5000 in the Tunisian capital, and again reiterated Hamas's position that it "will never give up its arms, its territory or its claims on Jerusalem on behalf of the Palestinians." Hamas' statements of defiance and intransigence have been made repeatedly and are abundantly clear, if only the M.S.M. would pay attention and process the implications for any "peaceful" end to the conflict.

Thus, Palestinian Arabs expect Israel to recognize their rights to a state, but deny that same right to Israel as the nation-state of the Jewish people. They don't merely desire a Palestinian Arab state in Judea/Samaria and Gaza, for they could have had this more than 60 years ago; their expressed goal is the total eradication of Israel and its replacement with an Arab-Muslim state. It is based on their rigid, deeply ingrained, life-controlling religious teachings finding a non-Muslim state to be abhorrent, especially a Jewish one, run by people whom Allah tells the Muslims in the Qur'an are to be hated. These despised people are, at best, to be minimally tolerated, condemned to live as *dhimmis* (second class citizens) under their hegemony; their survivability serves to repudiate what Allah forecasts. The success and prowess of this tiny state is perhaps envied, but it certainly cannot be tolerated (in their hostile midst) over a Muslim one, particularly when it is located on land that was once perceived as Muslim (conquered in offensive wars from other peoples); such land must always belong to Muslims, for the Middle East is felt to be "for Muslims only."

The hardened Arab/Muslim mind-set has produced terrorists who have demonstrated willingness to fight to the death to achieve the goal of destroying Israel. The unfortunate, cold reality is that this prevents any other scenario from prevailing, no matter how much the M.S.M. in the tolerant Judeo-Christian Western/democratic liberal tradition would wish it so.

Large segments of the international community and M.S.M. have ignored the evidence about Palestinian deception and still insist the conflict is merely about territorial claims, despite the fact that it is totally about the existence of a Jewish state in the perceived *Dar al-Islam* (realm of Islam). Rather than working toward peace, the P.A. is trying to internationalize the conflict. If interlocutors (E.U. and U.N.) were serious about ending the conflict, they would insist first that the P.A. end blatant incitement of violence, meanwhile confronting and containing the pattern of deception by Palestinian Arab leaders.

Sources:

P.A. Charter

Hamas Charter

Jewishvirtuallibrary.org

YNetnews.com

Peel Commission Report

The Jerusalem Post

"The Simplest Thing in the World to Understand: Why There Isn't Israel-Palestinian Peace" (Barry Rubin, RubinReports, October 18, 2011)

*Palestine Media Watch*

"Saudi Textbook: The Enmity between the Muslims and the Jews Is Everlasting" (*MEMRI*, December 8, 2011)

*The Fight for Jerusalem: Radical Islam, The West, And The Future of The Holy City* (Dore Gold, 2007)

"Finding Fault in the Palestinian Messages That Aren't So Public." (Isabel Kershner, *N.Y. Times*, December 20, 2011)

"The Palestinian Deception" (by Yochanan Visser and Sharon Shaked in *Ynetnews.com*, December 28, 2011)


# XIII. Opposition: Terrorists vs. "Militants"


The M.S.M. prefers to jettison the word "terrorist" in favor of the misleadingly soft, allegedly-neutral term "militant," as was exhaustively documented in Section 1. Instead, these moral relativists cite chestnuts such as "One man's freedom fighter is another man's terrorist."

The Merriam-Webster Dictionary: defines "militant" as:

1.     engaged in warfare or combat: fighting.

2.     aggressively active (as in a cause): combative.

A "terrorist" has been defined in federal law (U.S. Code, Title 22 §2656f(d), pertaining to the State Department):

> The term "terrorism" means premeditated, politically-motivated violence perpetrated against noncombatant targets by subnational groups or clandestine agents, usually intended to influence an audience.

And "international terrorism" has been defined in federal law (U.S. Code, Title 18 §2331(1), regarding criminal acts and criminal procedure):

> [T]he term "international terrorism" means activities that…involve violent acts or acts dangerous to human life that are a violation of the criminal laws of the United States or of any State, or that would be a criminal violation if committed within the jurisdiction of the United States or of any State; [and] appear to be intended…to intimidate or coerce a civilian population; …to influence the policy of a government by intimidation or coercion; or …to affect the conduct of a government by mass destruction, assassination, or kidnapping; and [which] occur primarily outside the territorial jurisdiction of the United States, or transcend national boundaries in terms of the means by which they are accom-

plished, the persons they appear intended to intimidate or coerce, or the locale in which their perpetrators operate or seek asylum.

The U.S. government has employed these definitions for statistical and analytical purposes since 1983. As a result, the U.S. Department of State has designated "foreign terrorist organizations" to include Hamas, Hizbullah, Al-Aqsa Martyrs Brigade, Palestinian Islamic Jihad, Islamic Jihad Union, Palestinian Liberation Front, and Popular Front for Liberation of Palestine; "state sponsors of terror" include Syria, Iran and Sudan.

Most Muslims are not terrorists, but most contemporary terrorists are Muslims. They are increasingly exporting Islamic terrorism—including to Muslim societies—around the globe: U.S., Russia, U.K., France, Spain, Holland, Australia, India, Sri Lanka, Thailand, Argentina, Columbia, and of course, Israel.

Here is a simple litmus test: those who perpetrate, commit, prep, train, assign, transport, target and dispatch mass-murder bombers of civilians on buses, roadways, restaurants, shopping malls, religious assemblies, schools and the like are not "militants" anytime anywhere, they are "terrorists" every time, everywhere.

Sources:

Patterns of Global Terrorism 2003 (U.S. Dept. of State, April 2004)

U.S. Department of State

# XIV. Politics: "Land For Peace"
## David Vs. Goliath

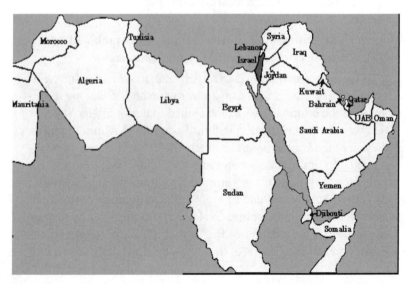

The M.S.M. reflexively buys into the notion that Israel should give up land so that the Arab/Muslim world will give it peace. Yet, how much smaller can she shrink, how much more of her land does she have to relinquish without sacrificing herself to her enemies – enemies who have openly/repeatedly/unambiguously declared their intentions to eradicate the Jewish state, have refused to recognize her right to exist, and have initiated five wars against her since her re-establishment in 1948? Unlike the Qur'an—which commands Muslims to engage in *jihad* to force the entire world to submit to Islam—the Torah promises the children of Israel a modest and reasonable allotment of land.

The map above shows that, geographically, Israel is one of the tiniest nations on the planet. She has a 112-mile coastline and is only 260 miles at its longest; she is 60 miles at its widest and 3-9 miles at its narrowest. Israel's land mass (8019 square-miles) is about 1/625 (1/6 of 1%) of the size of the Arab world; counting Iran the ratio is 650-1. She is 1/19 the size of California.

The M.S.M. generally shows a map (below) of Israel that magnifies her relative size to the disputed territories (Judea/Samaria and Gaza), misleadingly portraying her as much larger than she is (within the context of her Middle East neighborhood). Such magnification of her physical status – coupled with disproportionate M.S.M attention to her operational status (following incessant issuance of complaints from Arabs/Muslims) – compounds the challenge faced by Zionists when attempting to rebut the ongoing barrage of "unfairness" complaints.

*ISRAEL SAMARIA JUDEA*

*Courtesy of IRIS (Information Regarding Israel's Security)*

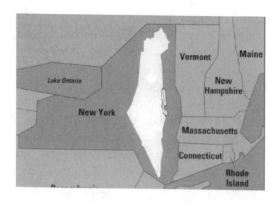

*Courtesy of AICE (American-Israel Cooperative Enterprise)*

Israel would fit 768 times into the entire U.S. and seven times into Florida. The U.S. is a large country surrounded by two vast oceans and bordered by two friendly countries, Canada and Mexico, in counterdistinction to Israel's geographic situation.

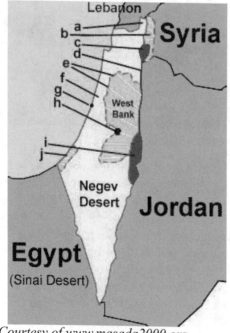

a. 3 miles wide here
b. Golan Heights
c. Sea of Galilee
d. Jordan River... Sea of Galilee to Dead Sea
e. 1967 territory beyond the "Green Line"
f. 9 miles wide here
g. Tel Aviv
h. Jerusalem
i. Dead Sea
j. Gaza Strip: 5 miles x 25 miles

*Courtesy of www.masada2000.org*

Israel is an oasis of Western Democracy and Judeo/Christian morality in the middle of a totalitarian Arab/Muslim Middle East. She is surrounded by 22 hostile Arab/Islamic dictatorships (not including Iran which is not an Arab country), including some very nasty and murderous Arab Islamic terrorist organizations. There are 56 Islamic countries and 1.4 billion Muslims worldwide; there are 49 nations where Catholicism is the official or dominant religion, 20 Protestant nations, 12 Eastern Orthodox nations, and 4 Hindu nations. But there is only one state with a Jewish majority—Israel. The total population of the 22 Muslim countries in the Middle East (including Iran) is 350 million; 5.7 million Jews live in Israel, yielding a regional population-ratio of 56:1. (Israel has 1.2 million Arabs living as full-citizens.) The Arabs/Muslims and M.S.M. blame the problems and political dissatisfaction of these Arabs (with their huge oil wealth and with their close ties to the Muslim world) on Israel's 5.7 million Jews and, to a lesser degree, on the world's 13.5 million Jews (almost 5 million fewer than in 1939). Despite opposite portrayals, it is tiny Israel who is the "David" fending against the Arab/Muslim world's "Goliath."

*Courtesy of www.masada2000.org*

The photo above shows a west → east view of northern Israel's Hula Valley from atop the Menara Cliffs. Behind the photographer (not seen) is Lebanon. Along the top of the photo (light area) is Syria with the Golan Heights rising from the Hula Valley. From Kiryat Shimona (a) to the base of the Golan Heights (b) is only 3 miles. Prior to 1967, these geopolitical realities had prompted construction of bomb shelters everywhere to protect civilians from Arabs attacking from the high-ground; these provisions remain mandated, noting the proximity of Hizbullah's missiles in Lebanon, which have been supplied by Iran and installed south of the Litani River (under the auspices of U.N.-sponsored "monitors").

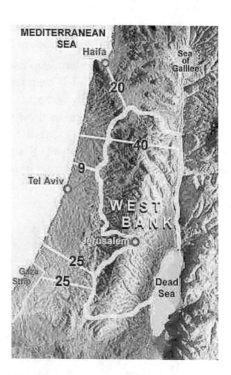

*Courtesy of www.masada2000.org*

The 1949 armistice lines separated Israel from her heartland of Judea/Samaria when Jordanian forces illegally annexed it. After the 1967 Arab-Israeli war, Israel regained that land, at which time the Arabs/Muslims (and then most of the world) began referring to Judea/Samaria as the "West Bank" to try to erase any Jewish connection to this historically Jewish land. Those who advocate that Israel relinquish Judea/Samaria so that the Arabs can form yet another Arab "Palestinian" state (the first being Jordan) should notice the topography that the Arabs/Muslims and the M.S.M. often overlook. The 2200-foot high Judean Mountains extend north-to-south for 60 miles along the entire length of Judea/Samaria. A Palestinian Arab terrorist, with a sniper or a rocket launcher, would have a bird's eye view of Israel's most densely-populated areas, including Israel's Ben Gurion International Airport which lies just a few short miles below from the border of a would-be "West Bank" Palestinian nation. And were the Gaza Strip and Judea/Samaria joined to form a contiguous "Palestinian" land mass, Israel would be literally cut in half.

Were such a dramatic retreat to be imposed on Israel, her capital city of Jerusalem would become nearly enveloped by Palestinian Arab territory and 65% of Israel's population (located within a 9-mile wide section around Tel Aviv) would be laid-bare. Israel would be reduced to a defenseless nation,    9-

25 miles wide at areas separating "Israel proper" from enemies on her eastern flank (let alone acute vulnerabilities to the west).

According to Mark Langfan, who has developed an invaluably illustrative "America-Israel Security" 3-D map (see below): "(T)he inescapable policy conclusions aren't politically correct....the American Jewish establishment is now asleep and in total denial as they were in World War II during the Holocaust. This map shows how a "demilitarized' Palestinian West/Bank/Gaza State will ultimately turn Israel from a U.S. strategic asset and bulwark against Middle East terrorism, into an albatross of sorts around the neck of the U.S.; a defenseless liability that invites attack and can no longer project American military superiority."

*Courtesy of www.MarkLangfan.com*

An Israeli capitulation and return of the vital high-ground terrirtory of Judea/Samaria to Palestinian Arab control would indubitably create indefensible "Auschwitz borders" for the "promise" of peace; this would be tantamount to Israel's suicide. Strategic land depth does matter, as recent history dramatizes. When Israel ceded territory, she has received increased unprovoked rocket, mortal, missle and terrorist attacks; southern Lebanon and Gaza have become terrorist launching pads, encroaching increasingly into Israel's heart.

It is almost unimaginable to envision Israel surviving thereafter, for a terrorist-based state situated high in the Judean Hills would endanger virtually the entire country (as was experienced repeatedly prior to 1967), rendering Israel's security to a level beyond "precarious." How can the M.S.M. proclaim that Israel is not the "David" in its epic struggle to survive against the vast Arab/Muslim world? How can the M.S.M. believe that by forcing Israel to concede any of its land to create yet another (22nd) Arab state, that peace will reign in the Middle East and end the Arab war against Israel?

Sources:

www.masada2000.org/geography

Israel Ministry of Foreign Affairs

www.Standwithus.com

American-Israel Cooperative Extension

www.Iris.org.il

www.MarkLangfan.com

*A Durable Peace: Israel and Its Place Among the Nations,* by Benjamin Netanyahu (2000)

# XV. <u>Politics: UNESCO - Against the Jews and Israel</u>

The Paris-based U.N. Educational, Scientific and Cultural Organization (UNESCO) is one of the U.N.'s most influential and prominent agencies; its mandate is to promote worldwide culture, education and science. Yet, over the past four decades, it has repeatedly adopted blatant anti-Israel policies. Examples include:

> **1974:** Voted "to withhold assistance from Israel in the fields of education, science and culture because of Israel's persistent alteration of the historic features of Jerusalem," and voted to exclude Israel from its European regional group. (This ostracism ended in 1978 when the U.S. withheld $40 million in payment to the organization in protest.)

**1989:** Claimed "Israel's occupation of Jerusalem "was destroying it by "acts of interference, destruction and transformation."

**1990:** Described "irreversible" changes to Jerusalem's architectural heritage due to Israeli "occupation."

**1993:** Boycotted an international conference on science in Jerusalem (by then-Director General Frederico Mayor).

**1995:** Rebuffed an Israeli request to mention the Shoah during the 50th anniversary of the U.N.

**1996:** Organized a symposium on Jerusalem at its headquarters in Paris, but failed to invite any Jewish or Israeli groups.

**1998:** Refused to meet with Israeli officials (by delegation visiting Jerusalem).

**2001:** Endorsed the "Cairo Declaration Document for Jerusalem Antiquities Preservation" which falsely accused Israel of demolishing Islamic antiquities on the Temple Mount and in the Old City, in a desperate attempt to deflect attention from Palestinian crimes defiling Jewish history and archeology at that site.

During the Second Intifada (2000-2005), UNESCO condemned Israel for "destruction and damage caused to the cultural heritage in the Palestinian territories" as a "crime against the common cultural heritage of humanity." However, UNESCO remained suspiciously silent when a Palestinian mob destroyed Joseph's Tomb, a major Jewish shrine in the P.A.-controlled town of Nablus—the Biblical Shechem—and built a mosque on the site. The Oslo Accords had placed the site under Israeli jurisdiction but, in 2000, then-Israeli P.M. Ehud Barak had ordered a unilateral retreat based on a Palestinian agreement to protect the site. Within hours, smoke was seen billowing from the tomb as an Arab crowd burned Jewish prayer books, ritual items and other significant objects. With pickaxes and hammers they desecrated the stone building, turning it to rubble. Two days later, the dome of the tomb had been painted green and bulldozers were clearing the area. This is further proof that Muslims cannot be trusted with safeguarding Jewish sites, recalling Jordanian destruction of over 50 synagogues in the Old City of Jerusalem and denial of Jewish access to the city and Temple Mount/Western Wall during its illegal occupation (1948-1967).

In 2009, UNESCO designated Jerusalem as "capital of Arab culture," working in concert with the P.A. and key Arab leaders to object to what they portray as "the Israeli occupation of Holy Jerusalem." This directly repudiated and denied 4000 years of Jewish history in Israel, including the 1000 years before Jesus after King David had designated Jerusalem the capital. It is a city which the Jews never entirely left voluntarily nor abandoned, even during times of occupations, deadly persecutions, pogroms, Muslim invasions and the Crusades. Coincidentally, since the beginning of the 20th century, the City of David in Jerusalem has been one of the hottest open archaeological municipal areas in the world, providing proof of an ancient Jewish presence with findings of Biblical artifacts, buildings, burial spots, water sources, jewelry, and royal seals. One would think UNESCO would value such non-political efforts.

Instead, in 2010, UNESCO ruled with the ultimate *chutzpah* and arrogance that "Muslim Mosques" now included Rachel's Tomb and the Cave of the Patriarchs (Machpelah) in Hebron, the burial location of the first family of the Jewish people (Abraham, Sarah, Isaac, Rebekah, Jacob and Leah) in addition to ancient judges, generals, and relatives of David.

In July 2011, it maliciously called upon Israel to cease all archaeological excavation and construction work in the Old City of Jerusalem immediately and, in particular, attacked renovation of the Mughrabi Bridge linking the Western Wall plaza and the Temple Mount. This decision was advocated by Arab states and endorsed by the consensus of Western members of the commission. In their mendacious view, these areas lie outside Israel and belong to (the fictitious) Palestine, and such activity allegedly threatens the heritage of Islam.

On October 31, 2011, the P.A. took its statehood road-show to UNESCO and, not surprisingly, found a receptive audience. UNESCO became the first U.N. agency to accept "Palestine" as a full member, its 195th. This action was taken despite the fact that the U.N. Security Council (which is the only U.N. body that can accept a state as a full member) has not voted in favor of the recent bid of the P.A. to admit "Palestine." By so acting, this U.N. organization recklessly defied a cutoff of U.S. funds under federal law with its vote, thus jeopardizing many of its worldwide programs; this step will cost UNESCO one-quarter of its yearly budget, the 22% contributed by the U.S. (about $70 million) plus another 3% contributed by Israel. The U.S. and Israel oppose the Palestinians' unilateral bid for recognition of statehood at the U.N. as premature without direct negotiations leading to a mutually agreed-upon settlement between the parties that address the issues of full mutual recognition, borders and security. By taking this route, P.A. President Abbas abrogated the Oslo Accords. Furthermore, he ensured Israel will not trust the P.A. as a negotiating partner for the foreseeable future, and he has expressly embarrassed and iso-lated the U.S. (which indicated it will use its veto power in the Security Council).

In short, this U.N. body has been engaged in an Inquisition-like campaign against Israel, the Jewish people, and their heritage.

Sources:

"UNESCO against the Jews" (by Giulio Meotti in *Ynet news.com*, July 19, 2011)

"Arab vandals desecrate Joseph's Tomb" in *World Net Daily*, February 25, 2003)

*UNESCO.org*

*Wall Street Journal*, (October 31, 2011)

# XVI.   Politics:   "Israel Lobby" v. "Arab Lobby"

Derisive reference is often made to the "Israel Lobby" or "Jewish Lobby" in an effort to illuminate Jewish political influence in the United States for Israel. These terms are vague and inadequate. Freedom-of-speech rights to organize and to attempt to affect legislation through the political process is a cherished American right available to all. One of these organizations, the American-Israel Public Affairs Committee {"AIPAC"} is a registered lobby that represents the policies and preferences of the democratically elected government of Israel to the U.S. government. The lobby, originally called the American Zionist Committee for Public Affairs, was founded in 1951 by I.L. (Sy) Kenen to appeal directly to Congress for legislation to provide aid to Israel to circumvent State Department opposition. Other groups, with various different viewpoints engage in direct lobbying (*e.g.*, B'nai B'rith, ZOA, AJC, JCPA, Hadassah, various Christian groups) on issues related to Israel and the Jewish community.

Support of Israel by the U.S. Congress has not been "bought and paid for" by the "Israel Lobby," as the M.S.M. and critics, such as Mearsheimer and Walt commonly suggest. Israel has near universal support in Congress, as a matter of conscience, a fundamental commitment to Israel's right to exist, a recognition that she is an asset of and her security is in the national interest of the U.S., and owing to her shared, democratic and Judeo-Christian   values.

However, the M.S.M. rarely, if ever, notes the pernicious effects of the in-sidious "Arab Lobby" on U.S. policymakers; it is at least as old, perhaps older, than the Israeli lobby. It is composed of what Kenen called the petro-diplomatic complex consisting of the oil industry, missionaries, and diplomats. According to Kenen, there was no need for a formal Arab lobby because the petro-diplomatic complex did the Arabs' work for them.

Mitchell Bard, in his exhaustively researched book, The Arab Lobby, documents how Arab states have poured billions of dollars—dwarfing the power of the so-called "Israel Lobby"—into influencing U.S. policy to pay disproportionate attention to their interests, assisting Arab countries (all of them dictatorial regimes with abysmal human rights records) that do not share our values, and often work to undercut our interests. The "Arab Lobby," historically, consisted of the oil industry, Christian missionaries, and current or former U.S. diplomats, and Arabists in the State Department, many of who were openly anti-Semitic. Since they failed to prevent America from recognizing Israel in 1948, they have waged a bureaucratic guerrilla war to undermine the alliance that formed between the U.S. and the only democracy in the Middle East. The most powerful member of the Arab lobby is Saudi Arabia, who from its earliest days when American companies discovered oil in the Arabian Peninsula have used a variety of tactics including threats and bribes to coerce U.S. policymakers to ignore their human rights abuses, support of terrorism, and      generally mask their opposition to American interests. Today, the Arab Lobby's goal is feeding America's oil addiction, obtaining more sophisticated weaponry, and weakening our alliance with a democratic Israel.

Several major differences distinguish the "Arab" and "Israeli" lobbies. The pro-Israel lobby openly emerged following Israel's re-establishment, whereas the pro-Arab lobby was initially fronted by interest-groups. The pro-Israel lobby is comprised mostly of volunteers, whereas the pro-Arab lobby depends upon paid foreign and domestic agents. The pro-Israel lobby adopts a positive approach towards the need to appreciate conjoint American/Israeli interests, whereas the pro-Arab lobby routinely adopts an obstructionist posture (i.e., against pro-Israel legislation rather than for pro-Arab legislation). The pro-Israel lobby overtly targets Congress, whereas the pro-Arab lobby covertly focuses on influencing the Executive Branch and its bureaucracy.

Sources:

The Arab Lobby: The Invisible Alliance That Undermines America's Interest in the Middle East (Mitchell Bard, 2010)

The Israel Lobby (John Mearsheimer and Stephen Walt, 2007)

# XVII. Israel Did Not "Deliberately" Kill Gaza Civilians During the 2008 War

The "war-crimes" charge that Israel deliberately killed civilians during the Gaza war in 2008 (Operation Cast Lead) is another of the Big Lies perpetuated by Palestinian Arabs and enabled by the M.S.M. Like the proverbial "pot calling the kettle black," it is the Palestinian Arabs who deliberately choose to adopt a policy that subjects Israeli citizens to terrorist attacks, and that concomitantly anoint as national heroes and martyrs (*shaheeds*) those who commit these murders of Jews, including those launching rockets and missles, and dispatching suicide-homicide bombers. Thus, as justified as was this campaign, Israel had to contend with claims that it was acting disproportionately to its provocation and, in particular, that there not be reciprocal targeting of civilians.

Gaza, through its elected government Hamas, had become a terrorist enclave and base from which it had fired over 7000 rockets and missiles against Israeli civilian targets— including towns and schools—before Israel finally responded in a large-scale military action. Notably, 20% of Israel's population was in range of these attacks (a figure that has grown following subsequent importation of more sophisticated weaponry from Iran).

But Israel did not in response deliberately and indiscriminately aim at civilians in Gaza; her targets were the terrorists and their leaders. During Israel's airstrikes on Gaza rocket sites, on average, one civilian died for every 30 terrorists. To place this figure into context, a 2001 study by the International Committee of the Red Cross found that the civilian-to-military death ratio of wars fought since the middle of the 20th Century was 10:1. In other words, in this war, Israel protected civilians at a rate 300 times greater than had any other national army and even did so when confronted by amoral enemies who routinely violated basic principles of warfare. (As an aside, intra-Muslim violence has killed more Muslims by far than during the Arab-Israeli conflict. In 2007, Gunnar Heinsohn from the University of Bremen and Daniel Pipes, director of the Middle East Forum, found that some 11 million Muslims have been violently killed since 1948, of which 35,000 (0.3%) died during the Arab wars against Israel, or one out of every 315 fatalities.)

Violating international law, Hamas committed multiple war-crimes, while showing abject disregard for public safety and deliberately causing casualties to undermine lawful military reaction taken by Israel, whose civilians had intentionally been attacked. In the process, Hamas glorified the sacrifice of their own people by: (1) using human (women, children) and structural (mosques, hospitals, schools, residences) shields, meanwhile firing rockets from homes and institutions doubling as arsenals; (2) wearing civilian clothing rather than military uniforms; and (3) traveling via emergency vehicles including ambulances for non-emergency purposes.

Yet, the M.S.M. chooses not to disseminate documentary and video proof of such actions (including hiding in U.N. schools). Also ignored was the unprecedented effort by the IDF to warn Palestinian civilians in Gaza—via leaflets and telephone calls—that the areas in which they were located were subject to being militarily targeted, to halt the rocket attacks, to bomb arms caches, and to root-out terrorists.

According to Harvard Law Professor Alan M. Dershowitz:

> So here is the legal dilemma faced by democracies such as Israel. They have every right under international law to take whatever military actions are necessary to stop the rockets randomly fired at their civilians. Their enemy uses human shields to prevent Israel from destroying the rockets without also killing Palestinian civilians. All the law requires under these circumstances is that Israel take reasonable precaution to minimize enemy civilian deaths in order to prevent the murder of its own civilians. Has Israel taken such precautions? Let retired British colonel Richard Kemp answer that question as he did in a recent BBC interview. He said that there has been "no time in the history of warfare when an army made more efforts to reduce civilian casualties and the deaths of innocent people than the Israel Defense Forces did in Gaza." To accuse Israel of "war crimes" under these circumstances is to distort international law and expose the bias of the accuser.

A soldier of Palestine          A soldier of Israel

From the cover of *The Case for Moral Clarity*, by Alan M. Dershowitz, CAMERA (Committee for Accuracy in Middle East Reporting in America), 2009.

Cynical, perhaps, but on-point is this rendition of the Hamas "dead baby" strategy: it is a "good day" when one of its rockets kills Israeli civilians, provoking Israel into attacking rocket-launchers near Palestinian civilians, causing accidental casualties in the crossfire. The more dead—on both sides—the more Hamas can exhort the M.S.M. into condemning Israel as the aggressor (conflating arsonist and firefighter) and exploit the conflict (exciting its native population). It is a win-win for Hamas, as it kills Israelis and whips-up loyalty from its electorate (and makes *shaheeds* out of some of them).

The cartoon above epitomizes the dichotomy between how Israel fights to protects its citizens versus how Palestinian Arabs/Hamas fights by hiding behind their most vulnerable civilians. The Arabs—and sanctimonious M.S.M.— expects Israel to exhibit higher moral standards and not to retaliate under these circumstances.

Even President Barack Obama, when he was a presidential candidate in 2008 visiting Sderot (an Israeli town near Gaza which has been the recipient of thousands of Hamas rocket, mortar and missiles) stated:

> I don't think any country would find it acceptable to have missiles raining down on the heads of their citizens. The first job of any nation state is to protect its citizens. And so I can assure you that if—I don't even care if I was a politician. If somebody was sending rockets into my house where my two daughters sleep at night, I'm going to do everything in my power to stop that. And I would expect Israelis to do the same thing.

On December 27, 2008, upon the commencement of Operation Cast Lead, Israeli P. M. Ehud Olmert said in an address to the nation:

> For approximately seven years, hundreds of thousands of Israeli citizens in the south have been suffering from rockets being fired at them. Life in the south under rocket barrages had become unbearable. Israel did everything in its power to fulfill the conditions of the calm in the south and enable normal life for its citizens in the communities adjacent to the Gaza Strip. The quiet that we offered was met with shelling. No country can countenance such a reality! The lives of our citizens are not forfeit. In recent days, it became clear that Hamas is bent on conflict. Whoever heard Hamas's statements understood that they decided to increase attacks on the residents of Israel by firing rockets and mortars indiscriminately. In such a situation we had no alternative but to respond. We do not rejoice in battle but neither will we be deterred from it….On Thursday, 25.12.08, I made it clear to the residents of

Gaza that we are not acting against them and that we have no intention of punishing them for the actions of Hamas. We will see to the needs of the population in Gaza and will do our utmost to prevent a humanitarian crisis that will impinge upon residents' lives....

Residents of Gaza, we are not your enemies and we are not fighting against you. This terrorist organization has brought disaster to two peoples. Israel is not fighting the Palestinian people but the Hamas terrorist organization that has taken it upon itself to act against the residents of Israel. Therefore, the targets that were attacked today were selected accordingly, with stress being placed on avoiding harm to innocents.

Our precise intelligence, from the I.D.F. Intelligence Branch and the Israel Security Agency, enabled maximum strikes at those involved in terrorism and minimized harm to innocents. This is how we will act in the future, as may be necessary. Israel is currently focusing on striking at the terrorist organizations that are operating to undermine stability in the entire region. I hope that no other element in the region will think that while Israel is fighting in the south, that it will it is inattentive to what is happening in other areas. We will not hesitate to respond to any aggression against us.

During the day, we spoke with the leaders of the main countries of the world and made it very clear that the situation cannot continue and that we were compelled to take action in order to halt the aggression against our citizens. We also made it clear that Israel will, at the same time, make every effort to prevent a humanitarian crisis in the Gaza Strip.

Sources:

*The Case for Moral Clarity: Israel, Hamas and Gaza* (Alan M. Dershowitz, CAMERA 2009)

Jewishvirtuallibrary.com

*The Jewish Policy Center* (PM Olmert's Remarks on the Operation in the Gaza Strip: December 27, 2008)

*Obama Defers to Bush, for Now, on Gaza Crisis*, (Steven Lee Myers and Helene Cooper in The *N.Y. Times*, December 28, 2008)

U.N. 2005 World Summit Outcome document

# XVIII.  Crossroads:  The Forgotten Refugees
## Jews From Arab/Muslim Lands

Dominant attention in Arab-Israeli peace process media coverage is directed towards the "plight" of "Palestinian Arab" refugees during the 1948 War of Independence – estimated at 472,000-650,000 – and their subsequent settlement in camps under U.N. auspices (*i.e.*, Palestinian Arabs insistence on "Right of Return"). Yet, little is mentioned of Jews who were forced to flee their homes from Arab/Muslim states through anti-Semitic ethnic cleansing campaigns. Most came from families that had lived in these lands for many hundreds of years, many predating the Muslim conquests. In 1945, there were more than 870,000 Jews living in various Arab countries, many communities dating thousands of years, and most pre-dating the advent of Islam. During the 1947 U.N. debates regarding the establishment of a Jewish state in Palestine, Arab leaders threatened Jews in their states with expulsion and violence if partition were to occur. For instance, Egypt's delegate told the General Assembly: "The lives of one million Jews in Muslim countries would be jeopardized by partition." Throughout 1947-1948, Jews were subject to increasing persecution (rioting, plus confiscation of their homes, businesses and property); in Iraq, Zionism was made a capital crime.

Approximately 600,000 Jews sought refuge in the fledgling State of Israel, traveling from around the world and arriving destitute armed only with a foreign language. But they did not maintain that status for long, for they were promptly absorbed into the fabric of the country and resettled in Israel at tremendous expense; they became an integral part of the state and full Israeli citizens. There was no offer of compensation from the Arab governments which had forced them to leave and had confiscated their possessions.

To the contrary, the vast majority of Arabs who fled their homes in Palestine never saw an Israeli soldier. In fact, thousands left in anticipation of a war, responding to Arab leaders' calls and orders to get out of the way of the advancing "victorious" Arab armies that would crush the Jews; most fled to avoid being caught in the cross fires, while a small number were expelled as a consequence of the war. Many who traveled a few miles over truce lines became, with their descendants, "refugees." They since have been kept in squalid camps—59 administered by UNRWA in Jordan, Lebanon, Syria, Gaza and Judea/Samaria—used as political pawns by their fellow Arabs for the subsequent sixty-plus years to prolong the conflict with Israel. They have not been absorbed by their Arab brethren to which they are akin, culturally, linguistically and ethnically.

In essence, an exchange of populations took place that has been neither fully nor fairly acknowledged by the Arabs and the M.S.M.

Below is a chart illustrating the Jewish refugees from Arab countries:

| Country | 1948 | 1958 | 1968 | 1976 | 2004 |
|---------|------|------|------|------|------|
| Aden | 8,000 | 800 | 0 | 0 | 0 |
| Algeria | 140,000 | 130,000 | 1,500 | 1,000 | < 100 |
| Egypt | 75.000 | 40,000 | 1,000 | 400 | < 100 |
| Iraq | 135,000 | 6,000 | 2,500 | 350 | c. 35 |
| Lebanon | 5,000 | 6,000 | 3,000 | 400 | < 100 |
| Libya | 38.000 | 3,750 | 100 | 40 | 0 |
| Morocco | 265,000 | 200,000 | 50,000 | 18,000 | 5,500 |
| Syria | 30,000 | 5,000 | 4,000 | 4,500 | < 100 |
| Tunisia | 105,000 | 80,000 | 10,000 | 7,000 | 1,500 |
| Yemen | 55,000 | 3,500 | 500 | 500 | 200 |
| **Total** | **856,000** | **475,050** | **72,600** | **32,190** | **c. 7,635** |

*From, "Jewish Refugees from Arab Countries," by Jacqueline Shields,*
*JewishVirtuallibrary.org*

Israel doesn't agree to limiting the refugee issue to "Palestinian" refugees. A December 9, 2011, *London Daily Mail* op-ed by Melanie Phillips ("The Algorithm of Malice") described a new video by Israeli Deputy Foreign Minister Danny Ayalon (http://www.youtube.com/watch?v=g_3A6_qSBBQ &feature=channel_video_title) as showing that "the widely-held belief that the Arabs were the only refugees from the Arab war against the newly reconstituted country of Israel (a war which started in 1948 and continues to this day)–is totally untrue." She found "Israel has begun to realize" the importance of awakening public awareness in the West that more Jews were displaced from vast Muslim lands than Arabs left tiny Israel. She explained:

> There were many more Jewish refugees from Arab countries. As a result of the 1948 war, some 500,000 Arabs left Palestine – most of them as a result of having been told to do so by Arab regimes certain of destroying the new Jewish state. But some 850,000 Jews were then attacked, stripped of their citizenship and ethnically cleansed from their homes in Arab states–causing the destruction of ancient Jewish communities in those countries which had well predated the arrival of Islam in the Middle East. And what happened to those refugees? They

were absorbed without fuss into Israel...., where they form around half of the population, and into other countries.

Others made this same point years ago.

Joan Peters in *From Time Immemorial,* p. 25:

> Arab propaganda has also managed thus far to direct all attention to one aspect of the Middle East refugee problem as if it were the only aspect of that problem, and thus to mask the overall reality. One crucial truth, among many that have been obscured and deprecated, is that there have been as many Jewish refugees who fled or were expelled from the Arab countries as there are Arab refugees from Israel, and that the Jews left of necessity and in flight from danger.

Samuel Katz, in his classic work *Battleground: Fact & Fantasy in Palestine* (p. 33):

> At the time of the rebirth of Jewish statehood in Palestine, approximately one million Jews were living in this area....Western statesmen have turned a blind eye to the fact that the Arab states, when they failed to destroy the Jewish state at birth, expelled or forced out large numbers of the Jewish citizens of their own countries. Of 900,000 Jews who were so driven out – and whose property was confiscated – Israel took in and absorbed nearly three quarters of a million. All these Jews were private citizens, most of them members of families that had lived in those countries for many generations, some of them for hundreds of years before their Arab oppressors. A central ethnic feature of the whole of what is now called the Middle East and of the North African coast for more than 2,000 years has been the continuity there of Jewish life.

These Middle Eastern Jewish refugees from Muslim lands have a three-fold significance:

(1) They form a critical second dimension of the "refugee" issue;

(2) Their absorption by Israel, with no help from UNRWA, discredits Arab "host" countries (including the P.A.'s) mistreatment of Arab refugees and their descendants;

(3) They and their descendants form a major segment of Israel's population, refuting the untruth that Israelis are "colonialist Europeans." This is not "right-wing propaganda." In 2001, the liberal Israeli author Amos Oz, wrote in a January 5 Peace Now press release:

> [Palestinian] leaders now openly claim the "right of return" for the hundreds of thousands of Palestinians who fled and

were driven out of their homes in the 1948 war, while cynically ignoring the fate of hundreds of thousands of Israeli Jews who fled and were driven out of their homes in Arab countries, during the same war.

A *J.T.A.* article in the November 8, 2007, issue of Philadelphia's *Jewish Exponent* covered a "major conference" held that week in New York. The conferees, "Justice for Jews from Arab Countries, an advocacy coalition of 72 groups," were meeting "to unveil documentation showing how Arab states conspired to persecute their Jewish citizens." The article stated that "in the aftermath of Israel's creation, hundreds of thousands of Jews fled Arab lands where they had lived for centuries, a total roughly equivalent to the number of Palestinian refugees that fled or were driven from Israel." It then cited an even greater than "roughly equivalent" number: "Estimates of the number of Jewish refugees range generally from 700,000 to 1 million, a majority of whom were absorbed by Israel."

The *J.T.A.* article continued:

> Leaders of the coalition insist that their efforts to publicize the rights of Jewish refugees—as well as the culpability of Arab governments in exacerbating their plight—have nothing to do with winning reparations. Instead, they say, they are seeking justice and establishing an accurate historical record...."We have one simple objective, and that is, in the context of peace, the issues for **both sides** must be addressed....Our objective is to ensure that **any explicit reference to Palestinian refugees is matched by an explicit reference to Jewish refugees, as a matter of law and equity.**"

Sources:

Mitchell G. Bard, *Myths and Facts: A Guide to the Arab-Israeli Conflict (2006)*
*Jewishvirtuallibrary.org*

Roumani, Maurice. "The Jews from Arab Countries: A Neglected Issue" (WOJAC, 1983)

# XIX. Crossroads: Christians in Peril in the Holy Land: The Story in the Shadows

The M.S.M. has inadequately reported the mistreatment of Christians in the Middle East (and around the world) by Muslim-dominated governments. The goal, here, is to summarize this "story in the shadows," place it into proper context, and illustrate the damage caused by M.S.M. indifference to the worldwide-war against this component of the Judeo-Christian Ethic by Islamic Fascists. The implications thereof are unnerving.

## The Current Problem

The Coalition for Responsible Reporting in Middle East has documented numerous instances of abuse and terror against Christians by Muslims in P.A.-administered regions of Judea/Samaria. Key-points in its report, "Christian Life Under the Palestinian Authority" (www.c4rpme.org) are as follows:

<u>Muslim groups imposed a "reign of terror" on Christians in the PA</u>

- On September 3, 2005, hundreds of armed Palestinian Muslims torched 14 Christian homes in Taybeh, a village near Ramallah, to punish the community because one of its residents was having a relationship with a Muslim woman from a neighboring village. The Muslim woman was murdered by her own family in what they termed an "honor killing."

- The militants who took over the Church of the Nativity in April 2002 had "imposed a two-year reign of terror (on Bethlehem Christians) that included rape, extortion and executions, according to Bethlehem residents. 'Finally the Christians can breathe freely,' said Helen, 50, a Christian mother of four. 'We are so delighted that these criminals who have intimidated us for such a long time are now going away.'"

- "In February 2002, Palestinian Muslims rampaged against Christians in Ramallah, burning apartments and stores owned by Christians and attempted to burn down the Greek Orthodox and Roman Catholic Churches." The PA failed to intervene, according to the Boston Globe.

<u>Muslim militants harass and rape Christian girls and coerce them to adopt Islamic clothing and behavior</u>

- Inaz Jiries Hanna Muslah, a 23-year-old Palestinian Christian teacher, said that "public harassment of Christian girls began when the PA came to power after 1993. Before, (there were) no things like this. We could go everyplace we wanted…(but now) I don't walk alone on the street because of this bad thing." (Interview, August 2002)

- Sana Razi Nashash, a 24-year-old Christian woman from Beit Jallah, said sexual harassment became widespread after the PA came to power. She feels she is a "virtual prisoner" in her own home due to the pervasiveness of harassment of Christian women: "So right now I could not go to the street, even 7 o'clock I cannot go to the street alone, but before (the P.A. came to power), I used to go and work with no problem at night." (Interview August 2002)

<u>Christian holy sites and cemeteries are vandalized, and worshippers are prevented from attending services</u>

• Muslim extremists have attacked Christian facilities and clubs, the Wall Street Journal reported in July 1994. Christian graves, crosses, and statues have been desecrated. Christian cemeteries have been defaced, monasteries have had their phone lines cut, and there have been break-ins at convents.

• In 1997, the Waqf (Muslim religious property) authorities attempted to break through into the Church of the Holy Sepulcher in Jerusalem, which is adjacent to the al-Hanaqa Mosque in order to install toilets on the roof of the church. The illegal construction was halted only after Israeli and world pressure. (Ha'aretz 5-11-97)

<u>Persecution is forcing Christians to flee the PA and its increasing Islamic radicalism</u>

• The Arab states in the Middle East all established Islam as their official religion and have "very serious issues of religious restrictions, discrimination, persecution... lack of tolerance and pluralism...(and) impose significant legal obstacles to religious freedom, contrary to the provisions of the Universal Declaration of Human Rights." (Steven J. Coffey, US Principal Deputy Assistant of State in the Bureau of Democracy, Human Rights and Labor,. testimony before the Senate Committee on Foreign Relations May 1, 1997.)

• "Life in (PA-ruled) Bethlehem has become insufferable for many members of the dwindling Christian minorities. Increasing Muslim-Christian tensions have left some Christians reluctant to celebrate Christmas in the town at the heart of the story of Christ's birth," according to a December 1997 report in the London *Times*.

• "The Christian rate of emigration from the Territories has accelerated and the Christian population of the Territories has dropped from 15% in 1950 to barely 2% today. Many fear that soon few if any Christians will be left in Bethlehem, the birthplace of Jesus, or in Nazareth though they once were

Christian majority cities."

## Muslim conversion to Christianity is a crime in the PA

• Muhammed Bak'r, a Muslim convert to Christianity, was jailed and tortured in a PA prison for distributing Bibles to Muslims. "His hands were tied behind his back to a rope connected to the ceiling and he was left hanging there for several days."

• The P.A. arrests Palestinian converts to Christianity. In late June 1997, the P.A.'s Preventive Security Forces arrested a convert to Christianity for regularly attending church and distributing Bibles. He is still in prison and has been subjected to physical torture and interrogations.

• In December 2002, Saeed and Nasser Salamah escaped from prison and from a death sentence for converting to Christianity in the PA and sought asylum in Israel.

• "[I]ncidents like these are known to be widespread, but most go unreported or are denied by the victims for fear of retaliation by the PA." (J.C. Watts, former U.S. congressman.)

• "Last week, five Muslims beat up a Christian boy. We are afraid. They have knives (and) guns and can do whatever they want. They can kill you simply(for) speaking bad about them." (Mar, a Palestinian Christian from Ramallah.)

• Palestinian Christians often say there are good relations with the PA because of fear of speaking the truth: "There is fear. If I lived in London, I would tell you (my real name). (Here), somebody will shoot me." (Abu Sumayah.)

• Former Florida Senator Connie Mack described the fear he found in Palestinian Christians. "Needless to say, these Christians met with me at considerable risk. They conveyed to me a message of fear and desperation."

• A Christian cleric in Jerusalem "compared the behavior of Christian *dhimmis* to that of battered wives and children, who continue to defend and even identify with their tormentor even as the abuse persists." You do not hear about this persecution because Christian leaders ally with the PA and are separated from their people

• Latin Priest Rafiq Khoury's "call to venerate the rule of Islam because it creates national unity ignores the heavy price Christians would pay... living under such a regime... It indicates acquiescence to an inferior position...and the abandonment of the Christian dream of a liberal, secular society that would accept them as equals." (Professor Tsimhoni)

- "You have to distinguish between the leadership (which was supportive of Arafat) and the people." (Christian resident of Bethlehem)

- "Our leaders are liars: They tell the newspapers that everything is OK. But when Christians go to the market, they're afraid to wear crosses." (Christian man from Bethlehem)

- "A public opinion poll performed by a Christian academic revealed that only 48% of Palestinian Christians trust their religious leaders."

In Bethlehem, Christian businesses in Bethlehem have been rapidly disappearing due to Muslim gangs associated with P.A. police and security forces. These thugs have promoted an economic boycott and have had official license, from top P.A. officials, to extort money from Christians. Failure to comply prompts Mafia-like punishment against their owners and families: arson, rape and murder.

International human rights lawyer Justus Reid Weiner, who teaches at Hebrew University and has extensively researched the plight of Christian religious minorities from the Middle East, told the Jerusalem Institute for Global Jewish Affairs that Christian Arabs have been victims of frequent human rights abuses by Muslims under the P.A.-Fatah regime:

> There are many examples of intimidation, beatings, land theft, firebombing of churches and other Christian institutions, denial of employment, economic boycotts, torture, kidnapping, forced marriage, sexual harassment, and extortion.

He has found that P.A. officials are directly responsible for many of the attacks, and some Muslims who have converted to Christianity have been murdered. As people with "*dhimmi*" status, Christians living in Palestinian-controlled territories are not treated as the equals of Muslims. Weiner states:

> They are subjected to debilitating legal, political, cultural, and religious restrictions. This has become a critical problem for the Palestinian Christians in the West Bank and Gaza. Muslim groups like Hamas and Islamic Jihad have built a culture of hatred upon the age-old foundations of Islamic society. Moreover, the P.A. has adopted Islamic law into its draft constitution.

Internationally-recognized holy sites in Judea/Samaria are being vandalized and desecrated by the P.A. without consequence. Weiner has further documented that Bethlehem has witnessed many forms of intimidation against Christians over recent decades. Perhaps the best-remembered is the IDF stand-off with dozens of armed Palestinian terrorists who had taken refuge in the Church of the Nativity in 2002, looting and desecrating this important holy-site while holding numerous Christian clergymen hostage for a month. Per Weiner:

> Christians in Bethlehem have been cursed and spat upon by Muslims. They have been beaten for eating in restaurants in violation of Ramadan, the Muslim month of day-time fasting. Islamic sharia law has been imposed in the curriculum for Christian children in public schools. Christian women have shunned modern Western garb to avoid being attacked for immodesty. Christian men have grown beards so they will be mistaken for Muslims. There is widespread bias against Christians in the Palestinian Authority's civil service hiring and promotion, as well as in the private sector. Church lands have been expropriated and mosques erected on them. Christians have been forced to sell historic family lands to Muslims at ridiculously low prices. Palestinian Authority officials have been exposed for taking bribes to record forged land deeds naming Muslims as property owners. Particularly infuriating has been imposed marriages of Christian women to Muslim men. In addition, Christian women have been raped and murdered with nothing being done to arrest or punish the Muslim perpetrators. The list goes on. Most cases of anti-Christian violence have gone unreported. So is anyone surprised why thousands of Palestinian Christians emigrate to any nation where they can obtain a visa?

He has found that Taibe, a village deep in Judea/Samaria, is the only all-Christian village left in the P.A. After a romantic relationship between a Christian man and his Muslim secretary was uncovered, she was forced to drink poison, the men of the village went on a rampage, beating people, burning houses, raping women. As a result of the perpetual violence, about 1500 Christians fled, and only 1300 remain. These Christians' situation has become grim.

## Population Statistics Document Christian Emigration

Weiner observed that M.S.M. reports consistently blame Israel for Christian-emigration, both from Judea/Samaria and Hamas-dominated Gaza Strip, ignoring the fact that Israel is the only nation in the region where the Christian population is growing. Christians now comprise less than two percent of the population of the Palestinian areas, compared to ten times that ratio before the 1948 War of Independence.

Of the more than 7.6 million people living in Israel (per the 2010 Statistical Abstract of Israel), there are approximately: 5,700,000 Jews; 1,286,500 Muslims; 151,700 Christians; 125,300 Druze. Approximately 24 % of Israel's population is comprised of non-Jews. Although defined collectively as "Arab" citizens of Israel, they include a number of different, primarily Arabic-speaking, groups, each with distinct characteristics. Christians constitute about 2% of the population (Jews 75.5%, Muslims 16.5 %, Druze 1.7%, and 4.4% not classified by religion).

In Judea/Samaria (*i.e.* "the West Bank"), the population is 2,568,555, comprising by religion: 75% Muslim (predominantly Sunni); 17%, Jewish; 8% Christian and other, according to the "CIA World Factbook" (July 2010), In the Gaza Strip, the population is 1,657,155, comprising Muslim (predominantly Sunni) 99.3%; Christian 0.7%. Combining the popultions of Judea/Samaria and Gaza, Muslims comprise more than 97%, while Christians made up just 2.3%; the average household size was seven. Given the higher fertility rate among Muslims, it is projected that, by 2020, the Christian population will shrink from 1.8% (currently) to 1.6% of the total population of Israel.

The population has never been large, but a significant drop in the Christian population in Judea/Samaria occurred under Jordanian rule from 1948-1967. Since 1967, however, when Judea/Samaria came under Israeli and later P.A. administration, the population increased, though at a slower rate than it would have increased without emigration. The percentage of Christians in Judea/Samaria, though, has indeed decreased markedly. This is due largely to the enormous increase in the surrounding Muslim population, with its far higher birth-rate, and Christian emigration.

According to OpenDoors.org, the most recent statistics available (in November 2006) for the number of Palestinian Christians in Judea/Samaria and Gaza were that the total was 40,000, of which 37,500 live in Judea/Samaria and 2,500 live in Gaza.

| | | |
|---|---|---|
| Greek Orthodox | 51% | 20,400 |
| Roman Catholic | 30% | 12,000 |
| Greek Catholic | 6% | 2,400 |
| Protestant | 5% | 2,000 |
| Syrian Orthodox | 3% | 1,200 |
| Armenian Orthodox | 3% | 1,200 |
| Coptic + Russian Orthodox | 2% | 800 |

Bethlehem and Nazareth are now primarily Muslim. Jerusalem is only 2% Christian.

At the end of December 2006, Israel's Christian population numbered 148,000 (2.1% of the total population). Most (~120,000) are Arabs, while 28,000 came to Israel with their Jewish families under the Law of Return, mainly during the wave of immigration from Russia and Ethiopia in the 1990's.

The Jewish Center for Public Affairs, in a 2011 "Background Paper" entitled "The Palestinian Christian Population" by Ethan Felson, provided "actual numbers" for the Christian population of Judea/Samaria, Jerusalem and Gaza as follows:

> 1945: 59,160
> 1961  45,849
> 1967: 42,494
> 1995: 51,163
> 2006: 48,800
> 2007: 51,710

These statistics, however, do not segregate Jerusalem (including the neighborhoods of eastern Jerusalem, which are under Israeli control), where the Christian population continues to increase (as it has throughout Israel).

Regarding Bethlehem, the JCPA study states that this is the area most commonly associated with Christian flight. In Bethlehem City, the Christian population dropped under Jordanian rule (1948-1967), but since 1967 (after Israel gained control after the Six-Day War) it has grown by 11% in the city and by 56% in the "district" as follows:

> 1945:  6,490/14,800
> 1961:  7,246/15,234
> 1967:  6,405/14,406
> 1995:  6,799/20,487
> 2007:  7,140/22,440

The JCPA study authors state the percentage of Christians in Bethlehem City has decreased from 71% (in 1945) to 28.3% (in 2007). In the "district," it decreased from 79.4% (in 1945) to 45.4% (in 2007). The authors note that a significant factor in this decrease is the growth of the Muslim population, "and if one factors in neighboring Arab villages, the drop has been even sharper."

Although statistics are limited and empirical data are sparse, community leaders have verified the increase of Palestinian Christian emigration. It is estimated that, during the past seven years, more than one thousand Christians have been emigrating from the Bethlehem area annually and that only 7,500 to 13,000 Christians remain in the city. This nadir is unprecedented during the past two millennia; it reflects how Chrisitans have fared throughout the Muslim world.

Indeed, this emigration phenomenon has been experienced most strongly in the Bethlehem, Nazareth, Jerusalem and Ramallah areas, where the Christian concentration had traditionally existed and where many Palestinian families were relatively prosperous until the Second Intifada. According to the Custody of the Holy Land, an order of Franciscans responsible for the Latin holy places in Israel and "Palestine," thousands of families have emigrated from the Bethlehem area since the 1993 Oslo Accords which created the P.A. Under Israeli auspices,Bethlehem's Christian population grew by 57%. But under the P.A., since 1995,those numbers have plummeted. In Bethlehem alone, the Christian population has slumped to 7,500 (2010) from 20,000 (1995). When the P.A. was established, Christians made up 80 % of Bethlehem's population but, today, they comprise less than 20% of the population.

Actual empirical data is scarce. Interestingly, the Palestinian National Authority publishes population and demographic data. In its 1997 Census, Table 21: "Population Report-Palestinian Territory," states that the total Christian population was 40,055. Table 22: "Palestinian Population by Governorate, Sex and Religion," states that the Christian population of Bethlehem was 22,318, and that of Ramallah and Al-Bireh was 11,140. The population of Jerusalem was 1,525, which "does not include those parts of Jerusalem which were annexed by Israel in 1967." There were much smaller Christian populations noted for Jenin, Tubas, Tulkarm, Qalqiliya, Jericho, Hebron and Gaza. The 2007 Census included Table 13: "Palestinian Population in the West Bank by Age Group, Sex and Religion," where the Christian population was 41,188. However, there was no comparable table, statistics or charts with similar categories to 1997 showing population by religion and region. This renders the database, therefore, potentially suspect.

## Interpretation of Population Statistics

The history of the Christian communities in the Land of Israel began with the life and ministry of Jesus of Nazareth. After his death, the early Apostolic Church, especially in and around Jerusalem, remained largely Judeo-Christian until the rebuilding of Jerusalem (c. 130 C.E.) by the Emperor Hadrian as the Roman city of Aelia Capitolina. From then on, the Church has been gentile in composition. By the time of the Muslim conquest in the 7th century, the Church in the East was already subdivided into various groups, but continued to share use of holy places. Christians encountered problems living in the land thereafter (through the Crusader Kingdom, the Mamluk and Ottoman periods, the British Mandate), but their contemporary challenges are truly existential.

Yet, the M.S.M. seems more concerned with alleged Israeli misbehavior toward Arabs in the defense of her citizens, or alleged Islamophobia in the West. According to OperationWorld.org:

Palestinian Christians find themselves attacked or betrayed from all sides. They are regarded as Arab Palestinians by Israel and as Western collaborators by extremist Muslims, and they are generally ignored or abandoned by the global Church. Yet they trace their roots back to pre-Islamic times. Their numbers in Palestine itself have declined at an accelerating rate, largely due to emigration. The pull to leave is strong, with a vastly greater quality of life available elsewhere, and with increasing pressures from Israel on one side and Islamists on the other.

The JCPA 2011 paper concluded:

The Palestinian Christian population faces multiple and significant pressures. These include the unresolved conflict, life as a minority among Muslims, a continued low birth rate and emigration. We should respect their condition. We should respect the connection our Christian neighbors have with their co-religionists in the Palestinian territories. We should join in advocacy with Christian friends for some of the concerns that Palestinian Christians face in the context of the as-yet unresolved Israeli-Palestinian conflict. We should do this because it is the right thing to do. We can, however, dispute the myth of a vanishing or almost extinct Palestinian Christian population, and the near exclusive association with Israeli actions. The most significant drop in Christian population in the region occurred prior to Israeli control of the Palestinian territories. The drop in percentage is a present reality, due mostly to the increase in the Muslim population that surrounds them. The story of Palestinian Christians is complex. They have many valid concerns that should be heard. But the part of their story that relates to their total population and the percentage they constitute should not be distorted to slander Israel the way it has been.

David Parsons, media director of the International Christian Embassy Jerusalem, notes:

It is farcical to pin the primary blame for the Palestinian Christian exodus on Israel's security fence or its "occupation," since the phenomena predates both by decades. More than 60% of the native-born Palestinian Christians had already fled the land long before the fence started going up three years ago. And most of that emigration occurred prior to Israel's entry into the West Bank in 1967, when the area was under Jordanian occupation. The last British census in Jerusalem, for example, found 28,000 Arab Christian residents in 1948, while Israel's first official tally in 1967 registered only 11,000.

## Implications of Chrisitan Emigration

Populist Islamic and Arab regimes have used Islamic religious supremacism and Arab racial chauvinism against Christians as rallying cries to their subjects. These calls have in turn led to the decimation of the Christian populations of the Arab and Islamic worlds. The Christian share of the Middle East's population has plunged from 20% a century ago to less than 5% today and falling. For example, at the time of Lebanese independence from France in 1946, the majority of Lebanese were Christians; today less than 30% are Christians. A decade ago, there were 800,000 Christians in Iraq; today, there are 150,000; since 2003, over 70 Iraqi churches have been burned. Under the Shah, Iran's Christians were basically free to practice their religion; today, they are subject to the whims of ayatollahs who practice Islamic triumphalism. In Turkey, the Christian population has dwindled from 2 million at the end of World War I, to less than 100,000 today. In Syria, at the time of independence a half century ago, Christians made up nearly half of the population; today 4% of Syrians are Christian. In Jordan, 50 years ago, 18% of the population was Christian; today 2% of Jordanians are Christian. Christians are prohibited from practicing Christianity in Saudi Arabia. The Coptic Christians of Egypt, whose presence there predates the establishment of Islam by several centuries, currently constitute 10-15% of the population; this total (~8 million) is declining precipitously, as increasing church-burnings reflect a government-sanctioned attack that has placed them under terrible siege (more so since the 2011 "Arab Spring"); 200,000 fled after beatings and massacres by Muslim mobs. In Pakistan, the Christian population is being systematically destroyed by regime-supported Islamic groups; church burnings, forced conversions, rape, murder, kidnap and legal persecution of Pakistani Christians has become a daily occurrence. In Nigeria, the Islamist group Boko Haram has targeted and murdered thousands of Christians, vowing to wage a religious war to drive them from the country's Muslim north.

Within Israel, the Christian population has grown considerably in recent years; **Israel is the only country in the Middle East where they thrive.** Just as Jews living in the    Islamic world fled persecution or were forcibly removed from their ancient communities by Arab rulers after the re-establishment of Israel in 1948, so Christians have been persecuted by Muslim radicalization and driven from their homes.

Christians have always been a minority in Israel, but it is the only Middle East nation where the Christian population has grown in the last half century (from 34,000 in 1948 to over 150,000 in 2010), in large measure because of the freedom to practice their religion. By their own volition, Christian communities have remained the most autonomous of the various minority communities in Israel, though they have increasingly chosen to integrate their social welfare, medical and educational institutions into state structures. The ecclesiastical courts of the Christian communities maintain jurisdiction in matters of personal status, such as marriage and divorce.

In fact, during the past two decades, a new Christian landscape has been created—shared by the realities of Israel—as Israel's native Arab-Christian populace (largely stagnated) has been enhanced by one of the most significant influxes of Christians into the Holy Land since the Crusades. The newcomers include guest workers from dozens of different countries (who fuel the economy with cheap labor) and asylum-seekers from Sudan, Eritrea and elsewhere from Africa (who bravely dare to sneak across the border or are smuggled into Israel by Bedouin from Egypt through the Sinai, where they would be killed or persecuted if they remained in Egypt). For the first time, there is also a significant population of non-Arab Christian Israeli citizens, mainly immigrants from the former Soviet Union who, unlike Arabs, are fully assimilated into the Jewish-majority Israeli mainstream and culture For example, among the 1 million immigrants who came from the former Soviet Union, about one-third were not Jewish according to Jewish law, but qualified for citizenship because they had a Jewish spouse or lineage; among them were an estimated 50,000 to 80,000 practicing-Christians, mostly Orthodox. In 1991, there were 5,000 Filipino workers, and today there are 40,000. There are now sufficient newcomers to have prompted construction of a Catholic cathedral in every major Israeli city; this has led to a shortage of clergy and places to pray. A Mormon center opened in 1989. If one counts all of the people in Israel who are neither Jewish nor Muslim, these newcomers outnumber Arab Christians by more than five to one. The Israel Ministry of Religious Affairs deliberately refrains from interfering in their religious life, but maintains a Department for Christian Communities to address problems and requests that may arise.

This contrasts with the status of Christians in the P.A.-controlled Judea/Samaria and Gaza. As Israel has relinquished control, Christians have became beleaguered, under the thumb of a Muslim-dominated government. This has prompted Christian flight from the Middle East, due both to universal factors (*e.g.*, economic hardship, housing and education uncertainty) and to Muslim persecution (*e.g.*, intimidation, incitement, torture, abduction of women, forced conversions, political uncertainty, threats to personal security, and challenges to religious identity, and taking of Christian businesses). The latter constitutes the major force prompting emigration—under-reported by the M.S.M—particularly noting that it has often occurred with the connivance of the P.A.'s secret police.

## Political Reactions to Christian Emigration

Both Christians and Muslims are responsible for the dearth of statistics regarding erosion of Christian society in Judea/Samaria. The Christian leadership (which wants to retain some semblance of power and influence) is hesitant to flesh-out limited information; the Muslim leadership (which likewise wants to portray itself as friendly toward Christianity and welcoming to Christian pilgrims and tourists) is reticent to release data that might reveal what is actually transpiring, for fear of inciting panic within the already struggling Christian community under Palestinian rule. The Palestinian Human Rights Monitoring Group endorses maintaining the emigration phenomenon as a well-kept secret because there are national interests at stake; the accepted wisdom is that the story should not be publicized because it would be detrimental to the narrative and the ethos of the coming Arab/Palestinian "victory" over the Jews and the destruction of Israel. Because so little is written about this phenomenon, it is very difficult to verify.

Western churches are similarly uninclined to defend the rights of their co-religionists in the Islamic world. The World Council of Churches (an umbrella organization for 349 Protestant and Orthodox churches founded in 1948) has devoted a significant amount of resources to broadcasting its biased, one-sided narrative about the Israel-Arab conflict, but has conspicuously failed to respond effectively to the ongoing campaign of terror against Christians in Muslim-dominated countries in the Middle East and North Africa and the documented decimation of those ancient communities. Few mainline Protestant churches (from the Anglican Church and its U.S. and international branches to the Methodists, Quakers and Mennonites) have organized sustained efforts to protect or defend the rights of Christians in the Muslim world. Instead, over the past decade, these churches and their related international bodies have repeatedly attacked the only country in the Middle East in which Christians have been free to practice their religion and whose population has increased in the past 60 years–Israel.

The one notable exception are Evangelical Christians, who have exhibited unprecedented support for Israel. According to one of the most outspoken Christian Zionists, Pat Robertson—the founder of numerous organizations and corporations including the Christian Broadcasting Network (CBN), the Christian Coalition, Regent University, and host of *The 700 Club,* a Christian TV program airing on channels throughout the United States and on CBN network affiliates worldwide—evangelical Christians support Israel because they believe that the words of Moses and the ancient prophets of Israel were inspired by God and that the emergence of the Jewish state in the land promised by God to Abraham, Isaac and Jacob was ordained by God. In a 2004 speech ("Why Evangelical Christians Support Israel"), Pat Robertson said the following regarding the people of Israel:

We are with you in your struggle. We are with you as a wave of anti-Semitism is engulfing the earth. We are with you despite the pressure of the "Quartette" and the incredibly hostile resolutions of the United Nations. We are with you despite the threats and ravings of Wahabbi Jihadists, Hezbollah thugs, and Hamas assassins.

We are with you despite oil embargos, loss of allies, and terrorist attacks on our cities. We evangelical Christians merely say to our Israeli friends, "Let us serve our God together by opposing the virulent poison of anti-Semitism and anti-Zionism that is rapidly engulfing the world."

Having affirmed our support, I would humbly make two requests of our Israeli friends:

First, please don't commit national suicide. It is very hard for your friends to support you, if you make a conscious decision to destroy yourselves. I hardly find it necessary to remind this audience of the stated objectives of Yasser Arafat, the PLO, Hamas, Hezbollah, and Islamic Jihad. Their goal is not peace, but the final destruction of the State of Israel. At no time do they, or their allies in the Muslim world, acknowledge the sovereignty of Israel over even one square inch of territory in the Middle East. If a Palestinian State is created in the heart of Israel with sovereign power to deploy troops, import modern weapons—even weapons of mass destruction—and operate with full secrecy and diplomatic immunity, the ability of the State of Israel to defend itself will be fatally compromised.

The slogan "land for peace" is a cruel chimera. The Sinai was given up. Did that bring lasting peace? No. Southern Lebanon was given up. Did that bring lasting peace? No. Instead Hezbollah rode tanks to the border of Israel shouting, "On to Jerusalem!" Now, as many as 10,000 rockets aimed at Metulla, Qiryat Shemona, and all of Northern Israel have been put in place throughout Southern Lebanon.

Arafat was brought up at the knees of the man who yearned to finish the work of Adolf Hitler. How can any realist truly believe that this killer and his associates can become trusted partners for peace?...

Second, the world's Christians ask that you do not give away the treasured symbols of your spiritual patrimony....

Other major Christian supporters of Israel include John Hagee, founder and

Senior Pastor of Cornerstone Church in San Antonio, Texas, a non-demoninational megachurch with over 20,000 members; former Republican presidential candidate, Governor Mike Huckabee; radio and former television host and author Glenn Beck; and Christians United for Israel, which has grown to become one of the largest pro-Israel organization in the United States and one of the leading Christian grassroots movements in the world.

The Vatican has abandoned the principled stand enunciated in 2006 by Pope Benedict XVI, when he laid down the gauntlet at a speech in Regensburg and challenged the Muslim world to act with reason and tolerance in its dealings with other religions. However, a true discourse of equals was been replaced by supplication to Islam in the name of ecumenical understanding. The Pope hosted a Synod on Christians in the Middle East, but persecution of Christians by Islamic and populist forces and regimes was not mentioned; instead, Israel was singled-out for criticism. Worse, whereas all E.U. ambassadors walked-out of Iran's Ahmadinejad's Holocaust-denying speech at the U.N.'s second Durban Conference in Geneva in 2009, the Vatican's ambassador remained in his seat. The Vatican has also embraced leaders of the Muslim Brotherhood in Europe and the Middle East.

Christians also feel intimidated by the P.A. and thus, in "public," blame the dramatic rise in Christian emigration on the continuing Israeli "military occupation" and the denial of the sovereignty of a Palestinian state where Christian Arabs could (theoretically) "feel at home" economically, politically, culturally and spiritually. Yet, many recognize in private that this constitutes, at best, wishful thinking; indeed, if/when the Palestinians were to get their own state, they appreciate the sad fact that Christians would be treated as second-class citizens, as they are in other Muslim states. Many also saw that their archbishops and patriarchs were covering for Arafat and were thus corrupted, though they could trust them for liturgy and baptisms and other religious ceremonies.

The fact remains that the P.A. adopted Islam as its official religion, uses *sharia* Islamic codes, and allows even officially appointed clerics to brand Christians (and Jews) as infidels in their mosques. One would think that Christians would gain little solace from the fact that the rulers in the Palestinian territories use militant Islamic rhetoric and endorse unadulterated terrorist acts of Hamas and Islamic Jihad. Christians have only recently begun to discuss the implications of how Muslim gangs appropriate Christian-owned land, simply coming and taking possession while Palestinian security services—almost exclusively Muslims—stand by.

But what has been verified is that since Hamas "liberated" Gaza from the P.A. in 2007, the area's ancient Christian minority has been under constant attack. With only 3,000 members, Gaza's Christian community has seen its churches, convents, book stores and libraries burned by Hamas members and their allies. Its individuals have been killed and assaulted. While Hamas has pledged to protect the Christians of Gaza, no one has been arrested for anti-Christian violence.

Stories about a vanishing Christian presence in the Holy Land have a deep emotional appeal, after all, it is the very place where Jesus is from. But it is a fundamentally complicated narrative, one from a Palestinian Arab perspective, which has been generally in opposition to Israel and Zionism. The case for a diminishing Palestinian Christian population is made on three fronts: population, percentage and narrative, which combine to form a platform from which to criticize Israeli government action and policies. Yet, while the predominant pressure facing Palestinian Christians comes from Muslims–as evidenced by a precipitous decline in Christian population from Muslim lands throughout the Middle East (except notably Israel)—persecution by Muslims is not the "narrative" presented by Palestinian Christians. They generally do not want to "rock the boat", thus while the tensions with the Muslim majorities are real and increasing, it is far easier to blame "Israeli occupation" for the radicalization of their Muslim neighbors, hosts and leaders. Unfortunately, they have been cowered into acting like *dhimmis.*

## Portrayal of Christian Emigration by the M.S.M.

On the rare occasion that the M.S.M. covers the plight of Christians in the Palestinian territories, it is often to denounce Israel and its security barrier. Yet until Palestinian terrorist groups turned Bethlehem into a safe-haven for suicide bombers in 2002, defiling the Church of the Nativity to escape from Israeli security forces hunting them after a series of vicious terrorist attacks on Israeli civilians, Bethlehemites were free to enter Israel. Tourism, the main source of income, is constantly subject to the whims of terrorism and a corrupt P.A. But even in Jesus' birthplace, there are reports of Muslims often standing in front of the gate of the Bible College and reading from the Qur'an to intimidate Christian students, and of Muslims rolling out their prayer rugs right in Manger Square. Any Palestinian plight not blamed on Israel is barely reported as it does not comport with its ingrained worldview.

On Sunday, April 22, 2012, CBS' "60 Minutes" aired a tremendously biased episode, "Christians of the Holy Land" by Bob Simon. This was yet another prime example of the MSM's imbalanced, unfair, and inherently distorted coverage seeking to blame Israel for all the ills of the Middle East without telling the full story. Simon only paid lip service to the violent persecution and flight of ancient Christian communities throughout the region- Copts in Egypt, Iraqi Christians, Syrian Christians living under Bashar al-Assad's slaughterhouse- which is the real historical tragedy unfolding in the Middle East, due in large part to Islamic persecution. Instead, he chose to bash Israel, the only Middle Eastern country that protects Christians. He failed to report how Israel is the only Middle East nation where the Christian population has grown in the last half century (from 34,000 in 1948 to 140,000 today), in large measure because of the freedom to practice their religion. He also failed to disclose that it was during Jordan's control of the Old City of Jerusalem from 1948 until 1967 when the Christian population declined by nearly half. Since then, the population has slowly been growing. Instead, the program scapegoated and demonized Israel, warping reality to censure Israel's security measures – checkpoints and the security fence -- for the suffering of Palestinian Christians. Simon interviewed biased and anti-Semitic sources, treating them as legitimate. The questions he asked were not inquisitive, but rather were leading. He dismissed the real reasons for the plight and flight of Palestinian Christians: persecution by Palestinian Islamists and the Palestinian Authority. This was not journalism, but shoddy and irresponsible propaganda, that Israeli Ambassador Michael Oren rightly called a "hatchet job" on Israel. "

In sum, the M.S.M. has failed to follow-up and report on these developments. The P.A. leadership maintains that it seeks peace, with guarantees of religious freedom. Unfortunately, these examples show otherwise. Some Christians are applying to move to Israeli-controlled areas, where they are assured the right to worship freely. If action is not taken to ease the plight of Christians in P.A.-controlled areas, it is likely that the presence of Christians in these areas will continue to dwindle until few will remain to guard their holy sites. It is unclear what Western governments and Western churches think they are achieving, with the complicity and apathy by the M.S.M., by turning a blind eye to the persecution and decimation of Christian communities in the Muslim world. As October 2011 events in Egypt against Christian Copts, Christmas Day massacres of Christians in Nigeria by Black Muslims, and other daily anti-Christian attacks by Muslims against Christians throughout the region have shown, the cowardly behavior of western governments and churches, and the M.S.M. is not appeasing anyone. What is clear enough is that, if these trends continue, Christians will likely have a bleak future in these lands.

Sources:

*Israel Ministry of Foreign Affairs*

*Central Bureau of Statistics, State of Israel* (CBS Statistical Abstract of Israel 2010)

*Palestinian National Authority, Palestinian Central Bureau of Statistics- Census 1997 and 2007* (website accessed September 2011)

*CIA World Factbook*

"The Palestinian Christian Population" (Ethan Felson, in *Jewish Council for Public*

*Affairs*, Background Paper 2011)

"Muslims Continue Pushing Christians Out of Bethlehem" (Gil Ronen in *Arutz Sheva,* September 12, 2008)

"The Forgotten Palestinian Refugees: Even in Bethlehem, Palestinian Christians are suffering under Muslim intolerance" (Daniel Schwammenthal in *Wall Street Journal*)

"Christian Life Under the Palestinian Authority" (*Center for Responsible Peace in Middle East*; www.c4rpme.org)

"Palestinian Treatment of Christian Arabs" (Meagan Williams, *Prism Group*, March 8, 2005)

"The Beleaguered Christians of the Palestinian-Controlled Areas" (David Raab in *Jewish Virtual Library*)

Report on Christian Emigration: Palestine (August 1, 2008)

"The Christian Exodus from the Middle East" (Jonathan Adelman and Agota Kuperman, in *Jewish Virtual Library)*

"Christians Suffer Under the Palestinian Authority" (Joseph Puder, in *Pajamas Media,* November 15, 2009)

"Apartheid in the Arab Middle East: How can the U.N. turn a blind eye to hateful, state-sponsored discrimination against people because of their race, ethnicity, religion and gender?" (*Facts and Logic About the Middle East* (FLAME) September 13, 2011)

"The Forgotten Christians of the East" (Caroline Glick, in *Jewishworldreview.com, October 11, 2011*)

Operation World.org (accessed October 5, 2011)

"Broadcasting a Lethal narrative: The World Council of Churches and Israel" (Dexter Van Zile, in *Jerusalem Center for Public Affairs*, August 2011)

"Q & A: Justus Reid Weiner on Palestinian Christians: If They're Not Sitting on Their Suitcases, They've Already Left" (*Christianity Today Magazine,* January 19, 2006)

"Bethlehem on the Rebound: Palestinian Christians Hope for Better Times, by Justus Reid Weiner" (*Jerusalem Post Christian Edition*, February 2011)

"Human Rights of Christians in Palestinian Society" (Justus Reid Weiner, in *Jerusalem Center for Public Affairs*, 2005)

"Bethlehem's Exodus: Christians Flee Muslim Pressure" (Benny Avni, *NY Post,*

December 25, 2009)

"In the Holy Land, a Changed Christian World" (Matti Friedman, *Associated Press,* October 27, 2011)

"The Plight of Christians in the Holy Land: How to remedy their distress and preserve a remnant" (*International Christian Embassy Jerusalem*, July 16, 2006)

"Why Evangelical Christians Support Israel" (Pat Robertson, 2004)

"Israel and the Plight of Middle East Christians," Michael Oren, Wall Street Journal, March 9, 2012

# CONCLUSION:

# THE MEDIA WAR: CAN ISRAEL GET FAIR COVERAGE?

The M.S.M. has generally skewered Israel's right to defend herself and has set for Israel a moral standard to which the world holds no other country and which no other country could hope to achieve. In doing so, the M.S.M. has provided an onslaught of inaccurate misinformation regarding Israel, and has done so in a manner that would be condemned as incompetent, unethical and unprofessional if it were reporting on virtually any other subject-matter.

In his book, *The Case for Moral Clarity: Israel, Hamas and Gaza*, Harvard Law Professor Alan M. Dershowitz asked in conclusion, "Can the whole world be wrong about Israel?" His response was that the "vast majority of people around the world engage in knee-jerk condemnation of Israel whenever it engages in self-defense…and even when it does nothing but exist. To the extent that most of the world engages in such automatic remonization of the Jewish state, the answer…is clear: Yes, when it comes to Israel, the world can be—and often is—wrong. Completely wrong. Immorally wrong. Sometimes anti-Semitically wrong." Which, he continued, should come as no surprise to anyone familiar with Jewish history. He further explains:

> Ignorance is the father and mother of bigotry. It is also its child. Because emotion based on prejudice rather than reason based on information often drives the reaction to Israel, many anti-Israel agitators deliberately dumb it down, substituting slogans for facts, chanting for thinking, and bigotry for fairness….Constructive criticism of Israel and its policies is healthy. It is ongoing in Israel and among its supporters throughout the world. Demonizing the Jewish state or subjecting its actions to a double standard is wrong and must be an-

swered in the marketplace of ideas.

Yet, it seems that no matter what actions Israel takes toward peace, including agreeing to implement the two-state solution, there are some for whom nothing less than Israel's elimination would suffice. And all too often, many in the M.S.M. who worship at the altar of "moral equivalence" go along with this. Thus, Israel's best defense must continue to be her steely determination to survive and her ability to defend her citizens against all forms of attack—bombs and bigotry, weapons and words—from those who cannot accept her as the democratic, independent nation-state of the Jewish people.

Israeli investigative journalist David Bedein explained why Israel cannot get fair and balanced M.S.M. coverage, even when it is obvious that she is defending herself against unrelenting terrorist attacks deliberately targeting her citizens; he elucidated this problem in an interview published in *Reform Judaism Magazine* ("Why the Palestinians are Winning the Media War") in 2002 and, unfortunately, his observations remain accurate:

> Q: Do you agree with those who say that "the Palestinians have been doing a better job than the Israelis on the public relations front?"
>
> A: Palestinian media professionals have no qualms about deceiving the media for political advantage….The Palestinians have an excellent track record in manipulating images that appear in the world media. They achieved an enormous propaganda windfall at the beginning of the second intifada, when a Palestinian film crew working for a French television network recorded the shooting of eleven-year-old Mohammed al-Dura as his father tried in vain to shield him during a battle at a road junction near Gaza. The video, edited to portray the IDF as heartless child killers, fit the Palestinian story line perfectly. The Israeli government fell into the trap, issuing an apology even before investigating the incident. Mohammed al-Dura, the "poster boy" of the second intifada, will go down in history as a celebrated martyr of the Palestinian people— and yet, the Palestinian version of al-Dura's death is a lie, an invention of Palestinian P.R. professionals. A thorough IDF investigation, which was issued three weeks after the incident and confirmed by a German TV crew, showed that the bullets fired at the boy had come from the direction of Palestinian gunmen who had attacked an Israeli guard post. But the world had "witnessed" the shooting of al-Dura, as the media scripted it—an atrocity committed by Israeli troops—and the damage could not be undone. It is impossible to put the toothpaste

back in the tube.

Q: When did these Palestinian P.R. professionals first come onto the scene?

A: Back in March 1984, Ramonda Tawill, a media professional (who six years later would become Yasser Arafat's mother-in-law), helped the PLO establish the Palestinian Press Service (PPS) to provide assistance to visiting journalists and conduct training seminars in media relations. The PPS then joined forces with the Palestine Human Rights Information Center (PHRIC) to change the image of the PLO from that of a sixties-style liberation movement to an organization fighting to protect the victims of Israeli human rights abuses. PHRIC seminars instructed their "students" to steer every media interview to the same themes—Israeli occupation, illegal settlements, human rights abuses, and the right of the Palestinian refugees to go home. Regardless of the question, these themes were to be repeated over and over again. I know this firsthand, because our agency made it a policy to assign our journalist interns to take Tawill's courses.

Q: Was the PHRIC widely perceived as a credible human rights organization?

A: Absolutely. By mid-1989, international human rights organizations routinely reproduced information developed by the PHRIC, which by then had secured funding from the Ford Foundation and had established offices in Chicago and Washington. Addressing the media in Jerusalem in November 1989, Amnesty International spokesman Richard Reoch acknowledged that his organization regarded the PLO, which works with the PHRIC, as an objective information source. "Since the PLO is not a government body," he said, "we feel comfortable with Amnesty using them as a source." And a U.S. embassy spokesman told me in February 1989 that the PHRIC had "impeccable" credentials.

Q: How have the Israelis countered this Palestinian strategy of portraying them as human rights violators?

A: The Israelis constantly find themselves on the defensive. They can't seem to get out of the box into which the Palestinians have put them. By framing the conflict as a human rights issue, the Palestinians have succeeded in convincing many journalists, on some level at least, that every act of terrorism against Israeli civilians is not a crime, but a legitimate response to human rights abuses.

Q: Do you believe the United Nations plays a role in advancing the Palestinian P.R. agenda?

A: Definitely. The United Nations Relief and Works Agency (UNRWA) maintains a professional media relations department and a news service called the UNRWA television network, both based in the Ain el-Helweh UNRWA refugee camp in Lebanon. UNRWA cooperates with the media services of the PLO and the Palestine Broadcasting Corporation (PBC) to provide the visiting press with information and services. Its literature focuses largely on the plight of the refugees who are being housed in camps until they can "return to their homeland"—which, according to their literature, includes not only the territories captured by Israel in 1967, but also all the areas that Israel annexed after Israel's War of Independence in 1948. The UN's agenda is to present the Palestinian Arabs as victims. In Witness to History: The Plight of the Palestinian Refugees, one of several primers distributed by UNRWA and published by MIFTAH, the Palestinian media agency run by well-known Palestinian spokeswoman Hanan Ashrawi and commissioned by the Canadian government, the UN asserts, on page 13, that all "refugees and their descendants have a right to compensation and repatriation to their original homes and land....

Q: Do you believe that many Western journalists harbor an anti-Israel bias, or are there other factors which work in favor of the Palestinian point of view?

A: I agree with the assessment of Dr. Mike Cohen, a Jerusalem-based strategic communications analyst and IDF reserve officer, who says that most foreign journalists are not inherently anti-Israel, anti-Semitic, or pro-Palestinian. They are, however, easily swayed by Palestinian manipulation, which relies on the reporters' and editors' lack of background knowledge, combined with the lack of time and desire to take a deep look at the facts. Another factor is the fear of losing access to Palestinian sources and logistical support if their stories are perceived as hostile. Moreover, non-Palestinian reporters are deliberately impeded and intimidated when trying to cover news that may embarrass the P.A. I know of several foreign journalists who had reported incidents of Palestinian incitement and were thereafter barred from P.A. briefings.

Q: In the final analysis, how important is the P.R. factor in the Israeli-Palestinian conflict?

A: Absolutely crucial. So long as Western journalists project an image of the P.A. as a defender of human rights and Israel as a brutal occupier, development funds from the United States and the European Union will continue to flow into the P.A.'s coffers with little public protest about some of that money being used to bankroll the intifada, including suicide bombers, as documents seized from Arafat's office during Operation Defensive Shield prove. So long as Palestinian P.R. professionals continue to dictate the story line to the media, Israelis will continue to be portrayed as the villains and the Palestinians the victims. It's time to change the script.

Further elucidating this concern, Cherryl Smith, Ph.D. (Professor of English in Rhetoric and Composition at California State University, Sacramento) examined the minds of the M.S.M. and how news consumers are influenced by its reporting ("Media Psychology 101 - Framing Israel: Is Fair Coverage Possible?" in *HonestReporting.com*):

Reporters and editors need to frame news, just as any communicator needs to frame information, in order to make sense of it. Framing makes streams of information coherent; it marks the implicit boundaries through which news events are viewed.

It will not surprise readers of *HonestReporting* that a dominant frame through which Israel is viewed is "the conflict,"— and a very particular interpretation of the conflict–presented through the other, connected frames. Probably the most apparent of these is the "cycle of violence" frame through which attacks on civilians are seen as the same as defense against attacks on civilians.

Along with "cycle of violence," other persistent media frames are "David and Goliath," with the state of Israel as Goliath and individual Palestinians as David; a frame of "Israel to blame" which allows for quite unbelievable reporting, for instance, days of "massacre" to be reported and then ultimately (and quietly) revised in 2002-2003; the accusation of "apartheid," and particular interpretations of the terms, "disproportionate response," and "settlements."

The frame of conflict blocks out the rest of Israel so that people who know about the country only from the news learn little of Israel's technological breakthroughs, its high standard of living, its thriving arts and culture, its scientific discoveries, or its social complexity. The everyday life of the country is obscured.

A narrative pattern using David and Goliath, for example, allows listeners/viewers/readers to feel empathy with David without the need for much evidence. Simply designating one player David and the other Goliath makes the case, makes a recognizable story even without a lot of detail or support.

If you are writing a novel, running a political campaign, or advertising your products, you will naturally work to trigger the appropriate responses in your audience—sympathy with the main character, voting for the candidate, buying what is advertised—not merely by providing evidence but by the way the entire discourse is framed. You are free to be as biased as you please.

Not so media in a democratic society. The public, and the press, itself, expect commitment to balanced and accurate presentation, so the limits of framing—what is left out, what is included—must be checked for bias. We expect to hear the whole story, to have the opportunity to draw our own conclusions; we expect political slant to be minimal or balanced in the reporting of the news. The whole range of ethical requirements for journalists demands that media seek a fair and truthful representation of events in their reporting.

Identifying and tracking the news framing of Israel is a promising way of addressing media bias. By focusing on the frames, we expose the underlying problems of biased reporting—bias that does not necessarily correspond to writers' or editors' own political views, since the frames, once well-established, become the conventional ways of reporting.

If we want to set the record straight about Israel, the facts are important, but focusing on the rhetoric may be even more important, since the frames through which Israelis viewed allow for inaccuracies to go unchecked. Media is expected, and expects itself, to report fairly, but often the current framing does not allow this to happen. Identifying these implicit frames reveals the incongruity between media's ethical standards and their reporting on Israel. If the frames are exposed perhaps fair coverage will become a possibility.

Such quasi-"subjective" views can be supplemented by objective data from an academic study by Roosevelt University that found that Middle East coverage by *Reuters* (the world's largest multi-media news agency) is tainted by systematic use of propaganda and violates its internal company principles. This analysis (published in the November/December 2011 issue of the *Journal of Applied Business Research*) finds that *Reuters* coverage is biased and influences readers to side with the Palestinian Arabs and Arab states against the Israelis. Researcher Henry Silverman analyzed a sample of 50 news-oriented articles published by *Reuters* for use of classic propaganda techniques, fallacies and violations of its own Handbook of Journalism (a manual of guiding ethical principles for its journalists). The study found over 1100 instances of propaganda, fallacies and handbook violations in 41 categories. In the second part of the study, a group of 33 university students were surveyed before and after reading the articles to assess their attitudes. The study found, on average, that sentiment shifted significantly following the readings in favor of the Arabs and that this shift was directly associated with the particular propaganda techniques and logical fallacies appearing in the stories. According to Silverman, "Governments have long used propaganda to whip-up public support during wartime and to demonize enemies. *Reuters* is adopting these same techniques to covertly shape audience perceptions and opinion in violation of its corporate governance charter." Silverman argues this is especially troubling since "the news agency promotes itself as a paragon of accurate and impartial reporting and its stories are read by millions of people who are led to believe they are being provided objective facts."

Coverage of Israel in the *N.Y. Times* has, since before Israel's re-establishment in 1947, been generously characterized as "less than favorable." (This may be explained by the fact that its publisher, Arthur Hays Sulzberger, was a charter-member of the anti-Zionist American Council for Judaism.) Its bias prompted Israeli P.M. Netanyahu, in December 2011, to "respectfully" decline an invitation to pen an op-ed piece for the paper. Netanyahu's senior advisor, Ron Dermer, in a letter to the *Times,* explained the degree to which they were fed-up with the paper's editorial policy:

> On matters relating to Israel, the op-ed page of the "paper of record" has failed to heed the late Senator Moynihan's admonition that everyone is entitled to their own opinion but that no one is entitled to their own facts.
>
> A case in point was your decision last May to publish the following bit of historical revision by Palestinian President Mahmoud Abbas:

*It is important to note that the last time the question of Palestinian statehood took center stage at the General Assembly, the question posed to the international community was whether our homeland should be partitioned into two states. In November 1947, the General Assembly made its recommendation and answered in the affirmative. Shortly thereafter, Zionist forces expelled Palestinian Arabs to ensure a decisive Jewish majority in the future state of Israel, and Arab armies intervened. War and further expulsions ensued.*

This paragraph effectively turns on its head an event within living memory in which the Palestinians rejected the UN partition plan accepted by the Jews and then joined five Arab states in launching a war to annihilate the embryonic Jewish state. It should not have made it past the most rudimentary fact-checking.

The opinions of some of your regular columnists regarding Israel are well known. They consistently distort the positions of our government and ignore the steps it has taken to advance peace. They cavalierly defame our country by suggesting that marginal phenomena condemned by Prime Minister Netanyahu and virtually every Israeli official somehow reflects government policy or Israeli society as a whole. Worse, one columnist even stooped to suggesting that the strong expressions of support for Prime Minister Netanyahu during his speech this year to Congress was "bought and paid for by the Israel lobby" rather than a reflection of the broad support for Israel among the American people.

Yet instead of trying to balance these views with a different opinion, it would seem as if the surest way to get an op-ed published in the *N.Y. Times* these days, no matter how obscure the writer or the viewpoint, is to attack Israel. Even so, the recent piece on "Pinkwashing," in which Israel is vilified for having the temerity to champion its record on gay-rights, set a new bar that will be hard for you to lower in the future.

Not to be accused of cherry-picking to prove a point, I discovered that during the last three months (September through November) you published 20 op-eds about Israel in the *N.Y. Times* and *International Herald Tribune*. After dividing the op-eds into two categories, "positive" and "negative," with "negative" meaning an attack against the State of Israel or the policies of its democratically elected government, I found that

19 out of 20 columns were "negative."

The only "positive" piece was penned by Richard Goldstone [of the infamous Goldstone Report], in which he defended Israel against the slanderous charge of Apartheid.

Yet your decision to publish that op-ed came a few months after your paper reportedly rejected Goldstone's previous submission. In that earlier piece, which was ultimately published in the *Washington Post*, the man who was quoted the world over for alleging that Israel had committed war crimes in Gaza, fundamentally changed his position. According to the *N.Y. Times* op-ed page, that was apparently news unfit to print.

Your refusal to publish "positive" pieces about Israel apparently does not stem from a shortage of supply. It was brought to my attention that the Majority Leader and Minority Whip of the U.S. House of Representatives jointly submitted an op-ed to your paper in September opposing the Palestinian action at the United Nations and supporting the call of both Israel and the Obama administration for direct negotiations without preconditions. In an age of intense partisanship, one would have thought that strong bipartisan support for Israel on such a timely issue would have made your cut.

So with all due respect to your prestigious paper, you will forgive us for declining your offer. We wouldn't want to be seen as "Bibiwashing" the op-ed page of the *N.Y. Times*.

Dermer's letter referred to the op-ed of famed *N.Y. Times* columnist, Thomas Friedman, who wrote that that the resounding ovation Netanyahu received in Congress when he spoke there in May 2011 had been "bought and paid for by the Israel lobby." Congressman Steve Rothman (D-NJ) released the following statement, which the *Times* did not cover:

Thomas Friedman's defamation against the vast majority of Americans who support the Jewish State of Israel, in his *New York Times* opinion piece today, is scurrilous, destructive and harmful to Israel and her advocates in the U.S. Mr. Friedman is not only wrong, but he's aiding and abetting a dangerous narrative about U.S.-Israel relationship and its American supporters.

I gave Prime Minister Netanyahu a standing ovation, not because of any nefarious lobby, but because it is in America's vital national security interests to support the Jewish State of Israel and it is right for Congress to give a warm welcome to the leader of such a dear and essential ally. Mr. Friedman owes us all an apology.

As reported by CAMERA, The New York Times published a report by its new Jerusalem bureau chief Jodi Rudoren on May 3, 2012, regarding Palestinian prisoners on a hunger strike. Number of quoted words by Palestinian supporters of Palestinian prisoners: 269. Number of words explaining the Israeli rationale behind administrative detention: 0. Number of paragraphs before Rudoren gets around to letting readers know that the stars of her article are members of Islamic Jihad: 14. Countries and groups that list Islamic Jihad as a terrorist organization: U.S., Canada, EU, UK and Australia.

Number of people murdered by Islamic Jihad: Hundreds Number of rockets fired at Israeli cities and towns by Islamic Jihad: Hundreds. Number of references in the article to those attacks: 0

Finally, the M.S.M. rarely, if ever, notes the pernicious effects of the insidious Arab Lobby on U.S. policymakers. Mitchell Bard, in his exhaustively researched book, *The Arab Lobby*, documented how – for decades – Arab states have poured billions of dollars (dwarfing the power of the so-called "Israel Lobby") into influencing U.S. policy by ensuring that U.S. officials pay disproportionate attention to Arab demands to assist Arab countries – all of them dictatorial regimes with abysmal human rights records that do not share American values, and often work to subvert American interests, including support for terrorism and threating the world oil supply.

The M.S.M. is mistaken in its focus on a single party, Israel, as the impediment to peace. Israel has repeatedly expressed its willingness to live peacefully alongside a Palestinian state. Since the rebirth of a Jewish state in 1948, Israel's democratic governments from across the political spectrum have repeatedly demonstrated an intent to make painful compromises in the interest of a peaceful resolution of this conflict, including recognition of a Palestinian Arab homeland for those descended from Arabs displaced during prior conflicts. Reciprocal recognition of Israel as the homeland of the Jews has yet to occur.

One thing Israel cannot do is make her enemies love and accept her. This is a hard truth for many to grasp, especially in the M.S.M. History has shown that good will gestures that Israel has made to its neighbors and enemies (*e.g.,* evacuating Gaza, southern Lebanon, releasing prisoners) have not led to reciprocal good will, but instead have made Israel's enemies more emboldened and hostile than ever. In the Arab/Muslim world, concessions and "good will gestures" are perceived as weakness to be exploited. It is Arab rejectionism and Muslim "supremacy" that are the obstacles to any true coexistence and peaceful settlement. The simple truth is that Israel has sought out peace for over 60 years with its neighbors, and the status can be stated like this: If the Arabs lay down their weapons, the conflict will come to an end, but if Israel lays down its weapons, Israel will come to an end.

On May 6, 2012, Israeli Ambassador to the U.S. Michael Oren told the Jewish Council for Public Affairs plenum in Detroit that the unity of the Jewish people should be a primary concern for all Jews: "Israel is our state, a work in progress in which every Jew can play a part. Of course, sovereignty is messy, and Jews can and will disagree about Israeli policies without necessarily loving Israel any less. Still, people often ask me, 'how do you define pro-Israel?' I have some elementary answers." A pro-Israel person "recalls what Jewish life was like without a Jewish state and works to ensure that there always will be a Jewish state." A pro-Israel person is also "grateful every day that he or she lives in a time in Jewish history when there is a proud and independent Jewish state." "The pro-Israel person also asks, 'how can I contribute to Israel, how can I enrich it and be enriched by it?'" Oren said a pro-Israel person is aware that Israel is a tiny country living under a massive threat. A pro-Israel person knows that making peace with the Palestinians constitutes a very real risk that Judea/Samaria/West Bank will devolve into a terror haven, just as Gaza did. The secret to the Jewish people's success, Oren stressed, is the unity of the Jewish people. That means that the Jewish State of Israel and the far-flung tribe that is the Jewish people must work together. "The great task of our generation is to preserve our unity."

Stand up and defend the sole Jewish state on the planet from being unjustly vilified. Speak out and fight back against the media's biased coverage. It is incumbent on those who value the truth to be an ambassador for truth, or the truth will be swallowed at the altar of political expediency, to the detriment of those who cherish freedom, Western, democractic Judeo-Christian values. The "Mission Impossible": Get the M.S.M. to change the frame, to ensure the game to blame Israel does not remain the same.

Sources:

"Why the Palestinians are Winning the Media War: An Interview with David Bedein   (*Reform Judaism Magazine,* August 17, 2002)

The Case for Moral Clarity: Israel, Hamas and Gaza, Alan M. Dershowitz, CAMERA (2009)

"Media Psychology 101 – Framing Israel: Is Fair Coverage Possible?" (Cheryl Smith, HonestReporting.c om, November 30, 2011)

"Academic Study Finds *Reuters* Middle East Coverage Tainted by Propaganda, Violates Company Principles" (PRWeb.com, December 6, 2011)

"Netanyahu 'Respectfully Declines' to Pen Op-Ed for New York Times" (Herb Keinon, Jerusalem Post, December 16, 2011)

"PM adviser's letter to 'New York Times' " (*Jerusalem Post*, December 16, 2011)

"Congressman Rothman: Friedman Owes Us An Apology for "Israel Lobby" Charge (Press Release, December 14, 2011)

*The Arab Lobby: The Invisible Alliance That Undermines America's Interest in the Middle East* (Mitchell Bard, 2010)

# DON'T FORGET TO TAKE A LOOK AT THESE IMPORTANT BOOKS:

***What's Legal by Lee Crane:*** A pointed look at various interpretations of the Muslim Shariah law with comparisons to American jurisprudence and the ramificaions for those who live under either.

***Black Fire*** by Jonathan Levitan: A riveting thriller rivalling *DaVinci Code* that reveals the end of a 3000 year rivalry between two families as they discard all the rules to employ murder and mayhem in order to possess a remnant of the original *Laws of Moses*.

***Lethal Rhythm and Deadly Rhythm*** by Dr. Peter Kowey*:* When it comes to medical murder, Dr. Kowey has no rival for spirited mysters and suspense. What happens when the sudden cardiac arrest of a loving wife causes the downfall of her doctor and the unfolding of deadly intent? This thriller and its sequel brings the whirlwind answer home.

***Pressing Israel*** by Jerome R. Verlin and Lee S. Bender: Once we recognize that an epic struggle exists between the culture of Islam and that of Enlightenment, we understand that the language of engagement controls the debate. This book will set the record straight and you can either take sides or at least understand.

***Survivor from an unknown War*** by Stephen Crane: The biography of Jay Narzikul, young lietenant in the Red Army, POW at the hands of Nazi Germany, high ranking officer of the Eastern Legions that fought against the USSR as allies of Hitler, romantic lover behind the iron curtain, and CIA agent will leave you breathless. Guarenteed.

***Jewish German Revolution: Saving Civilization in 400*** by Lee Crane: This book explores the military and political alliances that preserved and upheld the ideas that survived the Dark Middle Ages and emerged as Renaissance and Enlightenment. History buffs can now understand the momumental sturggles between Romans, Visigoths, Jews, minority Christians, Catholics, and Muslims.

***Israel 3000 Years*** by Jerome Verlin: A focused thorough research into the history of Jewish presence in Isreal since the time of Moses. This work sets aside the many lines of propaganda and misinformation to move through centuries of a people's relation to their homeland.

***Beware Your Friends Know Your Enemies*** by Joseph Puder: As a correcpondent and commentator on the Middle East, Mr. Puder cuts to the chase and explodes all fantasies and myths regarding the politics and history of the region. To read Puder is to be informed.